Isla
Marchena

Isla
Genovesa

EQUATOR ——— 0°

Galápagos
Islands

Isla
Baltra

Isla Seymour
Norte

Isla
Santa Cruz

Isla
San Cristobal

Bellavista

Puerto
Ayora

Isla Santa Fé

Puerto
Baquerizo Moreno

Puerto
Velasco Ibarra

Isla
Floreana

Isla
Española

© '02 jackie aher

Plundering Paradise

Plundering Paradise

The Hand of Man on the Galápagos Islands

MICHAEL D'ORSO

HarperCollins*Publishers*

Grateful acknowledgment is made to the following:

"The End". Words and music by The Doors. Copyright © 1967 Doors Music Co. Copyright renewed. All rights reserved. Used by permission.

"Ecuador: Beachhead on the Moon". Copyright © 1946 Time Inc. Reprinted by permission.

"Back to Nature" from *Newsweek*, October 6, 1934. Copyright © Newsweek, Inc. All rights reserved. Reprinted by permission.

"First-Hand Report on Galápagos Island Hunt" by Richard Meyer. Copyright © 1999 *The Hunting Report*. Reprinted by permission.

"Fire and Ice" from *The Poetry of Robert Frost*, edited by Edward Connery Lathem. Copyright © 1969 Henry Holt and Company. Reprinted by permission of Henry Holt and Co., LLC.

A continuation of this copyright page appears on page 348.

FIRST EDITION

Designed by Elliott Beard

Maps by Jackie Aher

Printed on acid-free paper

Library of Congress Cataloging-in-Publication Data

D'Orso, Michael.
    Plundering paradise : the hand of man on the Galápagos islands / Michael D'Orso.
      p. cm.
    ISBN: 0-06-019390-5
    1. Nature—Effect of human beings on—Galápagos Islands.
2. Environmental degradation—Galápagos Islands. 3. Galápagos Islands—Economic conditions. 4. Environmental protection—Ecuador. 5. Ecuador—Politics and government—1984 I. Title.
GF852.G35 D67 2002
304.2'8—dc21   2002023883

02 03 04 05 06 ❖/RRD 10 9 8 7 6 5 4 3 2 1

This is a work of nonfiction. The events on these pages occurred as described. The people are real, as are their words. No names have been changed to protect either the innocent or the guilty.

For Diane

We may infer from these facts, what havoc the introduction of any new beast of prey must cause in a country, before the instincts of the aborigines become adapted to the stranger's craft or power.

—CHARLES DARWIN,
Voyage of the Beagle

CONTENTS

PROLOGUE

Puerto Ayora, Santa Cruz Island
Galápagos, Ecuador

It was five years ago that a friend of mine, David, returned to his home in Brooklyn from a week-long tour of the Galápagos Islands. David could not stop gushing about the primeval purity of the place, the otherworldliness of the creatures that live there. These ungodly animals, he told me, have no fear of people because of their utter isolation, the absence of human predators on this cluster of oceanic volcanoes

I listened politely as David described how he had approached a blue-footed booby on a rocky plateau, reached out to feed the ungainly bird a twig, and the thing responded with no hesitation at all, devouring the snack with the eagerness of a calf in a petting zoo. David's eyes rolled back in his head as he talked of lying with his wife on a spit of sugar-white sand, gazing into the round, wet eyes of a baby sea lion that had cozied up next to them. It was, he said, "a religious experience."

I was glad he was so moved. But I had no great urge to visit the Galápagos myself. Sure, I'd heard of them. The iguanas. The tortoises. Darwin. All that. But until David mentioned his brief stay at the Hotel Galápagos—the *Hotel Galápagos*!—I had no idea anyone actually lived in this place. The only humans I had ever encountered in the magazine spreads and books and video documentaries that I'd seen in my lifetime—that we've *all* seen—were biologists, a guide or two, and maybe an on-camera narrator, someone like Richard Attenborough or Alan Alda.

There are the tourists, of course, tens of thousands of them each year, but they don't count. For these outdoor enthusiasts, the Galápagos are and have always been the ultimate theme park, a place where humans can step ashore from their cruise ships and walk the same lava-encrusted ground that the young Charles Darwin did nearly two centuries ago, which is essentially the same ground that thrust itself up from the ocean floor when these rocky islands first burst through the surface of the sea some five to ten million years ago, a blink of an eye in geologic time. For the ecowanderer, the Galápagos are and always have been a Holy Land.

But not for me. I've got nothing against nature. I live in an oak-shaded house on a quiet Virginia river not far from the Chesapeake Bay. I sit on my porch in the morning and read the newspaper while watching a crabber empty his pots in the pink light of dawn. I enjoy an occasional drive up to the Blue Ridge Mountains, especially in autumn when the leaves change. I even allowed a friend to convince me one winter to join him for a three-day hike in subfreezing temperatures along a spur of the Appalachian Trail—a mistake I will never make again. The hiking itself was just fine, but the two nights I spent cursing and praying for the sun to rise as I lay trembling in my pathetically outdated sleeping bag were the longest two nights of my life.

The point is, I take my nature as it comes but make no inordinate effort to reach out for it. As a journalist I've been lucky enough to see more than my share of the world. Wherever I've traveled, from Arctic Alaska to the swamps of South Florida, the one species of animals that truly excites me is the human. That's why I perked up when David mentioned the odd little hotel at which he had stayed on these islands.

"You mean there are people who actually *live* there?" I asked. "Even better," I added, "they're . . . *odd?*"

Now this indeed seemed like something to sink my teeth into. So I began some cursory research—a little poking around—and quickly discovered there's been a lot more going on in the Galápagos lately than simply snorkeling and bird-watching. At the time, I wasn't even sure where the Galápagos *are*. I knew they were located in the Pacific somewhere. When I learned that they sit directly on the equator, six hundred miles west of Ecuador—the nation that owns them—I imagined that might put them roughly due south of California, maybe even Hawaii. I pulled out a map and found I was off by roughly half a continent: The Galápagos are perched on precisely the same longitudinal line as . . . New Orleans.

Just as surprising were news briefs I found that told of poachers during the past decade invading the protected waters around these islands in pursuit of shark fins, sea urchins, and—I swear to God— sea lion penises, prized throughout Asia for their aphrodisiac effects. I read of a shoot-out between fishermen and Galápagos Park Service rangers. I read of local protesters seizing the tortoises at a scientific research station on one of the islands and threatening to kill the poor beasts if some demands were not met. Hostage *tortoises.* Who knew?

Who knew that the indigenous *Galápagueños*, the first permanent settlers on these islands, were not Ecuadorian, but Norwegian—a colony of expatriate fishermen and farmers who fled their homeland in the mid-1920s to sail to a new life half a planet away?

Who knew that the ensuing half-century would bring to the Galápagos a swirling array of nomads and grifters, dreamers and hermits, a wild stew of men and women from all over the world who shared one thing in common—a desire, for better or worse, to get as far as they could from the lives they'd been living. What better place for such an escape than to an honest-to-god desert island?

That is essentially what the fifty-some islands and islets that compose the Galápagos are—desert. Rocky and barren. Scorchingly hot. With cacti and lizards and no fresh water to speak of, other than the rain that occasionally sweeps down from the highlands. There are forests and farmland among some of those highlands, but that farmland is hacked out of virtual jungles, ridden with brambles and insects and volcanic stones.

It's easy to see why, when the Galápagos National Park was created in 1959, only a few hundred people lived there. Those scattered souls were allowed to remain, and the soil on which their homes stood—a few seaside villages and some farms in those highlands—a mere total of three percent of the archipelago's landmass, was set aside from the Park and from the restrictions created to protect and preserve the other ninety-seven percent of the Galápagos.

That unpeopled ninety-seven percent is what most of the world knows of these islands. It's what is portrayed in the books and magazines and TV documentaries with which we all are familiar. But it was that other three percent that I became eager to explore. I was hungry to learn how the hand of man has come to shape itself here, in Darwin's garden. And so, in late 1998, I booked my first flight to the islands for a one-week visit, a scouting trip to give me a taste of this place and these people. If things went as planned, this first trip would be followed by subsequent stays.

It isn't easy getting to the Galápagos by oneself. Flying from the United States to Ecuador is a snap; several major airlines routinely come and go daily from Miami to the capital city of Quito or to the industrial seaport of Guayaquil. But the only planes that fly on to the islands are Ecuadorian-owned, and those owners are intimately aligned with the nation's tourist industry, which controls almost all seating on the aircraft. Foreigners booking a trip to the Galápagos through a travel agency in their homeland (say, an American in the United States) can do so only by purchasing a package deal, which includes not just airfare but also the cost of joining a tour group on one of the ninety or so boats currently authorized to circle the islands—vessels ranging from six-passenger sailboats to 100-berth cruise ships. These one- or two-week junkets, which include the price of meals, guides, and shipboard lodging, typically cost from two to six thousand dollars per person.

If you'd rather get to the Galápagos on your own, I found out, you must first buy a ticket to Ecuador, then, through a travel agency in Quito or Guayaquil, reserve an individual seat—if it's available—on one of the two island-bound flights that leave the continent each day. Most of those individual seats are filled by Ecuadorians themselves, mainlanders traveling to visit kin on the islands, businessmen jetting out to close a deal, or *Galápagueños* themselves, returning home from a trip to the continent.

At the time I made my arrangements that winter of 1998, the Ecuadorian economy was manic. The value of the nation's currency—the *sucre*—was plunging every day. A year earlier, the *sucre* had been worth 2,000 per American dollar. By the time I booked my seats that November of '98, the figure had ballooned to 5,000. Two months later, as I boarded my flight from Miami to Quito on a bright January afternoon, the value of the *sucre* had plunged to 7,000 per dollar.

After an overnight stay at a small Quito hotel, where the desk clerk shouldered an automatic rifle and the smell of burning automobile tires hung in the air from an antigovernment demonstration staged downtown earlier that day, I boarded an Ecuadorian TAME Airlines Boeing 727 bound for the islands. TAME is owned by the Ecuadorian military and dominates virtually every route flown within the country. As the sun rose over the Andes behind us, the Pacific coast, glowing apricot in the warm morning light, soon loomed ahead.

We landed briefly at Guayaquil's grim international airport, where half the passengers deboarded. Those of us heading on to the islands were instructed to stay on the plane because the city was currently under martial law and not even the terminal was considered safe ground.

When we again lifted off forty-five minutes later, we were soon soaring over nothing but azure ocean, the coastline of Ecuador disappearing behind us, and the distant serenity of the Galápagos lying ahead. Even with all I had learned from my months of preparation, it was hard to imagine the turmoil and rot of this decaying nation stretching its tendrils across these hundreds of miles of open sea to invade those ageless islands. From the outside looking in, it seemed impossible. But soon I would be on the inside looking out, through the eyes of the people who live there.

This is their story.

ONE

The Village

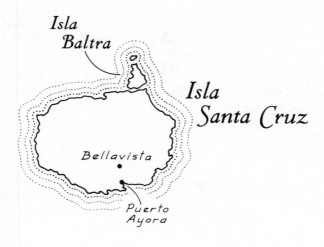

JANUARY 18, 1999

Jack Nelson, off Puerto Ayora

The midwinter sun has just begun to climb above the flat, blue Pacific, and already the cobbled pavers that form the streets of Puerto Ayora are warm to the touch. Marine iguanas, as common here as house cats, have crawled up from the sea to begin their day-long naps on the black lava crags that rim this island of stone.

They are outside Jack Nelson's front door as well, dozing on his concrete stoop as Jack steps into the white morning light. He shuts the door softly behind him, careful not to wake his partner Romy and their young daughter, Audrey. The mottled black reptiles lie undisturbed as Jack loosens the bleached red bandanna knotted around his neck, slips a sweat-stained Panama hat on his head, adjusts his knapsack, and checks his watch.

The march is set to begin at nine, but Jack's in no hurry to get there. Nothing begins on time on these islands. If there's one thing Jack Nelson has learned in his thirty-odd years in this place, it's that nothing in the Galápagos happens when it's supposed to. This was one of the first lessons his father taught him when Jack arrived here in the summer of '67. Patience, flexibility, the capacity to adapt—these are the qualities the old man said a human must have to survive on these islands. They are the attributes that allowed Forrest Nelson to settle this point of land nearly forty years ago, carving a couple of cement-block shelters out of magmatic debris and sun-scorched brush and calling them a hotel. The guests back then were mostly field scientists in search of a cot and some shade, or the occasional yachtsman and his crew bound west to Tahiti, or the hustlers and con men who, to this day, arrive on these islands seeking a place where neither the law nor the truth will follow.

Tourists, per se, did not yet exist here in 1961, when the Hotel Galápagos first opened for business. Six years after that, when Jack Nelson showed up, weeks still might pass between one guest and the next. Jack never dreamed he'd stay in this godforsaken place for more than a year or two. There were fewer than one thousand people on this entire island when he first set foot here. The Norwegians on their small cattle farms up the vine-tangled slopes of that extinct volcano had been around the longest, nearly half a century. Then there were the Germans and Belgians in their little hamlet across the harbor; most of them had come just before and after World War II. And here on this side, in what was no more than a scattered settlement, were the Ecuadorians, their fishing dinghies anchored in the turquoise shallows of Ninfas Lagoon.

Of course there were the scientists, always the scientists, coming and going from their base camp at the southeastern tip of the island, just beyond Jack's father's hotel. Forrest Nelson had helped build that camp for the scientists in the summer of 1960, kicking up clouds of dust as he gunned his small three-wheeled tractor up and down the dirt trail to the site. The scientists stayed at his hotel while the gravel road was put in and the first Charles Darwin Research Station dormitories were put up.

There were no paved roads back then. No electricity. The only fresh water to be found was that which fell straight from the sky, collected in downspouts and barrels and stored beneath layers of scum and dead insects. The closest mainland was six hundred miles east, where the beaches of Ecuador baked in the equatorial sun. A ham radio might be able to pick up a station now and then from Guayaquil or maybe Quito, the deejays chattering in Spanish over the buzz of the static. To hear an American voice, Forrest Nelson had to fiddle with the knobs of his shortwave, typically late at night, when the skies were clear and he just might connect with a farmer in Nebraska, or a college kid in New Orleans, or once in a blue moon, with someone closer to home, up in Southern California, the place he had left when he sailed here in the '50s. People still talk about the time old man Nelson hooked up with a guy in a garage in Long Beach, where Nelson's ex-wife and kids had continued to live after he'd left them a decade before. He asked the man for a telephone patch, gave him the number, then told the man who he was calling.

"Jack and Christy Nelson?" repeated the voice in Nelson's headset.

"That's right," said Forrest.

"Just a minute," said the voice. Next thing Nelson knew, he could hear the guy shouting at the other end of the line. "Jack! Christy!" And in a minute or two, Nelson's son and daughter were on the wire. Turned out this man lived next door to Christy and Jack and Nelson's ex-wife Bawn.

Who could believe it? Who could believe any of this life the old man had cobbled together, here in this place where tortoises the size of refrigerators and the age of sequoias roamed through moss-festooned mountain forests, where schools of hammerhead sharks darkened the crystalline sea like squadrons of B-52s, where the shadows of Darwin himself lurked among the lava-bouldered beaches and cactus-stabbed seaside slopes.

It was a universe away from Haight-Ashbury, where Jack Nelson had been shacked up with a girlfriend that summer of '67, the Summer of Love, dropping acid and working the streets, making ends meet by selling a lid or two of grass when circumstances demanded. This was before the vampires arrived in the Bay Area— the straight press with their hunger to label and devour, and the posers, the losers, the wanna-bes who showed up wherever the next new thing was supposed to be happening. The tour buses had not yet begun crawling through the Haight at that time, with their megaphoned guides pointing out the head shop on the left *"where Janis Joplin is said to have shopped"* and the soup kitchen there on the corner *"still run by the Diggers"* and the free clinic just down the block *"where you might like to stop and make a donation when your tour is completed."*

This was all still beyond the horizon at the start of that summer, and by the time it rolled through, Jack Nelson was long gone. It was a short letter that drove him away, a notice from his draft board telling him he was 1-A for Vietnam, which was not a place Jack intended to visit, not in this lifetime. Canada was out of the question—way too cold for his blood. But the Galápagos Islands, now could there be a better place on this planet for a man on the run?

And so Jack Nelson came here to join his father for a year, maybe two. But two years became three, and the cat-and-mouse game with his draft board grew more tiring until Jack finally said "screw it" and had his friend Fiddi Angermeyer take a snapshot of Jack perched on the summit of the island's Devil's Chimney volcano, an impish smile on his full-bearded face and not a stitch of clothing on his darkly tanned skin. He signed the photo "Best wishes," and mailed it to his draft board in Long Beach, which brought a return envelope containing a letter of indictment.

All was forgiven when Jack returned to the States in '75 to pick up his amnesty from the Ford administration. By then he was entrenched; so much of himself and his sweat was sunk into the hotel that leaving was out of the question. Not that he wanted to leave. The islands had begun to seriously shift, with the seeds of tourism finally starting to sprout. The first cruise ships—fishing boats, really, fixed up with some cots, some hammocks, a cook stove—had begun circling the islands, ferrying passengers ashore for close-ups with the boobies and finches and sea lions. The airstrip up on the island of Baltra, left to the rats and weeds after the U.S. military shipped out at the end of World War II, was now cleaned up and reopened, bringing one flight a week from the Ecuadorian mainland. Most of the people aboard those flights were Americans. Most still are today, and if they run into problems, the person they turn to is the U.S. Consulate warden for the province of the Galápagos, a man once wanted by the FBI for draft evasion, none other than Jack Nelson.

It's been ten years now since Jack was named warden, and that's part of the reason he's risen so early this mid-January morning, to check out this march in case something happens. Given a choice, he'd just as soon skip it. He was up until two last night, working his way through a week's worth of e-mail—reservations, cancellations, invoices for kitchen supplies and laundry equipment from the mainland. He still wasn't done when he finally fell asleep.

He strolls toward the hotel's main building, a long, low-roofed lodge, its walls made of whitewashed cement blocks, its rear floor-to-ceiling windows looking out onto the ocean. The walkway is lined with artfully arranged shards of driftwood, thickets of red-blossomed bougainvillea, and dense clumps of *opuntia* cacti. Ahead, through the structure's open-screened windows, Jack can hear the clatter of pots and the laughter of women, the lilting Spanish voices of his small kitchen staff.

There are only two guests this morning, a young Japanese couple who checked in late last night. They are finishing their fresh mangoes and toast as Jack steps through the dining room door. He nods good morning, moves past the bar and the pegged-wood-and-leather furniture, the reed matting on the cement floor and the broad wall of glass that looks out onto the glistening water of Academy Bay, then ducks into his office to check the reservation book.

Good. The tour group scheduled to arrive this afternoon have confirmed. Their cruise ship, the *Lobo de Mar*, should reach its anchorage sometime around three, in the harbor outside the room where Jack now sits. Sixteen passengers. That means just about all fourteen of the Hotel Galápagos' cottages will be filled come this evening.

Maybe, Jack muses as he grabs some keys from a hook on the wall, he'll untie his skiff later on—the fourteen-footer—and take it out past Punta Estrada for some fishing. Perhaps he'll ask Fabio to join him. The guiding has been slow this week, so Fabio should be free.

Yes, Jack decides, that's what he'll do. He sticks his head in the kitchen and, in a fluent burst of Spanish, tells Betty, the cook, to plan on preparing fish for the guests' dinner tonight. Probably tuna; word is the bigeyes have been running out near Estrada.

Then he heads in toward town. It's a short stroll down the worn, brown pavers of Darwin Avenue, past the cemetery, the El Bambu boutique, and the Media Luna café, where Jack sends guests who ask where they might find a decent pizza. It's not like the pizza they may be used to back home, he warns, but for the Galápagos, he tells them, it isn't half bad.

He passes the ramshackle docks of Pelican Bay, where the slim, sleek *pangas*, painted the colors of fruit, their outboard engines droning like hornets, slice in and out of the channel, some pointed toward a day of fishing, others already returning, their holds heavy with slick, silvery *bonito* and *bacalao*.

"*Buenas,*" a small dark-haired boy says with a grin as he clambers barefoot over the black shoreline rocks to help his mother empty a basket of mullet.

"*Hola,*" answers Jack. He has seen the boy before, though he does not know his name. There was a time, not long ago, when Jack knew nearly everyone's name in this village. But no longer. There are far too many names to know.

As he approaches the hub of the waterfront, the buildings grow larger, more numerous, squeezed more tightly together. Some are two, even three stories high. There is the Banco del Pacífico, a satellite dish planted on its roof and a line of men and women—local *Galápagueños*—queued up on the sidewalk out front, waiting for the windows to open. Some are here to cash paychecks, but most carry sacks stuffed with *sucres* and U.S. dollars, the weekend's take from the tourist trade at the restaurants and shops that rim the harbor. This day the exchange rate is 7,000 *sucres* to a dollar. Two months ago it was 5,000. Two years ago it was 2,000. Next year, next *month*, say the locals, cursing the thieving politicians back on the mainland, who knows what the *sucre* will be worth? Better, they say, to take the dollars straight from the foreigners' pockets whenever you can.

It's not quite nine, and already the taxis are trolling for business, the rusted Toyotas and pale yellow pickups tapping their horns each time they pass a pedestrian. The Rincon del Alma has thrown open its shaky screen doors, and a couple of old men sit at one of its terrace tables, each nursing a cold, brown bottle of beer. Tonight, after the tour boats pull in, this café will be pulsing with customers—Swedes, Germans, and Italians, in their silk shirts and fine linen skirts. But right now the old men have it to themselves.

And here the avenue ends, at a row of souvenir shops, their makeshift shelves heavy with key chains and paperweights, their windows adorned with hand-painted T-shirts. The tourists, who step from their water taxis to the wharf here at the waterfront, are confronted with a vista that is much more a city than the village they had imagined. Houses by the hundreds slope down toward the sea like waves of tossed boxes. Freshly washed laundry pinned to rooftop-rigged clotheslines flaps dreamily in the mild ocean breeze. Bursts of bright yellow *muyuyo* blossoms and ruby hibiscus hang over dry, dusty alleys and cobblestoned streets. Powerlines dangle like webbing, looped between high, cement stanchions.

Jack hears it all the time from his guests when they first come ashore from their ships. It's all so much huger, they say, much more sprawling than the place they'd envisioned. In the brochures and ads pitched by the tourism industry to tout the Galápagos, this town doesn't exist. Nor is it seen more than in passing in the documentaries and books and magazine spreads done on these islands— such as *Sports Illustrated*'s 1998 swimsuit issue, which was shot in the Galápagos and featured supermodel Heidi Klum on its cover, posed on a remote sandy beach, her cleavage, as the headline declared, "straddling the equator."

This is the Galápagos shown to the rest of the world: a place far out there, beyond this town and this harbor, among the unpeopled coves and volcanic uplands where the tortoises creep and the scientists camp and the echoes of Darwin abound. Puerto Ayora does not fit into that picture, and so it is largely ignored.

But it's here, and anyone with eyes can see that it's growing. The main road that rises toward the north end of town, up toward those cloud-shrouded peaks, is lined by scaffolded buildings of cinderblock and stone, bleached by the sun to the mildew-gray shade of old bones. The buildings house shops and *kioscos*, dark inside but for the daylight that slants through their windows. Thrown-open doorways display hardware and clothing, groceries and toys, shelves stocked with dated goods dusted by age. On the sidewalks outside, men sip *cervezas*, women nurse babies, and children on bicycles dash madly around corners. The faces are Latin, almost all of them locals.

Jack has heard it a thousand times, and he does not disagree: The Galápagos is no longer here, say the true natives, those who have been in this village longer than the shops and the bars and the discotheques. It is still out there, they say, among the inlets and coves where the cruise ships circle, where the tourists are put ashore to hike and to swim and to sun in a place like no other on Earth, a place alive with creatures that know no fear, birds and animals that do not flee at the approach of a human. To reach out for a finch that hops into your hand, to swim among sharks gentle as dolphins—these are transcendent experiences, say those who have had them. It is still a virtual Eden out there, they say, a timeless place of balance and harmony.

But that place is no longer here, not in Puerto Ayora. And not in the other three villages on the other three islands where the people of the Galápagos dwell. There was a time, say the old-timers, and it has not been that long, when these streets were serene, when there were no sidewalks, no traffic, when a single supply ship came through perhaps four, maybe five times a year. Jack remembers those days, when months would go by between the arrival of one hotel guest and the next. He and his dad would stay busy, building or repairing, or simply launching a party that would drift on for days, friends coming together from the town and the hills, drinking and dancing and howling at the moon, diving for lobster at sunrise, sharing stories and music and rum through the course of the day, some sharing each other at night, then doing it all over again the next morning, and the next. They had beaches, *playas*, back then, but not anymore. The sand is all gone now, used for cement. The nearest *playa*, out at Tortuga, is an hour's hike west from the west end of town.

Only twenty years ago, the old-timers recall, no more than three thousand souls lived in this village. You were born here and you married here, had children and died here. Now that number is close to ten thousand in this village alone, and nearly that many again in the rest of the islands. Now more than ninety tour boats ply these waters, not the mere two dozen or so that existed only two decades ago. The crews on those boats, as well as many of the owners, are largely strangers to one another, men and women who have recently fled with their families from Quito and Guayaquil, where the streets are awash with poverty and crime and the air stinks of corruption and despair. The mainlanders have heard how these islands are booming, how the tourists flock here by the tens of thousands—sixty thousand last year alone. And so these families with so little to lose have come here as well, bringing all they own, which, the old-timers are quick to point out, is often nothing at all.

With this influx of newcomers has come an influx of crime, though not of the sort that infects the mainland. The muggings and murders and rapes routinely described on the news broadcasts beamed from the continent out to these islands through Puerto Ayora's newly installed cable television system have not yet reached the Galápagos. But there has been a sharp rise in break-ins and vandalism, mostly by teenagers who, Jack understands, know and care nothing about the ocean, who have never been in a boat other than the one that carried them here, who have never journeyed beyond this island or even outside of this town. They have never beheld the albatrosses nesting down on Española or the frigate birds mating among the rocky cliffs of Genovesa. They have never hiked through a foggy caldera in the highlands of Isabela or climbed to the lip of Fernandina's still-steaming volcanic crater. They don't know what it's like to swim with the bottle-nosed dolphins in the clear cobalt waters off Santa Fé. And if they have seen a six-hundred-pound tortoise, it would be on the road just above town, where the large lumbering beasts sometimes cross the asphalt to get to their feeding grounds on the forested slopes.

Up that very road, away from the waterfront, toward the section of the village that few tourists visit, Jack now hears chanting. Clapping and whistling. Hooting and shouts. He cannot believe it. The march has begun, on time, and without him.

He hurries to catch up. He can see them now, a throng of perhaps sixty men, women, and children, crowding the boulevard from curb to curb, walking shoulder to shoulder. They wave homemade placards and hand-scrawled signs, laughing, joking, urging the onlookers they pass—their friends and neighbors—to leave the storefronts and stoops and small dusty yards and to join them in the march.

A small girl, too young to wear the uniform of the town's main Catholic school, leaps on her bicycle and pedals into the procession. A shopkeeper locks the front door of his *farmacia* and falls into step with some friends. Block by block, by twos and threes, the crowd swells, and their rhythmic chanting grows louder.

> *"Out! Out! Out!*
> *The judge is corrupt!*
> *Our town is united!*
> *Together we struggle!*
> *Avellan! Avellan!*
> *Take him away!"*

They move north, toward the top of the town, where the homes and *bodegas* dwindle and Puerto Ayora ends but the road keeps rising, a lone ribbon of asphalt disappearing into the mist-draped peaks of the highlands. They call the mist the *garúa*, and it is almost constant up there, in the hills that form the northern horizon. Even on a morning like this, with the cloudless sky a brilliant blue and the sun beating fiercely on the shoreline below, the *garúa* hovers over the highlands like a gray shroud of cotton.

By the time the marchers reach the top of the town, their number has doubled. Jack is with them now, staying to the rear. Ahead, to his left, strides a group of biologists from the Research Station. Among them, naturally, is Godfrey Merlen. Jack had no doubt Merlen would be here. Chanting in Spanish along with the crowd, thrusting a tanned, weathered fist into the air, shocks of wild, wiry hair bursting from his head and his chin and a fiery rage filling his eyes, Merlen could seem like a madman to someone who knew no better.

But the townspeople know him, at least those who are marching this morning. They know him, although they have not read the guidebooks Merlen has written, if they have heard of his guidebooks at all—biologic rosters of the fish and animals that inhabit these waters. They have seen Merlen board the boats of the poachers, leaping like an ecologic Captain Blood onto the wet wooden decks of those dinghies to hurl their illegal catches—strangled hammerheads and mangled sea turtles—back into the ocean, slice the green mesh of the lawbreakers' nets, and curse the bandits in their native tongue.

They have all heard how this British scientist, who looks like no scientist they have ever seen, led a raid not long ago on an illicit camp on a beach out at Fernandina, where a gang of the poachers were chopping down mangroves to build the fires to cook their *pepinos.*

Pepinos. Sea cucumbers. The wormlike creatures that cover the ocean floor around these islands by the millions. Headless, tubular grubs no larger than good-sized dog turds.

A decade ago the *pepinos* meant nothing to the locals who fished the Galápagos. But then the trawlers appeared on the western horizon, massive vessels from Taiwan and Korea, hungry to fill their holds with these creatures, which are prized as a delicacy on dining tables in Hong Kong and Singapore, and as an aphrodisiac in bedrooms from Bangkok to Tokyo. The money those boats were prepared to pay—75 cents per *pepino*—put to shame the ten or so cents a pound the local fishermen earned for their traditional catches of mullet and grouper.

And so began the gold rush, as some islanders call it. Every boat that could float was put in the water to harvest the bounty. Skin divers, *pepiñeros,* took to the sea bottom in droves, breathing through crude rubber tubing as they crawled along the ocean floor, picking *pepinos* as if they were mushrooms. At first there were perhaps a hundred *Galápagueños* who became *pepiñeros.* But as the price of *pepinos* climbed toward $2 apiece by the end of the decade, and as the islanders saw that a three-man crew could make as much as several hundred dollars each in a single day—this in a nation where the average per capita annual income was less than $1,600—the business exploded. Soon there were four hundred *pepiñeros* in Puerto Ayora alone. Then more than a thousand. Most of the newer *pepiñeros* came from the mainland, but it was hard to say how many, because most worked the waters without a license.

But who needed a license? Everyone knew that the laws were a joke. Eliecer Cruz certainly knew it. When he was named the province's Park Service director three years ago, he understood all too well how the law works on these islands, which is the same way it works throughout Ecuador. The local judge, whomever he might be, sits in his office, where he receives a steady stream of visitors who pay cash for his verdicts. Here, in Puerto Ayora, the *pepiñeros*, or the mainland fisheries for whom many of them work, pay often and pay well.

And so, although laws had been reluctantly written in recent years by the Ecuadorian Congress to protect the fragile marine food chain of the *Encantadas*—the "enchanted islands"—everyone knew that the laws had no teeth. The politicians on the mainland had more pressing matters to worry about: students and Indians rioting in the streets of Quito, martial law declared in Guayaquil, an economy gone to hell with no hope in sight, an exiled madman ex-president lying poolside at a hotel in Panama City, plotting with his stooges to return to the nation he so recently pillaged.

The Ecuadorian government would have passed no laws at all were it not for the pressure that mounted from the international community of scientists and naturalists who reminded them that if they did not give a damn about the food chain in these delicate island waters, perhaps they might consider the chain of tourist dollars that would be broken if the ecotourism industry were to be alerted to the slaughter taking place. If the sea cucumbers weren't enough, warned the caretakers from afar, maybe the world would like to hear about the Galápagos sharks being butchered for their fins or the growing black-market demand for yet another Asian aphrodisiac—the penises of sea lions. The very idea of boatloads of camera-wielding tourists rounding the bend of a sun-speckled cove only to be confronted by a heap of wet carcasses with their balls hacked away—this was not good for business, not good at all.

So the Congress passed laws. But the Park Service wound up with just one boat to enforce them, a boat that came not from the government but one that was donated by an Asian billionaire with Yakuza—Japanese organized crime—connections. One boat to patrol a watery region the size of Pennsylvania (the Galápagos Marine Reserve is the second-largest area of protected ocean on Earth, next to Australia's Great Barrier Reef). And that boat rarely had enough fuel to fill its tanks. The Park Service's joke of a budget left no room for fuel, and so most days the *Guadalupe River*, an aluminum-hulled 100-footer built for sheer speed, could be seen bobbing harmlessly in the gentle harbor swells just beyond the lobby window of Jack Nelson's hotel.

It was so easy to see why, despite the laws, the *pepino* industry in these waters grew like the drug trade on the mainland. Almost overnight, sea cucumbers became the cocaine of the Galápagos, and the number of fishermen on these islands multiplied like crack dealers in the Bronx, with the same attendant violence. Locals still talk about an encounter in the spring of 1997 between a crew of *pepiñeros* and a team of park wardens who stumbled upon the poachers' clandestine camp on an Isabela beach. Guns were pulled, and one of the wardens took a bullet through the liver. He survived only because a military helicopter happened to be visiting a nearby islet, answered a radio alert, flew the fifty miles to where the man's wounded body lay, lashed the victim—Julio Lopez was his name—to the aircraft's struts (there was no room for the hemorrhaging body inside) and medevaced him back up and over the volcanic craters of Isabela and across ninety miles of open sea to a clinic on the southeastern island of San Cristobal, where he was then stabilized and rushed by plane to the mainland.

Not quite two years before that, a mob of fifty machete-wielding local fishermen invaded the Research Station itself. They were enraged by the government's latest *pepino* fishing restrictions. Which do you value more, the fishermen asked, us or these animals? For three days and nights, encouraged by a town politician urging them to break windows and sack buildings, the masked protesters brandished Molotov cocktails, threw the scientists out, then drank and played poker and waved machetes at the station's resident animals, including Lonesome George, a penned-in poster-child of sorts for the Galápagos' famed giant tortoises, the only survivor from the thousands of saddlebacks that once roamed the far northern island of Pinta. Just a year earlier, in the spring of 1994, some of these same *pepiñeros* had slaughtered seventy-two tortoises on Isabela in response to an earlier tightening of the laws—slit the poor creatures' throats and left them hanging from trees. So this threat to the station was taken seriously. Government negotiators flew out from the mainland to talk to the fishermen.

Jack remembers that scene, how surreal it all was. The masked fishermen barking in Spanish, waving tourists and scientists off the property. The roadblock erected at the entrance to the Park. The campfires that burned through the night. After three days of discussion, the officials decided to sit tight, to refuse the *pepiñeros'* demands. And with that the siege ended, on the bright early morning of its fourth day, with the protesters departing as they had arrived, swiftly, silently, via the ocean, in their *fibras*—their fiberglass dinghies.

Jack was not happy with what happened that week. It didn't help business, the dispatches going out on the news wires about guns and terrorists here in the Galápagos. But he understood the fishermen's feelings, the frustration and anger they felt watching so much money washing around them, those gleaming cruise ships berthed in the harbor, their colored deck lights twinkling each night as if it were Christmas, the hotels and restaurants sprouting like seedlings along the waterfront, their tables filled with big-spending foreigners, the bank changing hundred-dollar bills for the never-ending lines of tourists cradling sacks of souvenirs in their arms.

And what did the fishermen come home to? The more recent arrivals lived in hovels no better than what they'd left behind in the ghettos of Guayaquil. As for those who had lived here for years, many of them still slept in lean-tos and shacks made of hardwood hauled down from the highlands, rough-hewn homes built by their fathers when only their fathers were here. Those homes had seemed fine when there was nothing beside them but more of the same. Now, though, the village had become a town, and the town was becoming a city. And those homes? They now felt like slums.

Was it a crime to want more? Who could blame a man who hungered to give his wife and children and himself some of the things they saw others enjoying? To see the Europeans and *Norte Americanos*, so well dressed and wealthy as they stepped ashore from those ships, and to turn on the television—television!—and witness a world so much richer and more radiant than the one that existed on the backstreets of this village—who could blame a man for wanting some of that? So what if some sea slugs had to die to provide it?

Jack understood such emotions. He was torn by his central role in the chain of tourism that was now choking these islands and by the reverence he felt for the sanctity of this place, the closest he had come in his life to a sense of the holy. That feeling, beyond anything else, was why he had stayed here in the first place. The wonder of this untouched paradise had gripped him, crept into his soul. It wasn't just the purity that appealed to him, the ancient innocence, although that beauty was certainly something to be adored, something he expressed in his paintings and sculptures, in the odd pieces of art that adorned the walls and rafters of his hotel's lobby. That beauty was mighty, but it was these islands' harsh brutality that entranced Jack even more, the tests that a creature—every creature—had to pass to survive here.

Life had to be earned in this place. It was that simple. It had to be fought for, especially if you were human. These islands were simply not made for people. Those who came and survived understood this. They arrived armed with the strength, the resourcefulness, and most of all with the humility it took to carve out a life here. Among those who stayed and perservered, there was an unspoken respect for one another simply because they had endured, unlike the fools whose bones were scattered among those mountains and beaches, the dreamers and wanderers who had perished here over the centuries. Entranced by the primitive allure of this place, they did not comprehend its fierce lack of mercy, and so, through the unyielding calculus of indifferent nature, became casualties.

This was what separated those who belonged in the Galápagos from those who did not. Jack liked that. He had always been a man who could take care of himself. He had built this hotel, he and his father alone, cobbling it together piece by piece. There were no plumbers to call. No welders. No carpenters, except for the odd neighbor who knew how to handle a hammer and saw and might help you out. For the most part, if you needed something done, you did it yourself with whatever you had or could find on your own.

Now, though, there were plumbers in this town. And electricians—electricity! Now there were people who lived here who did not know how to do for themselves, who did not need to know. That bothered Jack. He knew that in his own way, with his hotel and its role in the growth of this town, he was part of the problem as well as of the solution.

Yes, Jack understood the townspeople's frustrations, those of the deep-rooted fishermen and those of the freshly transplanted *marginados*, the waves of newcomers to the Galápagos who have no niche at all in the islands' economy.

Eliecer Cruz understood them as well. Cruz was born and raised *Galápagueño*, on the island of Floreana, at the southern edge of the archipelago. Life there—only seventy or so people live on the entire island—is rustic even by Galápagan standards. Other natives refer to the residents of Floreana as Robinson Crusoes and shake their heads at the isolation of life in that insular place.

When Cruz was given the job of Park Service director in the spring of 1996 and announced, in his soft, unassuming voice, that he was honored to accept the responsibility of preserving the integrity of this province, no one took him seriously. This is the same speech every official gives, everywhere in Ecuador. Judges, police chiefs, bureaucrats, and, yes, Park Service directors, make speech after speech in such lofty language, then simply sell their services to the highest bidder.

But Cruz was different. No sooner did he put on the government-issue white cotton shirt and green khaki shorts of the Park Service than he overhauled his staff, sending away the mainlanders who had worked for his predecessor and hiring native Galápagans like himself as his lieutenants. Then he took that single patrol boat, the *Guadalupe River*, tuned it up, topped off its fuel tank, and actually began roaming the islands looking for lawbreakers. When his men made their first arrest, hauling in a small *panga* filled with illegally harvested black coral, eyebrows were raised. But when the town's judge immediately handed the boat back to its owners, with not even a fine imposed, the villagers shrugged. Business as usual. They watched with mild curiosity as a handful of Cruz's staff, along with a few scientists from the Station, responded to that release with a small protest, gathering in the street outside the judge's office and chanting for justice. But when the judge, a man named Avellan, came out, chiding them like children and sending them home, they went. And the townspeople just smiled. Nothing was different.

Still, Cruz kept pushing. He gathered support, went to the mainland, met with politicians and urged them to create laws that would protect these waters while also allowing the people who lived here to make a decent living. Keep the outsiders away, he told the congressmen, but take care of our own.

Then he and his staff went back to the people and talked to them about vision, about realizing that any future they might have depends upon preserving what is around them, not destroying it. The staff from the Station spread the same message, at meetings, in the schools, even in the churches, where anti-Park feelings were often the strongest. The choice, they said, does not have to be between these animals and yourselves. The fact, they said, is that one cannot survive without the other.

Some of the people listened. Not all, but some. Cruz and his wardens continued to make seizures, small arrests here and there. And the judge continued to turn around and release both the boats and their owners.

Then came the *Magdalena*. A big boat—a barge, really. A pirate vessel roaming the seas of South America and filling its hold with whatever contraband was available. No one was certain what nation it belonged to; it flew the flag of whichever country's coast it approached: Peru, Chile, Colombia, Venezuela—it didn't matter.

The *Magdalena* was flying an Ecuadorian flag on the March afternoon that it was surprised and seized in a channel between Fernandina and Isabela by the *Guadalupe River*, with the help of an Ecuadorian Air Force spotter plane. In the ship's hold were forty black plastic sacks of cooked sea cucumbers, a thousand cucumbers per sack.

That seizure made national news. Television crews from the mainland arrived in Puerto Ayora to tape the arrival of the barge and its illegal cargo. Cruz and his men made a show of unloading the huge bags of black crusty *pepinos*. The *Magdalena*'s crew was handed over to the Puerto Ayora police, and the barge was hauled into the harbor's inner lagoon, where it was anchored a stone's toss away from the souvenir shops.

Two years went past and still the barge sat there, its dark blue paint peeling from its brown rusting hull, its waterline crusted with barnacles, the chain of its anchor slick with algae, creaking as the Pacific tide rose and fell. The *Magdalena*'s crew was long gone, released almost instantly by the police upon orders from Avellan, just as everyone had expected. The barge, too, was ordered to be returned to its owners. But Cruz, not the police, was in charge of the boat, and he refused to give it up.

Now this was something new. No one had directly defied a judge in this way before. Avellan himself could not believe it. He issued another order. Again, Cruz refused. And so the judge then issued a warrant—this one for the arrest of the Park Service director himself.

With that, Cruz disappeared. Rumors flew. Some said he had fled the country. Others said he was down on Floreana, hiding at his family's highland farm. Some believed he had flown to the mainland to gather support.

Wherever Cruz had gone, he eventually returned. And when he did, he was embraced by a coalition of his staff, of scientists from the Station, and of local businessmen, including Jack Nelson. They met and talked late into the evenings, in one home or another. They finally framed a list of demands and decided that a demonstration, a march—*this* march—would be the best way to deliver them.

"Avellan! Avellan!
Take him away!"

The chant rings like an anthem as the crowd continues to swell. This is the demand the march planners agreed upon—that the judge be ordered to leave the island. Nothing less will do, they decided. Jack shares their emotions, their sense of drama. There is no way, of course, that it will actually happen. Even now, as the marchers turn back toward the center of town, with Cruz himself leading the way, flanked by members of his staff, Jack knows there is no way the judge will actually go. But that isn't the point. It's the sheer drama of simply making the demand. Jack has seen this sort of thing many times before. Here. On the mainland. Even back in Long Beach in the '60s.

He knows what these marches are really about. They're part politics, part catharsis, part street theater. A carnival of emotion. No matter how somber the subject, there is always a sense of giddiness that takes root in a crowd of this size, an infectious air of elation. You could sell refreshments if you wanted.

In fact, as the throng, now numbering close to three hundred, arrives at its destination, fanning out in front of the whitewashed two-story building that houses the office of the judge, a street vendor rolls up with his umbrella-shaded cart, breaks out his colored bottles of syrup, and begins crushing the ice for the sno-cones that will sell as fast as he can make them.

Jack finds a spot beneath the feathery limbs of a *flamboyant* tree, pulls a bottle of water from his knapsack, and takes a long swallow. He looks at the crowd. They are laughing, singing, jeering. He looks at the police arrayed on the building's front steps. There are seven of them, a fourth of the town's entire force. They are young, each dressed in gray-and-black camo fatigues and caps, combat boots on their feet, loaded pistols in their holsters. They face the crowd, expressionless. Behind them are two heavy, steel-barred doors.

Jack knows what will come next, speeches. One after another, men—all men—step forward to orate, until, finally, Cruz takes his turn. He is lighter-skinned than the park wardens who stand beside him. Where their hair is jet-black and straight, his is brown and soft. His voice is gentle, and the crowd hushes to hear him. There is no emotion in his tone, no anger. But his words are angry, and by the time he is finished, the crowd is whipped into a fury.

The mob pushes forward. The police push back. There is jostling, but it is restrained, all in slow-motion, as if it were staged. One officer loses his cap, but no one comes close to touching the doors.

Then they recede. There is no sign of life within those windows and doors, no sign that anyone is actually inside that building. The moment, whatever its purpose, seems lost. The crowd begins to break apart. Small knots form in the narrow street and in the shade. A group of young men find a spot by a wall, not far from where Jack stands. They light their Larks and their Belmonts and wait for something to happen.

A group by the steps shake their fists toward the second-floor windows. They are certain the judge is up there. They shout for him to show his face.

"Where *is* the little turd?" hollers a stout, white woman with a British lilt to her voice. She wears a ball cap and a worn, cotton smock. Sandals are strapped to her sunburned feet. Jack knows her well—Georgina Cruz, who lives with her husband, Augusto, and teenaged son, Sebastian, across the harbor, in the place the towns-people call *El Otro Lado*—"the Other Side."

"Romeo, *Romeo!*" the woman shouts toward the barred windows above. "Wherefore *art* thou?"

Jack smiles. Through the building's ground-floor windows he can see two American movie posters tacked to a wall. The posters are old, their colors bleached by the sun to a lifeless blend of purples and white. Billy Crystal. Leonardo DiCaprio. The room is a video rental shop, leased from the building's owner, just as the judge leases his office above.

The crowd mills, watches, waits. A small girl on her bicycle leans against a wall, slurping the red juice from her cup of flavored ice. Above her, in the distance, dark clouds gather beyond the highland *garúa*, billowing skyward like plumes of volcanic ash. It's raining up there in the mountains, but down here it's clear, and the midmorning heat is blistering.

Nothing is happening. The protest is all but over. Jack can feel it. But the crowd is in no hurry to leave. Most have nowhere else to be. For a few minutes more, they will joke and laugh and gossip, and then, in the same way they came together, by twos and threes, they will disperse, drifting back into the rhythm of another day.

Then there is a sudden burst of shouts, a clamor of movement up by the steps. The police look startled, alarmed. One steps back, waving his arms. Another stumbles, reaching for his holster as he falls to his knees. They are shouting in Spanish for the people to stop, to get back. But no one listens.

And then there are screams, cries of pain.

"*Jesus!*" exclaims a young man near Jack, a thin, suntanned blond wearing a torn dive shop T-shirt and a shoulder tattoo. "They're using pepper gas!"

It's true. The protesters in front are now reeling back. One, a small, wiry, brown-skinned young man, stumbles from the throng, clutching his face, gasping for air as he gropes his way out into the street.

My God, realizes Jack, it's Fabio.

In an instant Jack is beside his young friend, grabbing his forearm and guiding him into the shade of a small grocery's front door. From his knapsack, Jack pulls out his bottle of mineral water, turns Fabio's welt-mottled face toward the sky, and carefully, clinically, dribbles the cool liquid over his friend's clenched, seared eyes.

Someone yells out to build a fire. Smoke, they shout, is good for eyes burned by gas. Within seconds, a small pile of protest signs has been set afire, the yellow flames licking and crackling as the cardboard blackens and curls.

"Wow," says a small woman gazing through wire-rimmed glasses at the flames and the smoke and the crowd. Her accent is American. "It's been thirty years since I've seen something like this." Then she pauses. "At Berkeley," she says.

As Fabio's eyes, red and swollen, begin to open, yet another clamor arises from a nearby side street. A massive wooden pole appears, a log really, cut from giant tropical bamboo. It's more than twenty feet long, nearly a foot in diameter. It seems to levitate, rising above the crowd, then slides along a sea of upraised hands toward the barricaded doors.

The police hold their ground but do not resist as the pole is passed over their heads. They apparently have had enough. This fight is now the judge's, if indeed the judge is around.

A second pole appears, and the mob surges forward, its momentum bringing the full weight of their battering rams smashing into the doors' iron bars with a shattering clang. They pull back and charge again. And again. The bars begin to bend. The aged hinges loosen. And then, with one last blow, the doors fall open.

The people roar. The leaders, those in front, pour into the building's darkened front hall. Cruz is among them. Several of his staff stay behind, stationing themselves at the entrance, ordering the crowd to move back and wait while the judge is being located.

Word soon emerges that Cruz and the judge and both of their

staffs are upstairs, negotiating. For ten minutes, then twenty, the people wait. No one is about to leave.

Then, stepping from the blackness of the unlit front hall out into the bright morning sunlight, Cruz appears. He stops at the top of the steps, waving the cheering crowd silent as three of his colleagues, wearing the same Park Service uniform as he, fan out behind him like sentinels.

The judge, Cruz announces, has agreed to leave the island. The audience explodes with applause. He will be gone, says Cruz, by sunset. Another burst of cheers.

The judge, cautions Cruz, has asked only that he not be touched. And with that, Avellan appears, flanked by four of the same policemen who had earlier confronted the mob. He is a small, portly, elderly man, his snow-white hair slicked straight back on his small, globe-like head. He wears a casual tropical shirt—a *guayabera*—white, silk, expensive, untucked. In one hand he clutches a black briefcase; in the other he holds an umbrella. His shoulders are hunched. His eyes show terror.

The crowd pushes in. The police push back. An egg cuts a long, lazy arc through the air. It sails past the judge's head and breaks against the building.

Then comes another. A policeman swats it aside. A flurry of eggs and tomatoes fills the sky as the judge is rushed into a waiting pickup truck. Two policemen with shotguns in their hands leap onto the vehicle's rear bed, raising their weapons as the truck lurches away.

Now it really is over. By sunset the judge will indeed be gone, on an airplane bound for the mainland.

The street empties. A mound of black ash smolders near the curb. Yellow egg yolk oozes down the building's front wall. The iron doors dangle on broken hinges.

It's almost noon now, time to find shelter from the sun. Jack Nelson heads back to his hotel, his friend Fabio by his side. Jack has his e-mails to answer, and later he's got fish to catch for the evening meal. Then, after that, sometime this evening, he'll make a couple of phone calls. If the judge is truly gone, it would be nice to know who's going to take his place.

TWO

El Loco

NOVEMBER 2, 1999

Soldier at Baltra Airport

A bank of low, ashen clouds scuds across the northern Virginia sky, grazing the treetops as sheets of soft morning rain sweep over the gridlocked traffic below. Bumper-to-bumper headlights bend from one horizon to the other, like a necklace of wet, glimmering beads. A soft autumn breeze lifts swirls of amber leaves from roadside thickets as bleary-eyed commuters inch their sedans through a suburban crossroad called Falls Church.

Ahead to the east, across the Potomac, lies the low-sprawling skyline of Washington, D.C., where most of this traffic is bound. Drive-time radio crackles with the morning's top stories: Divers have begun searching for the wreckage of a downed Egypt Air jet in the ocean off Nantucket Island; Disney executives have announced plans to build an amusement theme park in Hong Kong.

At this asphalt intersection in downtown Falls Church, across the street from a Christian bookstore, on the second floor of a bare redbrick building, down a carpeted corridor past a row of identical doors, each marked with the nameplate of the occupant—an accounting firm, a family counseling service, a commercial realtor, a Weight Watchers franchise, the National Association of Bail Enforcement Agents—sits the office of the executive director of the Charles Darwin Foundation, Inc., a woman named Johannah Barry.

This is not a good morning for Barry. The principal at her son's elementary school is on the phone, and Barry is listening silently, her elbows propped on her desk, her lips pursed. She's a redhead, and this morning her hair is pulled back in a bun. A pair of black slacks and a vermilion sweater drape her slim, angular frame. She peers out through wire-rim glasses.

The principal talks for some time. Barry's staff, a man and two women, come and go from a set of small cubicles near the door, silently laying sheaves of documents on her desk. A framed photo of Lyle Lovett is perched on the bookcase behind her. A Polaroid of

Andy Warhol is pinned to her bulletin board. On a shelf of their own sit a neat row of videotapes, their titles hand-penned in black Magic Marker: "Incident on Tower Island"; "Sea Cukes"; "CNN 12/22/95"; "Invasion Pescadores."

The rain is falling harder now, pelting the office's lone window, which looks down on an empty parking lot and a franchised restaurant.

"I understand," Barry finally speaks, glancing out at the darkening day. "Thank you." And then she hangs up.

The papers on her desk are not heartening—news reports from Ecuador, where students and Indians are burning tires in the streets of Quito, and armed soldiers have been dispatched to guard every ATM in town. The volcanoes surrounding that capital city have been erupting for weeks now, spewing nine-mile-high columns of smoke and fine ash, closing off major roadways and shutting down the airport. Tourists waiting to fly into Quito, including dozens bound for the Galápagos, are turning away as terrorist threats have been issued by the Colombian rebel army to the north, which is incensed that Ecuador has allowed U.S. antidrug forces to establish outposts on the border between the two nations.

Just another day in the life for Barry, who is a soldier of sorts herself, an officer in the environmental army fighting to protect the fragile little cluster of islands called the Galápagos. As ecowarriors go, Barry is an odd bird. She's not really the outdoors type, never has been. She might join her husband Dave now and then for a hike up on Skyline Drive, but when he packs his gear to go climb cliffs out in Joshua Tree in the California desert—where he's headed this very weekend—he does it alone.

They've been together twenty-three years now, half of Barry's life. They got married the day after she received her master's degree in medieval literature from the University of Virginia. Her thesis, "Alchemical Parallels in Book One and Book Three of Edmund Spenser's Fairie Queene," was not the sort of work that would point toward a career in wildlife preservation. But it taught her two things: how to read with the eye of a hawk and how to write with the clarity of water. Before long, she learned that those two skills led to a third:

raising money. That was what the Weyerhauser Foundation—the timber people—asked Barry to do when they hired her to join their development branch back in the late 1970s. She and Dave were living in Seattle at the time, but before long they moved to D.C., where Barry spent the next decade carving a niche as someone with a knack for pipelining dollars into naturalist causes. The World Conservation Union, the Wilderness Society, Rails to Trails, the Belize Audubon Society, American Rivers—these groups and others enjoyed Johannah Barry's golden touch.

"There are lots of ways to be an environmental activist," she told the reporters as her reputation grew. "Some people tie themselves to trees, and that works. Some spend their time on Capitol Hill, and that works. And some of us write proposals and get the movement underwritten, and *that* works. That's what I know how to do. That's how I contribute."

Barry knew as much—or as little—about the Galápagos Islands as most people when she got a call from the Darwin Foundation in December of 1990. They wanted her, naturally, to raise cash. And naturally, before she would say yes, she needed to know what she was stepping into.

It wasn't pretty. The Foundation itself had an honorable, even noble history. It was created in 1959, the same year the nation of Ecuador declared the Galápagos Islands a national park, exactly a century after the publication of Darwin's *On the Origin of Species*. Such a park had long been a dream to an international network of scientific and environmental organizations, all of whom regarded the Galápagos as a fragile, priceless crown jewel of nature, an undisturbed petri dish of biologic adaptation and evolution, the mecca of natural scientists from every nation on Earth. To Ecuador, however, which had owned the archipelago since annexing it in 1832 (three years before young Charles Darwin passed through), this cluster of volcanic outcrops had long been little more than a worthless pile of rocks. It had provided a handy garbage dump, a nice target for Ecuador's small navy to take artillery practice, and a convenient location for penal colonies. Other than that, as far as the

Ecuadorian government was concerned, the Galápagos Islands were essentially useless.

It would seem that somehow the Ecuadorians were suddenly struck by the light when they made the move to create that Park in 1959. But they would never have done so if wads of cash—more specifically, the promise of tourist dollars—hadn't been waved in their faces. The word "conservation" meant virtually nothing at that time to the military generals, bureaucrats, and businessmen who controlled this country, the second smallest nation in South America, roughly the size of Nevada. These power brokers cared little about the esoteric needs and desires of the foreign scientists wringing their hands over the fate of the Galápagos. The question that mattered to the Ecuadorians was, what were *they* supposed to get out of this deal? The answer, included in the very language of the charter that was eventually written for the Park—a charter hammered out behind closed doors by representatives of the Ecuadorian government and by leaders of an international coalition of conservationists that included UNESCO's Julian Huxley, a German ecovisionary named Irenaus Eibl-Eibesfeldt, and an American zoologist named Robert Bowman—was tourism.

Until then, the only tourists who visited the Galápagos were occasional millionaire yachtsmen bound west toward the Marquesas Islands. They would pull into a cove, drop anchor, snap a few photos, maybe swim with the sea turtles. They were free, if they had the room and the resources, to grab an iguana or two, a flamingo, or even, God forbid, a tortoise to take home with them as a living—or dead—souvenir. Anything they liked. Rules and restrictions were few, and enforcement was nonexistent.

Outrageous, said the scientists, that these precious islands should remain such a killing ground, even as humankind was launching missiles into space. A treasure such as the Galápagos should be closed off to humans forever, they said. The planet was shrinking, they warned, and places like this, pockets of nature still virtually untouched by human hands, must be protected, preserved at all costs.

The Ecuadorians saw things a bit differently. If they had *their* way, if the forecasts of a tourist boom just around the corner were correct, the best use of these islands would be to throw them wide open, allow the construction of luxury hotels, beachfront cabanas, roadways up to volcanic overlooks, with cafés and restaurants perched on the craters of those mist-enveloped peaks. The Caribbean couldn't hold a candle to something like this.

The agreement finally reached in that summer of 1959 was a compromise. The ninety-seven percent of the islands still uninhabited at that time would remain so forever, patrolled and protected by the government of Ecuador. The Galápagos National Park Service would be created to provide that protection. The newly formed Charles Darwin Foundation, spearheaded by a Belgian professor named Victor Van Straelen (which explains why the group's operational headquarters were placed in Brussels and why, to this day, the King of Belgium puts his signature on all CDF statutory procedures) would be permitted to establish a "Research Station" on the islands, a command center for the handful of scientists who fanned out each year to conduct studies there. The Station would also serve as a watchdog, helping the Park Service protect this natural treasure. The three percent of the Galápagos where people lived— those four fishing settlements and a smattering of highland farms— would be free to go on as they always had.

For a time, things went as intended. The seedling ecotourism industry indeed began to take shape, in much the same way as both sides had foreseen. The Foundation had proposed early on that a system of boat-touring be created, with the vessels serving as self-contained hotels and restaurants. Along with its crew and passengers, each ship would carry at least one naturalist guide, trained and certified by a coalition of National Park and Research Station instructors. These guides would accompany each group of visitors as they journeyed ashore. Specific landing sites would be established, to provide the tourists with a wide range of experiences while disturbing the islands as little as possible: Only eight percent of the islands' 4,500 square miles of land would be open to tour groups.

The Ecuadorian government, in exchange for agreeing to such restrictions, created a Park "entrance fee," collected in cash from each visitor. That money, along with the taxes and licensing fees paid by the tour boats, would go straight to the mainland and into the government coffers, where it would supposedly then be funneled back to protect and maintain the islands.

Not a bad plan—on the face of it.

But things haven't turned out quite as planned, which surprises no one with even the slightest knowledge of what a cesspool the government of Ecuador is and always has been. On the face of it, Ecuador should be racing headlong into First World status rather than mired as it is in the muck of Third World disarray and confusion. It has the agriculture: verdant plantations of coffee and bananas, sugar, and cocoa. Its forests are thick with timber; besides being the world's largest exporter of bananas, Ecuador also produces more balsa wood than any nation on the planet. The country's coastline, fed by frigid Antarctic currents, embraces some of the richest fishing waters in the world, especially for shrimp. Minerals, particularly gold, are abundant. Vast deposits of oil, discovered in the 1960s beneath the Amazon forests along the nation's eastern border, have pumped billions of dollars into . . . well, into *somebody's* pockets.

And then there is tourism. The sheer geography of Ecuador has long been a beacon for travelers. From the snow-coned peaks of the inland Andes, to the rain forests, to the ancient towns and cities rich with their blends of Indian and Spanish cultures, to the beaches along the coast, and—most significantly, as they have emerged since the 1960s—to the Galápagos Islands, Ecuador has established itself as a prime destination for South American vacationers. More than half a million tourists cross its borders each year.

With such riches, there seems to be no reason for this nation to be spiraling downward like the swirl in a flushing toilet. No reason, that is, except for a government that has become so horrifically convoluted and corrupt that onlookers have taken to calling this country "Absurdistan."

Ecuador is supposed to be a democracy. It has been since 1973, when its military rulers, who drafted that '59 deal with the Darwin

Foundation, handed the government over to the people. It has a constitution. It has courts. It has a congress and a president, all directly elected by the nation's roughly thirteen million citizens. But in survey after survey conducted during the past thirty years, Ecuador has consistently ranked among the ten most corrupt countries in the world.

Estimates are that eighty-five percent of Ecuador's wealth belongs to roughly fifteen families, most notably the Noboa clan, whose fortune was built during the mid-twentieth century on bananas (this is, indeed, a "banana republic"). Today, the Noboas have not only cornered the country's fruit market, but they also own several hundred Ecuadorian businesses, ranging from banks to department stores to shipping conglomerates.

Little of the cash flowing into the bank accounts of families like the Noboas is cycled back into the nation's economy. Tax collection in Ecuador is a joke. The rich avoid paying by bribing inspectors, hiding ownership of property, and spiriting away millions of undeclared dollars into overseas deposits. The poor, watching this cash drift away while they receive next to nothing in terms of government support—education, health care, land reform—refuse as well to pay taxes, creating a downward spiral of evaporating public resources and services.

Stoking these flames of instability and corruption is the office of the presidency itself. Typically, an Ecuadorian presidential candidate campaigns as a populist, seizing on public unrest, aligning himself against the rich who control the congress, and promising the poor majority of Ecuadorians that he (and it is always a "he") will overhaul the system with reforms and justice. Once he takes office, he is either overwhelmed and ultimately rejected by the fractured, feuding congress, or he simply joins the system and lines his own pockets as swiftly as he can during the time he has, which is usually not much. The Ecuadorian public is as impatient as it is passionate. As soon as they see little or no change occurring in their own largely lamentable lives, the people, typically with the encouragement of the congress, take to the streets, call for the president's head, and begin hunting for another.

More often than not, their behavior is justified. The roster of Ecuadorian presidents during the past quarter century includes a dizzying array of lunatics and thieves, spinning in and out of the presidential palace as if it has a revolving door. One, a white-haired heavy drinker named Leon Cordero, who held office in the mid-1980s, went nowhere without an automatic pistol—"my best friend," he called it—openly strapped on his hip. The low point of Cordero's term in office was when he was kidnapped by his own troops, of whom he was supposedly commander in chief.

Ecuador has had as many as three presidents in one day. Few have survived an entire term. But none can compare to the one they call *El Loco*, or "the Crazy One," a former mayor of Guayaquil named Abdala Bucaram.

"I do as I damn well please," Bucaram spat at the press and the public when he was criticized in the mid-1980s for extorting payments from Guayaquil's wealthiest businessmen during his tenure as that city's mayor. Those charges of corruption finally chased him out of the country in 1990. It took six years for Bucaram to return, but when he did, it was with a bang. He launched possibly the most bizarre campaign for a nation's presidency in the history of man.

Rotund, balding, sporting a tightly trimmed moustache reminiscent of Hitler's (he did, in fact, once declare that *Mein Kampf* was among his favorite books), the forty-four-year-old candidate took to the presidential hustings and . . . sang, backed by a Uruguayan rock band. He toured the poorest provinces of the nation by bus, passing out free bags of rice, his face dripping with real tears as he emotionally denounced the "oligarchy" that was running the nation into the ground and derided the current administration as a herd of "burros." It was a classic populist campaign, spiced with Bucaram's blatant showmanship.

"Do you want me to sing or talk?" he would ask the roaring crowds at each rally. They would always shout back for him to sing. His unabashed whiskey swilling and skirt-chasing only made the cheers louder. Bucaram won that 1996 election in a landslide, carrying twenty of the nation's twenty-one provinces.

Bucaram as a candidate, however, was nothing compared to Bucaram as a president. In the classic tradition of patronage that typifies embryonic democracies and that plagues Ecuador to this day, Bucaram's first act was to fill his cabinet with family and friends. He appointed his brother Adolfo, who had no political experience to speak of, as minister of social welfare. He put his eighteen-year-old son, Jacob, in charge of the customs service (the Ecuadorian Customs Service has always been a lucrative channel for bribes and kickbacks), then threw a lavish party six months later (with reporters and photographers invited) to celebrate the boy "earning" his first million dollars. He pardoned and brought home from exile in Panama his sister, Elsa, who, like him, was also a former mayor of Guayaquil and, like him, had fled the country several years earlier in the face of charges that she had stolen millions from that city's vaults. He named his best friend, Alfredo Adum, a man who made his own tainted fortune in Guayaquil's notorious La Bahía black market district, as minister of energy, then immediately dispatched Adum to spring Bucaram's brother Gustavo from a police station where Gustavo had been held after being found in a stolen Jeep outside the U.S. Consulate's office. (The Jeep, it turned out, had been used extensively during Bucaram's campaign.)

Upon taking office, Bucaram immediately shunned the presidential palace—"too gloomy," he called it—and moved his family and a cadre of close friends into a cluster of suites in Quito's most expensive hotel, instructing the manager to bill his personal account rather than the government.

And then Bucaram partied. He skipped a cabinet meeting to spend an afternoon drinking and dancing with Ecuador's "Miss Banana." He cut a music video featuring himself crooning a tune titled "A Madman Who Loves." He invited Ecuadorian-born Lorena Bobbitt to the presidential palace and hailed her as a "a national heroine" for cutting off her husband's penis. "She would be a better ambassador to the world for Ecuador than anybody we've got," he proclaimed to the press. "I welcomed her to the palace, just as I would have welcomed the Pope."

When Bucaram's energy minister, Adum, stirred up a ruckus by detailing his sexual appetite to an Ecuadorian magazine reporter ("I would have liked to have lived in the caveman era when there was more freedom, less prejudice. Then if I liked a woman I could grab her by the hair and drag her off to my cave and eat her."), the president defended his good friend by proclaiming his own healthy lust. "I admit I love women," said the married commander in chief. "Besides, what's so bad? What would be terrible would be if I loved *men*."

Bucaram's act was entertaining for a while, but soon it wore thin. Contrary to his campaign promises, the inept administration he assembled simply worsened the lot of Ecuador's poor, few of whom were earning the then-minimum salary of $30 a month. And he alienated the already splintered congress with his embarrassing behavior and his erratic handling of the nation's economy. By early 1997, the people took to the streets by the hundreds of thousands, banging pot covers, burning garbage, and demanding the resignation of *El Loco*. Forty-four of the eighty-two members of the congress responded by voting to remove him from office for "mental incapacity." The Ecuadorian supreme court issued a warrant for Bucaram's arrest on grounds of misuse of presidential funds, but by then, after a mere six months in office, Bucaram had already skipped the country. He fled to Panama, taking with him between $100 and $300 million of the government's money and leaving the manager of that chic Quito hotel with more than $50,000 in unpaid bills.

A new president named Jamil Mahuad was elected that same year, prompting hopes among many observers that decades of governmental rot and ruin in Ecuador might finally be turned around. Mahuad, a former mayor of Quito, was Harvard-educated, dignified, and respected as an honest, effective public servant. The candidate he defeated that summer, banana tycoon Alvaro Noboa, was supported loudly and strongly by the exiled Bucaram, who was now spending his days playing blackjack and lying by the pool at a Panama City hotel famous for taking in deposed despots. (Among recent guests who have enjoyed asylum in the sweet sunshine of this Central American sanctuary are Haitian strongman Raoul Cedras, accused of hundreds of killings committed by troops under his command, and former Guatemalan President Jorge Serrano, who packed his bags in 1993 after a Guatemalan court accused him of lifting $22 million from a presidential fund.)

But Bucaram's backing wasn't enough to give his good friend Noboa the presidency. Instead, the Ecuadorian public offered the forty-nine-year-old Mahuad his chance. In his inaugural address, Mahuad raised hopes by pledging to create nearly a million new jobs, to build new housing for a quarter-million of the nation's people, to improve education, and to bring water and sewage services to the many towns and neighborhoods throughout Ecuador that did not have them, including those in the Galápagos.

Less than a year later, however, Mahuad's popularity was already bottoming out. The belt-tightening he demanded in order to restore some solidity to the nation's ever-more-worthless *sucre* was too painful for most Ecuadorians to endure. Mahuad was not stealing from them. He did not fill the government with members of his family. But neither was he able to stabilize the sinking value of his nation's currency. Day by day, thieving political leaders and corporate executives continued to sink their teeth into their own nation's coffers, transferring millions of U.S. dollars into overseas bank accounts, with more than a few of those accounts being in Miami. Economic sirens sounded throughout the country. International newspaper reports described Ecuadorian banks defaulting in droves on foreign loans, to the point where the cost of bailing them out came to equal a third of the country's gross domestic product. In response to the crisis they had created themselves, the bankers jacked up their interest rates to nearly 150 percent, prompting individual Ecuadorians to descend like rabid dogs on their shrinking savings accounts, pulling their devalued *sucres* out of the banks and stuffing them in private safety boxes or under mattresses in their bedrooms.

This is the situation that confronts Johannah Barry as she riffles through her paperwork on this rainy autumn morning. It is the situation she foresaw when she was hired by the Darwin Foundation back in the spring of 1991. It was clear even then that the Galápagos were under siege on a variety of fronts. Tourism had exploded during the 1970s and '80s, and with it had grown issues of crowding, control, and safety. Projections made in the 1960s had warned that no more than 12,000 tourists could ever visit these islands in a single year without causing damage; by 1990 more than 40,000 people a year were boarding those tour boats. Where a study done in the early 1970s warned that these waters could safely sustain no more than fifty such boats at most, *ever*, by the turn of the '90s more than sixty vessels were licensed to tour the archipelago, with more being added each year.

Some of those ships carried but four or five passengers; others were full-fledged cruise liners, with swimming pools, elevators, carpeted dining rooms, lavish buffets, and live music. More than a few of those ships, large and small, were hardly seaworthy, and the Ecuadorian Navy inspectors responsible for licensing them were notoriously inept. The results were occasional nightmares, such as the *Bartolomé* disaster.

The *Bartolomé* was a seventy-four-footer, fitted for sixteen passengers, which was what she was carrying on the evening of October 26, 1990. It was around four A.M. The guests were asleep in their berths below deck, and the boat was moving from Genovesa, where its passengers had spent that day hiking, to the island of Baltra. This is how almost all Galápagos tour boats travel—at night. When the sun sets, they are at one island; when it rises, they are at another. In between, while the guests sleep, the ship sails.

But on this night the passengers on the *Bartolomé* were awakened not by the gentle voices of the crew, but by the stench of oily smoke in pitch-black darkness, the sounds of clamoring on deck, and slivers of flickering light crackling through the ceilings above them.

The boat was on fire. What none of these passengers knew when they'd booked this tour months earlier, was that the *Bartolomé* had caught fire several times before. Those mishaps had been electrical, nothing to worry about according to the inspectors who continued to license the ship and allow it to sail. The boat's owner, a woman well known on the islands, was "ordered" after each incident to fix the ship's wiring. In response, she not only ignored the repairs but did not even bother to replace the burnt hull; she simply had her crew paint over the scorched, blackened wood.

The fire that began that October evening was sparked by a short circuit in that unrepaired wiring. The crew, rather than disturb the sleeping guests, tried quelling the flames with extinguishers. When that didn't work, they panicked, flung the extinguishers aside, reached for the boat's lifejacket supply, and began buckling the jackets on themselves.

A dinghy was tied to the stern of the ship, and the first man to board it was the captain. By the time the lifeboat was loaded with crew and those passengers lucky enough to climb out through the flames—some wearing pajamas, others half-naked, burned, and in shock—the heat was too intense to untie the line securing the skiff to the ship. They had to wait for the fire to melt it away. The last man off was an American guide named Richard Polatty who, unlike the crew, had stayed aboard to save what passengers he could.

As the survivors looked on in horror from their *panga*, they could hear the screams of people still trapped inside the boat's burning, buckling shell. One passenger burst out from below, his body in flames, his arms flailing as he stood for a moment, outlined against the night sky, before collapsing to the deck.

Six people perished that night; an Austrian couple, an Ecuadorian crew member, and three women from the United States. Lawsuits ensued from the survivors of the Americans, but in the tangled legal and political web that connects two nations like the United States and Ecuador, those lawsuits vanished like smoke. To this day, the woman who owned the *Bartolomé* is still running cruises in the Galápagos. Her insurance money from that loss allowed her to buy a bigger boat.

Tour boat safety remains a hot-button issue in the islands. One or two go down every year . . . the *Albacora,* the *Resting Cloud,* the *San Juan.* The list goes on and on. But just as important to Johannah Barry and the Darwin Foundation, to the scientists manning the Station, to the Park wardens patrolling those forests and shores, and to anyone with the slightest concern for the fate of these islands, is the impact on the Galápagos not from the tourists or the $120-million-a-year industry built around them, but from the people who inhabit this place and will do anything they must to survive. That small handful of souls who called these islands home in 1959 now numbers close to 20,000, a figure undreamed of when the officials who created this Park allowed that slivery three percent of inhabited land to remain so. Even more mind-numbing are predictions that the Galápagos population, which has been growing at a rate of six percent a year for ten years, will swell to more than 30,000—half again what it is today—by the year 2010.

It is these people, the residents of the Galápagos themselves, who hold the fate of these islands in their hands. Or so virtually everyone with a stake in the future of this place believes. They all say that the people who inhabit those four seaside communities are the best hope for these islands' salvation. But they are also the greatest threat. Outsiders—from the burgeoning worldwide ecotour industry to international industrial fisheries to the mainland Ecuadorian businessmen and politicians eager to get their slice of the Galápagan pie—ceaselessly bang at the door of these islands, but it is the islanders themselves who choose whether and how to let them in. It is the Galápagos people who decide whether to make these outside forces their partners, their foes, or a combination of both.

Right now, by all indications, they are making these forces their partners. Barry can spread out a map on her large conference table and point out two fronts in the war that she and her colleagues are fighting.

"This is where the people are," she says, tapping her forefinger on the town of Puerto Ayora. "And *this*," she says, sliding her hand over to the western island of Isabela and the village of Puerto Villamil, "is where the trouble is."

The people she refers to are the flash flood of migrants who have arrived from the Ecuadorian mainland during the past ten years, half of whom have settled in Puerto Ayora. The "trouble" is the rampant introduction of life-forms—animals, plants—that don't belong among these islands, along with the wholesale slaughter of life-forms that do. These are the Foundation's top two concerns at the moment: "Getting rid of what's there," says Barry, "and stopping what's coming in."

"What's there" are nonindigenous animals (feral goats, rats, dogs, cats and pigs), insects (wasps, cockroaches, fire ants), and plants (*mora* blackberry vines, lantana, quinine and guava trees) introduced over the years by unthinking or uncaring humans. Like toxic waste, these life-forms have oozed out across the islands, wreaking havoc among the native wildlife that get in their way. The goat problem on Isabela alone has become an apocalyptic nightmare relatively overnight. Just seventeen years ago, scientists were alarmed by the appearance of a handful of goats left behind on the northern part of the island by local fishermen. Today, the feral goat population of Isabela Island numbers more than one hundred thousand. Hillsides that were once lush with green foliage now stand denuded, stripped bare by ravenous leaf-eating goats, and littered with the carcasses of dehydrated, malnourished tortoises.

Mounting counterattacks to such assaults costs money, much more than the dues collected from the memberships of the web of well-meaning organizations created worldwide to support the Galápagos, groups ranging from the Friends of the Galápagos to the Darwin Foundation itself. And that's where Barry comes in. Her fund-raising targets are the heavy hitters—international agencies and organizations for whom a couple of million dollars is no great shakes. Sitting on her desk this very morning is a grant for $10 million from a group called the Global Environmental Facility Fund. That money has almost made its way through the bureaucratic pipeline. When it does, the Darwin Foundation will send it down to help fund the extermination of those Isabela goats, to help pay for the helicopters, sharpshooters, automatic weapons, and supplies for dozens of ground troops that will constitute the saturation-spray assault on that island. The "eradication," as the scientists call it, is not set to actually begin until the fall of 2002, but word has slipped out, and animal rights groups in several nations have already begun to launch protests against the slaughter of the innocent creatures—just one more headache Barry and her colleagues must deal with.

They're in a tough situation, delicately balancing themselves on a tightrope between diplomacy and the truth. Their priority, of course, their very reason for being, is the preservation and restoration of these islands. It's helped that international organizations such as UNESCO, which declared the Galápagos a "world heritage site" in 1978, thereby throwing the considerable weight of the United Nations behind efforts to preserve the islands, have over the years joined the battle. But what makes things sticky is the unfortunate fact that the primary threat to the mission of all these agencies (the Darwin Foundation and all of the others) is the ineptness, instability, and ignorance of the powers-that-be who control the nation to which these islands belong.

It was not until 1998 that the Ecuadorian government reluctantly responded to the burgeoning crises in the Galápagos by passing a package of legislation that had real teeth to it. The Special Law, as it is called, is aimed at such issues as stemming the flood of immigrants from the mainland, extending the authority of the Park Service, educating the islanders about the necessity of conserving the resources that too many of them have been plundering, placing limits on local fishing, widening the boundaries that protect the islands' waters from industrial fleets, and establishing an effective quarantine system to block the invasion of nonindigenous plants and animals.

These laws faced stiff resistance from some Ecuadorian congressmen aligned with such powerful lobbying forces as those mainland industrial fishing fleets, which have sharpened their teeth for decades at the prospect of casting their longlines and drift nets into the rich waters of the Galápagos. Such fleets became absolutely voracious at the turn of the '90s when their own coastal waters—like heavily fished waters all over the world—became depleted and they had to look elsewhere for prey. Those forces continue to work in direct opposition to the goals of people such as Barry and her colleagues, the scientists down at the Research Station, the Park Service staff, and those among the islanders committed to protecting what remains of the Galápagos' purity.

Few of these people can openly criticize the true sources of their problems and fears (the politicians and private businessmen to whom the islands mean nothing but short-term profit) because it is by the permission of those same institutions and individuals that these outsiders are even allowed to be there. The very existence of the Station depends entirely on the good graces and support of an Ecuadorian government that is riddled by bribes and backroom deals. It could change hands at the snap of a finger. It is, at the moment, facing an economy in utter collapse. And it is reeling from a recent war with Peru on one border and continual clashes with Colombian guerrillas on another. The Galápagos remain low on the list of Ecuador's priorities, but still, people like Johannah Barry must mind every word that they say—at least openly—lest they anger the bureaucrats, who, for all their rancor, still control these islands. The last thing anyone wants is for an angry Ecuadorian administration to repeal those hard-won laws or even worse, and entirely conceivable, to simply throw all the foreigners out, putting the Galápagos back where they were fifty years ago.

None of this makes Barry's job any easier. She was heartened, on the one hand, to hear about that protest march down in Puerto Ayora at the start of this year. It was encouraging to see the islanders themselves, at least some of them, taking a stand for their own future. Who could have imagined that they would actually throw that judge—what was his name, Avellan?—off the island?

But on the other hand, it's been ten months since then, and the judge still has not been replaced. No one knows who will eventually fill his seat. It could be someone even worse. Avellan has powerful allies on the mainland, and they were angered at his ouster. Retribution is not out of the question.

So the march was a mixed blessing, certainly for Barry. It's hard asking for money under such unsteady circumstances. In fact, on this November morning, murmurs of concern are arising from some of the islands' chief benefactors, who are alarmed at recent events in the Galápagos and at the increasing shakiness of the Mahuad presidency. They're happy to give money to help protect those islands, but if they can't be assured of where that money will actually wind up; if they can't be certain that it won't be swept up overnight by the greedy hands of corrupt island officials or by a new national regime in the wake of a coup—an entirely possible scenario, and one that has played itself out all too often—well, then they may just want to hold back for a while, until things settle down.

But things are not settling down. The protests in the capital are growing more intense each day, as the last Christmas of the century approaches, and the Indians and peasant farmers and oil field workers continue to pour into Quito, camping in the parks and the streets and demanding that Mahuad step down. The nation's top military leader, a general named Carlos Mendoza, just this week made a less-than-reassuring statement to the press. "The elements which make up the structure of the state," said the general, "are under threat to the point where the possibility of its survival is under question."

Meanwhile, the volcanoes continue to burst open, with each morning's newspaper carrying red alert warnings for the people of Quito to stay in their homes. To the north and east, the Colombians are stretching their tentacles further into Ecuador each day. Just last month, four tourists and eight oil workers were kidnapped in the jungle near the Colombian–Ecuadorian border, where American-financed oil operations are centered. The Colombians are unhappy about any American presence in Ecuador at all, and their warnings have lately turned into action. The U.S. Embassy in Quito is concerned enough that a bulletin has been drafted, warning American travelers to steer clear of this country. The bulletin has not yet been issued, but with Christmas approaching and the millennial New Year after that, the warning is ready to go.

Just one more thing to keep Johannah Barry awake tonight.

THREE

Año Viejo

Isla Santiago

NEW YEAR'S EVE, 1999

Christy Gallardo

Midnight is not yet an hour away, and already the streets of Puerto Ayora are in flames. The fires cast flickering shadows across the shuttered fronts of the village's shops and *bodegas*. The broad fronds of the coconut palms and the feathery branches of the *flamboyant* trees glimmer against the overarching blackness of the Pacific sky.

The flames are fed by rag-stuffed effigies of the politicians and bankers, the oilmen and fruit barons, the dealmakers and millionaires on the mainland who, as far as these islanders are concerned, are robbing the people of Ecuador blind. Just one Christmas ago, the *sucre* had seemed to bottom out at 7,000 to a dollar. No one could imagine it sinking any lower. But now, tonight, it is at 20,000 with no bottom in sight.

No one can keep pace. The prices on the menu at the Garrapata restaurant down by the harbor have been rewritten so often they are now inscribed on tape, for easy removal. For tourists, of course, this has become a bonanza. A T-bone steak dinner, the meat sizzling and thick, its seared edges draped off the plate, is selling this night at the Garrapata for 75,000 *sucres*—less than four dollars. Including trimmings.

The tourists, mostly Americans, snap photos of one another posing with their insanely cheap meals. Just twelve days earlier, the U.S. Embassy in Quito had closed in response to threats from a vaguely identified Marxist organization, most likely attached to the Colombians. A warning had been issued citing "credible information that terrorist attacks are planned specifically targeting U.S. citizens during the period before New Year's . . ."

Undeterred by the danger, these travelers have come, and their reward is now spread before them. They laugh and they crow and they order more beers, while the locals walk past drinking beers of their own. Or jugs of red wine. A few carry jars filled with *puro*, the fiery, clear moonshine distilled from the cane that grows up in the highlands. Their faces, glinting crimson and gold in the glare of the firelight, are ecstatic. Packs of them pass, heaving like waves in a heavy sea, shouting and singing, lurching one way, then another. The din of their glee echoes out over the harbor.

The thick scent of cologne and perfume merges with the stench of smoke and sweat, of liquor and sex, as the thump of Latin rap booms from a pair of speakers perched atop a battered pickup parked down by the wharf. There, by the waterfront, a couple embraces in a darkened alley; two teenagers, her back pressed against an adobe wall, her eyes squeezed shut, one leg wrapped tightly around the boy's thigh as he buries his face in her neck. A stereo pulses from the window of a nearby villa: "*Sí, señor! . . . Sí señor! . . . Sí señor!*"

A man dressed as a woman, a widow—a *viuda*—his lips painted pink, his sun-beaten face framed by an ungodly, blond wig, his thick clumsy body squeezed into a tight black minidress and his feet wobbling in a pair of stiletto heels, stumbles from person to person, cradling a plastic infant in one arm and thrusting out an open palm with the other. This is a tradition, men dressed as *viudas* on New Year's Eve, and this man is insistent, wailing in mock misery as he weaves through the crowd, cornering passersby as if he really is the widowed mother he pretends to be on this night of nights. Around him race children, licking candy and ice cream, screaming with delight as they chase one another through the shadows in the utter abandon of this forbidden hour.

They call this night *Año Viejo*, the "Old Year." Among these islands, across this nation, throughout this entire culture, it is a tradition. The effigies, the *muñecos*, are reminders—some goodhearted, gleeful; others fierce, filled with rage—of issues and events of the year just gone by. Tonight the effigies are sadly familiar, hardly different from last New Year's Eve.

Across the street from the police station and the jail, arranged like a grotesque nativity scene, stands a figure of President Mahuad, pink-faced, leering, propped by a curb, wearing a garish tuxedo, grinning and showing the way to a stuffed, smiling banker lugging a briefcase bulging with *sucres*, bound for a chartered flight to Miami.

Up by the hospital, near a rusted chain fence, sits a faux fishing trawler fashioned from cardboard and scraps of old wood, a hooked hammerhead figurine dangling from its bowsprit, a dead sea turtle and tuna pulled onto its deck. All of them are smeared with red paint like blood, while a figure of Uncle Sam stands nearby, counting out dollars to pay to the pirates. The word "MANTA," the Ecuadorian port city that's home to the nation's largest industrial fishing fleets, is painted on the boat's stern.

But it's not only mainlanders who suffer the taunts of the villagers' creations. The gas man, Lenin Ortiz, who runs the petrol pumps up at the north end of town, the only gas station in the entire Galápagos, is there by the curb, his likeness propped in a manger of straw, an extortionist's grin smeared on his coal-black papier-mâché face, a gas nozzle clenched in his fist like an upraised saber. The black islanders call him *Familita*—"Loving Little Family"—because more than a few are his relatives. For years now, *Familita* has managed to charge his customers for fifteen gallons of petrol each time he fills their twelve-gallon tanks, pocketing the difference for himself and his kin.

Even Eliecer Cruz, the Park Service director, is not spared on this night. An elaborate booth, with a painted backdrop of erupting volcanoes, displays serape-cloaked Indians, the word *"ILEGAL"* scrawled on their backs, sneaking through customs while effigies of the islands' immigration officials and Park Service wardens—Cruz's men—swig bottles of wine and clutch handfuls of money.

Down below, in the star-speckled harbor, dozens of yachts and cruise ships swing at anchor. Strings of twinkling holiday lights line their masts as a ceaseless parade of water taxis crawls among them, crammed with tourists eager to join the celebration in town, to ring in the new millennium, here on the belly of the planet.

To the tourists, this *Año Viejo* is impressive. But to Christy Gallardo, it's just one more sign that the islands are truly going to hell in a handbasket. Five, ten years ago, this show was really something to see, she says. Back then, the townspeople put their *souls* into it. They'd get started days before New Year's, constructing intricate, elaborate creations that would blow your mind.

"But now, well *geez*," says Christy, "most of these things weren't thrown together until this *afternoon!*" They look like they were put up by drunks—which, when she comes to think of it, most of them were. Of course, she can't really blame them. With no money, no morale, with the country falling apart *again*, with the villagers seriously talking about bringing back Bucaram—New Year's masks of *El Loco*'s tear-stained face, at a buck apiece, are outselling Mahuad's, two to one, in the shops along Darwin Avenue—well, there's really not much juice left for a celebration.

Even Christy's son Jason's booth is not much to look at. Jutting out from the bambooed entrance to the Galápason nightclub is a massive, sea-blue, papier-mâché wave with a nice-looking curl at the top and a longboard attached to its face and the words *"CONTAMINACIÓN VISUAL"* painted on a sign to the side. The phrase is a jab at the Park Service, which lately has been hounding Jason and his buddies, warning them to stay away from the waters of the outer islands, telling them the tourists didn't pay all that money to come down here and see surfboards.

Some people think it's kind of amusing that Jason, a thirty-one-year-old man, a grownup, for god's sake, spends so much of his time with the teenage surf rats who trail in his wake. He's talented, educated, and good-looking, with those tumbling dark ringlets and that carved Tarzan body. Why, ask some of the townspeople, would he waste so much of his time with kids who could be his little brothers?

The answer is simple, says Jason. He loves to surf. He *lives* to surf. And as far as he's concerned, those aren't kids climbing into his speedboat every time he takes it out to the breaks at Las Palmas or over to Cerro Gallina. They're surfers, and that's all that matters.

Christy had hoped to see Jason tonight, but he's nowhere in sight. Word is he's hooked back up with his girlfriend, Monica—*again*, Christy says, shaking her head. Tomorrow, first thing in the morning, he's setting sail with some friends for the island of San Cristobal. They've been planning this trip for months, a four-day getaway to some of the biggest waves in the Galápagos. They say there's a swell moving down from the northwest, from Hawaii. Within the next twenty-four hours there should be double-over-head sets breaking off the north coast of Cristobal. Jason was so excited earlier tonight that he could hardly eat.

Christy's husband, José-Luis, used to surf this sea when he was a young man. At the end of a long day of work, and they were all long days of work back then, José and a few of his friends would grab some nice planks of wood, maybe some balsa, and swim out off the point where the Research Station now sits, then ride the waves in.

Of course that was some forty years ago, when José was working for Christy's dad, Forrest, over at the hotel. José did everything back then: plumbing, carpentry, sheet metal work. Christy will never forget the first time she set eyes on him. It was the summer of '67. Her dad was dying, or so Forrest said in the brief message he sent home to the States. So Christy came quick, flew down from L.A. to Quito, where her brother Jack joined her, and that's where they found out their father just had a bad case of kidney stones. He would be all right. He just *felt* like he was dying.

Since she'd traveled that far, Christy decided to go all the way with Jack and Forrest and hang out on the islands for the summer. The day she arrived on the Research Station's sailboat, the *Beagle II*, a dinghy motored out into Academy Bay to greet them. At its stern was a small, hard-muscled Ecuadorian man with a smile to die for.

By the time Christy packed up to return to L.A.—Jack would be staying behind to work the hotel with their father—José-Luis was packing up, too. Christy was twenty-three at the time, three years older than Jack and seven years younger than José-Luis. It had been almost a dozen years since her parents had split up. It had been longer than that since she'd last *seen* her dad before this. Even when Forrest was home, he was gone. Christy still holds it against him today that he moved out for good and left her and Jack and her mom in the lurch, just like that. It was a pretty turdy thing to do, Christy will tell you. That's the word she uses when she thinks of her father and the way he took off—turdy.

But it wasn't traumatic, she says. There's hardly a thing in this world that could happen to Christy that she'd call traumatic. Not after all she's been through. Just getting their family started, she and José-Luis, was an odyssey. It took months for her to get him up to L.A., months of hassling with the immigration officials, because she was a woman trying to bring a man, a foreigner, into the States at a time when a woman's place was behind her husband, not beside him, or—perish the thought—out in front of him. Now if Christy had been a man bringing his new Ecuadorian wife home to the United States, there would've been no problem, no problem at all.

But they managed, Christy going ahead to the United States, and José-Luis eventually getting the papers in Guayaquil that allowed him to join her in L.A., where he landed a job on the aircraft radar assembly line at RCA. Meanwhile, Christy, who'd picked up her undergraduate degree at USC (in international relations, as a matter of fact) and had tried grad school in Ann Arbor before taking that first trip to the Galápagos, had grown weary of academia. She was a wife now, soon to be a mother, so she left school behind and became a typist for a publishing firm.

That was in 1968, the year Jason was born. By '72, with Christy pregnant again, they decided they'd had enough of America. Neither she nor José cared much for the direction the country seemed to be going in—its politics, its values. What was happening in Vietnam made both of them ill. José had joined Christy at one antiwar protest, but the two of them weren't really much for marches. Groups, zealots of any kind, made them nervous. All they wanted was to live their own life, a clean, simple life, and they weren't getting that in Los Angeles. Jason was four years old now, and he hardly ever saw his dad, what with José's job at RCA, where he'd risen to a high-level engineering position. That and José's night school classes in electronics left him hardly a sliver of time to spend with his family. He was working his ass off, which was what he had done all his life, but it didn't seem worth it anymore, not there in L.A. So they decided to leave, to come back to the Galápagos, where they'd be working their asses off even harder, but at least they'd be doing it together, at home.

After stopping in Quito for Christy to give birth to their daughter, Corina—named, Christy says proudly, after that folk song, the one Bob Dylan recorded—they went on to the islands, moved into an old wood-plank house right on Academy Bay, next door to the hotel. The place had been built in the '40s with panels of pine carried down from the closed U.S. airbase up on the island of Baltra. There are still a few houses left standing around town made out of that stuff, but most of the old cabins are long gone.

Christy and José-Luis's place, built by a Norwegian, Jacob Lundh, son of one of the island's first settlers, was torn down in late '97. It served Christy and José-Luis well, giving them twenty-five good years. But the weather and termites finally had their way, forcing Christy and José to rebuild the place from the ground up. For months they hauled pinelike *amarillo,* cedarlike *cedrela,* and slabs of matazarno as dark as mahogany and dense as concrete down from the highlands. As the new wood went up and the old wood came down, the pests finally went away, including the rats.

Christy can't help but smile when she thinks of the rats. Mention a subject like this and her face just lights up. Because this opens the door to a story. And on these islands, where televisions, radios, and even electricity are fairly recent arrivals, storytelling is more than a mere pastime.

Annnybody who lived here in the old days, Christy will tell you, her voice rising high like a cartoon canary's, has a thousand rat stories to share. Trap 'em, poison 'em, shoot 'em, stomp on 'em—Christy can't tell you how many rats she and José killed just in their home alone. There was one that got wounded and ended up in the bathroom. Jack happened to be visiting that evening and followed it in there, a hammer clenched in his fist. He locked the door behind him. Then came the kicking and screaming. The whole house was shaking. You couldn't tell who was winning or losing. God, Christy will tell you, she went in there when it was over, and you *still* couldn't tell who had won.

It's getting near midnight, and the crowd's heating up. Christy pushes her way through, a familiar figure to the people around her, in her faded, print frock and those beat-to-hell sneakers. Her face— broad, round, and freckled—is fixed with a purpose, as is her pace. Her mousy-gray hair is cut short and simple—a long way from the blond locks that hung far down her back when she first met José. A pair of thick glasses covers her sparkling blue eyes. She looks like an eccentric librarian, but she strides like a warrior. And the villagers know her, making way as she nears.

Walking beside her is José-Luis. He is short, squat, with the soft roundness of late middle age and the broad open smile of a child. As they move through the throng, he is stopped by almost everyone they pass. He is treated with deference, with respect and affection. Many of the people he greets are his relatives: sisters, brothers, uncles, cousins. He is one of ten children. José has family all over this island, and those who are not his kin have at least heard of his courage, how he has spoken out against the authorities time and again over all of these years, how even right now he is helping rally the farmers' cooperative, the *Granja*, to fight for their rights.

In this country, for all of its failings, there is one thing the people respect, one thing that they have always understood about themselves: An Ecuadorian *works*; he or she holds nothing back when it's time to sweat or shed blood. Just ask the Peruvians, who lost two thousand or so of their best men in that brief, one-month border war between the two countries back in 1995. Ecuador's casualties totaled only two hundred. They may seem docile compared with their more violent neighbors in Colombia and Peru, but when aroused, the Ecuadorians will fight. And it is precisely this that most troubles the people of Ecuador about the bankers, businessmen, and officials who control their country: Few of these privileged classes have ever had to actually fight for anything. Few of them know what it means to work, to really *work*. They make all of that money, the people complain, but they do so little to earn it.

Most every morning and late into each night, José-Luis is up at the hardware store he and Christy opened years ago, the Bodega Blanca, taking the inventory with Jason or programming the computers José has assembled piece by piece in their small attic office. At lunchtime he walks home in the heat, has a sandwich with Christy, or maybe some soup, then loads two buckets of food scraps in the back of his pickup. He then drives into the highlands up to their farm, the old Hendrikson place, where he dumps out the buckets for the chickens to eat and then roams through the woods with a machete in hand, hacking the weeds away from the elephant grass so his cattle can get to it and graze. He stays there till sunset each day, then drives back down to town for dinner with Christy. When that's done, he might take a short nap, then stroll back up to the store, where he stays until two, sometimes three in the morning. That's the best time to get on-line with the computer, he will tell you. The island has only a single server (a phone line that runs through the bank) for all its PCs, which, in just the past year, have sprung up the way TVs did five years ago. There were maybe a half dozen personal computers on the whole island just last year. Now there are seventy, which means a wait of an hour—busy signal after busy signal—is not uncommon if you try logging on during the day.

It's been almost half a century since José-Luis was a boy of fifteen, in 1952, back on the mainland, driving fruit trucks down mountain trails from farms high in the Andes, pumping the brakes that his legs hardly reached, hurtling around steep hairpin turns, the bed of the truck piled high with bananas. The peaks of the volcanoes would rise around him as he rushed down to the market before the bananas went bad. He would pull to the shoulder when the sun began setting because driving at night was simply too risky. He would sleep there, on the ground under the truck, a tarp draped over his body to keep the mosquitoes away. The temperature beneath that thick, heavy canvas was as hot as an oven, but there was really no choice. Better to bake than to be eaten alive.

At eighteen José was drafted into the Ecuadorian Army. The men were fed next to nothing, the meals so small and scarce that the first thing you did when you were actually served your food was to openly spit on it, to discourage the soldier sitting beside you from stealing a swallow. José would never have made it through that year without the *machica* his family mailed him, the bags of coarse barley flour that he'd mix with some water and force down his throat. The brownish gray paste didn't taste half bad, but even better, it stuck to the belly, and that was what mattered.

José was twenty when he first came to these islands, to visit some uncles and cousins, and he never left. He found a job in the salt mines over on Santiago, where the men did the work that the donkeys refused. All they wore were gloves on their hands and shoes on their feet—better to be naked than encumbered by sun-dried, sweat-encrusted clothing that tore at one's skin like sandpaper. José tried starting a farm up on the high, jungled slopes where the old Norwegians had first settled, the Hornemanns and Graffers, who had carved homesteads out of those vine-tangled forests more than four decades earlier. Those Norwegians were something, sharing their lives with the lizards and tortoises. Their livestock—hogs, cattle, horses—fed on the fruit that fell from the trees. The thump of a fallen avocado was enough to trigger a small stampede. The Norwegians ate those avocadoes as well. And papayas. And bananas. The jungle was relentless, pushing back up at their windows and doors, the coffee and *guayaba* and *níspero* branches reaching out to reclaim what the humans had hacked away. Both old man Graffer and Hornemann carried machetes wherever they went. So did their wives.

But José couldn't make it up there, not by himself. It was just too much for one man to go it alone. No roads. No food. And so he gave up, moved back down to the village, where, in the summer of 1960, word came that the *gringos* were building a place for the scientists and a road would soon run from the town to a "station." And that's how José Gallardo met Forrest Nelson, working together on that crushed-coral road and constructing those buildings. From that summer on, until Forrest's daughter Christy and his son Jack sailed into José's life seven years later, he worked side by side with the American, Nelson, as if they were brothers.

Midnight is now only minutes away. There is a bang from the harbor, from out on the water, and everyone turns to see an arcing red flare rise from one of the cruise ships. The boats anchored all over the bay shimmer red as the flare rises higher, a shower of sparks raining out from its tail. The *viudas* are dancing with a group of small children, holding hands in a circle as the crowd cheers them on. The one with the wig—the blonde with the doll—swats at a man who is poking his nose at the back of his dress, like a dog sniffing under another dog's tail.

On the steps of the waterfront chapel where the Catholics wor-
ship, a small man—the priest—stands all by himself, his chocolate-
brown robe and glimmering crucifix lit by the street fires below.
Behind him the sanctuary beckons, its long rows of pews waiting for
the worshipers to take their places for the Mass that will begin in just
minutes. But the people aren't coming, not on this evening. The pews
sit empty, forsaken, and the priest is furious. His dark brow is fur-
rowed as he glares at the revelers. They're not coming, he knows,
because just a short week ago, at the *Misa del Gallo,* Christmas Eve's
"Mass of the Rooster," the priest preached and prayed for almost three
hours. The people felt tortured, like the convicts old Señor Cobos
used to flog in the fields over on San Cristobal. Those prisoners eventually rose up as one, descended on Cobos, and hacked him to death.
No one was going to beat the priest like that, of course, though their
thoughts might have wandered to just such an image. But some did
sneak out. Others simply fell asleep, and when it was over, blessedly
done, they left, vowing to themselves that they'd be damned if they
would allow him to put them through that again.

And so as the hour draws near, the priest stands alone. But he is
not about to relent. This behavior, this drinking and dancing and
lewdness, it is godless. It's evil. And if the people don't hear him
tonight, they will certainly hear him tomorrow on their radios, where
he holds court every day, broadcasting his speeches and sermons and
political rants on the town's largest station, one of just two on the
island. The other is owned by the Swiss brothers, the Schiesses, who
run the Garrapata along with their sister. Their station is newer, with
far fewer listeners, and the priest only hopes this will always be so. He
thanks God that for most of the islanders, his church station remains
a matter of habit. And so, though they might avoid him tonight,
tomorrow their ears will be his, and those ears will be blistered, he
swears to himself, for the sins that these people are committing
tonight.

And now the church bells are ringing. And the night sky glows
orange from the flames in the streets. And the end of the century is
just seconds away.

"Diez!"

"Nueve!"

They are counting down, thousands of voices rising as one along the entire waterfront, faces turned up toward the December sky, where fireworks arc and trail curtains of sparks, the smoke from the street fires spreads like a gauze, and the stars blink and sparkle in the swirl of it all.

"Tres!"

"Dos!"

An elderly Indian—his face bronze and cut deeply with canyon-like wrinkles, his long, jet-black hair tucked under an old porkpie hat and tied in a braid that hangs down to his trousers—stands next to a tourist wearing red plastic eyeglasses shaped in the number 2000, a noisemaker pressed between his wet grinning lips, a half-empty bottle of beer in his hand. They are both gazing skyward, their shoulders just touching.

"Uno!"

The night sky turns brilliant, pinwheels of white fire whirling over the harbor, whistling and bursting as the crowd dances and screams and young men leap through the flames in the street.

For Christy and José-Luis, this is enough. They watch for a few minutes, then turn back home to avoid the madness that will go on until daylight. Jack and Romy are already over at Fiddi's place, where the champagne is flowing and the Christmas lights twinkle around the palm-shaded swimming pool. The mangroves throw shadows across the inky lagoon. A hired deejay plays American rock-and-roll, old songs from the fifties. The scientists and their children dance barefoot on Fiddi's wide-open living room's waxed wooden floor. Jason is there, in the kitchen, mixing drinks for some friends while Monica hangs on his arm.

The party's just starting, as are parties throughout the village, where for at least this one evening, there is nothing to worry about. The tourists aren't worried, spilling out of the taxis lined up at the gate to the Galápason, where James Brown's "Sex Machine" thrums from the open-air sound system, and strobe lights mounted in tree-hung tortoise shells flicker madly upon the dancers below. The dee-jay's mix segues into the guttural growl of that *gringo*, Jim Morrison, and his band from the United States, The Doors. A trancelike guitar riff snakes out of the speakers, wrapping around the revelers and rising up through the treetops into the black sky above and out over the velvety waters of Academy Bay:

> *This is the end.*
> *My only friend, the end.*

The fires in the streets are now burning down, but the ashes continue to smolder.

FOUR

Fire and Ice

Isla Santa Fé

JANUARY 1, 2000

Jason Gallardo

A lmost noon, New Year's morning, and they haven't left yet. Not that it's the end of the world, but Jason would have liked to have lifted anchor when planned, which was six hours ago. Now that it's this late, there's no way they'll make San Cristobal by sunset, not with a seven-hour sail in front of them. And that means they won't make San Cristobal at all, not today. No way would anyone in his right mind try entering that island's harbor in darkness. First, there are the reefs: wicked black outcrops larger than the ships that they threaten, lurking a mere meter beneath the sea's smooth surface. Then there are the currents, cyclones of sea-water sweeping this way and that, churning with the force of sub-merged river rapids. It's with good reason that the harbor at San Cristobal is known on the charts as Wreck Bay. Its murky bottom is strewn with two centuries of good reasons, their masts grown green with algae, their holds now home to fish.

If the group had left when they intended, more than half the jour-ney would be behind them by now. But the Balfour brothers, Andrew and Robert, were still in bed when Jason called there at eight. And the Cruz kid, Sebastian—Jason just got off the CB with Sebas' mother, Georgina, and she says he's still packing. So now they will have no choice but to drop anchor this evening at the island of Santa Fé, about halfway to Cristobal, and spend the night there.

Not that Jason minds. Half the point of this trip, as far as he's concerned, is just getting away from this town with all of its peo-ple, just surrounding themselves with the dolphins and seabirds and no sign of man. There are moments right here in Puerto Ayora when Jason feels like he's back in the city of Quito, where Christy and José-Luis sent him to boarding school the year he turned twelve. There are nights, with the clubs and the discos that crowd Darwin Avenue, when Jason feels like he's back in the States, up in Chattanooga, barhopping with his college pals.

Now those Tennessee boys could drink. Night after night they'd sit in their frat houses and pound bottles till they passed out or puked. Jason never cared much for that. Even the language they used—"smashed," "trashed," "wasted"—didn't sound like much fun. But eating good food, *that* was fun. After growing up on this island with nothing to eat some days but beets and carrots and carrots and beets, to arrive in a place where there were dozens of restaurants and cafés to choose from, with hundreds of items on their menus—anything you could imagine—well, it was as if Jason had died and gone to heaven.

He eats well these days, in his harborfront house there on Pelican Bay, with its lofted living room and vaulted ceilings, its wine rack stocked with cabernets and merlots, the espresso machine beneath Jason's rack of restaurant-grade skillets and pans, a flamenco guitar CD cued up on his state-of-the-art stereo system, and the bed—oh yes, the bed—facing out toward a drop-dead view of the sea.

And behind all of this, the garage, which Jason has set up as a gym, with a weight bench in the corner and an inversion bed for his bad back, and six surfboards mounted on the wall, in bright neon colors, three made by Klima himself—Roberto Klima, the top surfboard shaper in all South America.

Across from the boards, on a wall of their own, are tacked autographed photos of Miss Argentina ("A terrible shot," Jason will tell you. "She looks so much better in person than that") and Miss Brazil ("Geez, she has *everything*. Fascinating. Fun. I didn't sleep for a week after I was with her").

Ah yes, the women. They are like food, Jason says, so many flavors to choose from. He admits they're his weakness. His ex-wife was the most gorgeous thing in the world, at least through his eyes. Six years they were married, and it still hurts when he speaks of her. He still calls her the love of his life, though that's long past him now.

Now there is Monica, to whom Jason swears he'll stay true this time around. No more straying. She's taken him back more than once in the past, but she's made clear in no uncertain terms that this is Jason's last shot.

Jason loads two of his boards and a tightly stuffed pack in the back of a pickup and heads down toward the wharf. A samba beat drifts through the trees from some homes up the hill where parties are still going on. The remains of the bonfires have been swept in neat piles to the side of the boulevard—a half-burnt mask here, a charred sneaker there—but people are nowhere to be seen.

As Jason pulls up at the wharf, the water taxis sit tied to the dock, empty and bobbing in the bright morning sun, with pelicans perched on their bows. The only souls in sight are Jason's pal Bico and Bico's girlfriend Petra, loading supplies into a gray, rubber dinghy. It's Bico's sailboat, the *Symbol*, anchored out among the large tour ships, that the group will be taking to San Cristobal.

They've known each other almost all of their lives, Bico and Jason. Their fathers worked together building the road to the Research Station, back before either of the boys had been born. To this day the whole island knows that by all rights and logic, Bico Rosero should never have been born. Or his mother, at the very least, should never have survived.

There was no bona fide doctor on the island back then, not in 1964. The only man who came close was a villager named Moises Brito, and that was because Moises knew how to make do. He was a schoolteacher by trade, but his hobby, if you could call it that, was surgery. As a mechanic tinkers with carburetors or a fisherman feels for the depths and the tides and the shape of the shallows, Moises Brito just had a knack for healing hurt bodies. If you needed a tooth pulled, or a bone set, or a baby delivered, you sent word for Moises, and you hoped he was sober.

Which he was not on the night Bico was born. There was actually an intern on the island that month, a medical student sent out from the mainland to finish his training. The student was young, unseasoned, and nervous. By the time he arrived at the Roseros' house, Bico's mother was in great pain. She needed a C-section, which the student had never done. He tried, but he panicked, slicing the knife across the infant's face as he cut into the womb. To this day, Bico wears that scar on the side of his cheek.

With the bleeding baby finally pulled out, the doctor hurried to finish. He sewed up Bico's mother and all but ran from the house. Bico's father, Abraham, sat by the side of his wife, who was still in great pain. As her pain grew even greater, Abraham realized something was wrong. So he rushed to find Brito.

But Brito was not home. He was up in the highlands, at a party in the small village of Bellavista. The only way there was by burro, and so Abraham went. It was a five-mile ride, and when he arrived, he found Brito stinking of *puro*. It was hard lashing a drunk on the back of a donkey, but Abraham did it, and by the time they arrived back at Abraham's home, Brito's eyes were open and his mind was half-clear.

That was enough to do what was needed. Brito had no surgical instruments, so someone found him a razor. When he reopened the belly of Bico's mother, he saw that the intern, in all of his haste, had neglected to sew up her uterus. She was hemorrhaging badly, but still hanging on. Brito stitched the womb closed, and the bleeding subsided. He then restitched her belly, and Bico's mother fell blessedly to sleep. Brito slept too, once Abraham helped him home to his own bed.

It's been thirty-five years since that night. Moises died years ago from a bad liver. There is a street by the lagoon named after him, and the story of Bico's birth is still told now and then by almost every person in town except Bico himself. Bico has never been much of a talker. As a boy, he would sit with his friends among the mangrove trees by the water; four or five of them waiting for hours for a tug on their fishing lines, hoping that one of the yard-long *robalos* swimming lazily by would go for their bait. Jason and the boys would go off to play soccer or go belly-boarding out at Tortuga, and Bico would be there among them, but he hardly would speak. Not that he had nothing to say; he was just not one to waste words.

And in the way that silence so often can do, it brought Bico Rosero a strange kind of respect. When he returned to the islands in the mid-1980s, after leaving for high school and college in Quito, it was to work as a guide. His timing was perfect. Ecotourism in the Galápagos was exploding, and a guide's salary (plus tips, and tips are where the big money is made) put to shame what an electrician like Bico's father was paid, or what any man earned at a traditional job on the islands. Competition for guide jobs had become fierce among the Galápagans.

Bico had no trouble getting hired because the tour operators knew he was one of those islanders to whom every inlet and cove, every insect and animal, was a familiar and deeply felt friend. The operators respected him, they wanted him, and they paid top dollar to get him. After less than a decade, Bico was at the high end of the Galápagos guides' pay scale, earning more than five hundred dollars some weeks. By then he and his girlfriend, Petra, had saved enough to buy their own boat, and they had no doubt about the particular vessel they wanted.

The *Symbol.* A solid thirty-nine-footer, with a hull made of carvel-planked pine and a deck of sweet teak. Its hatches and portholes were trimmed with cedrela the color of cocoa, with a galley below and berths that slept seven—the perfect size for the kind of tour-sailing Bico had in mind when he bought it. He knew what those big boats were like, the 100-foot yachts and the huge, steel-hulled cruise ships with their squadrons of uniformed cooks, maids, and maintenance men, and their battalions of guides, herding the passengers ashore as if they were cattle. Bico wanted something smaller, more intimate. Six guests, no more, sailing the islands a week at a time, he or Petra at the wheel, the passengers eating meals that Bico and Petra cooked, sleeping in beds Petra made, going ashore to hike the same ocean cliffs Bico hiked as a boy—the *Symbol* was perfect for that.

As Bico and Petra toss the last of the supplies into the *panga*, Jason unloads his boards and his backpack, climbs in beside them, and the three race full throttle out to the sailboat.

The boys—Andrew, Robert, and Sebas—are all there with their own boards and gear by the time Bico's dinghy pulls up. The *Symbol* looks stately, its white hull striped red at the waterline and the deck. The list of its previous owners reads like a who's who of the islands. Among them is old Karl Angermeyer, who fled with his three brothers to the Galápagos in 1935 to escape Hitler's Germany. After the Angermeyers came the Wittmers, whose name is entwined with stories of sex slaves and scandal and death on the island of Floreana. It was from Rolf Wittmer that Bico and Petra bought the *Symbol* in the autumn of 1995.

They had met—Bico and Petra—just eight months earlier, on the rim of Isabela Island's Volcán Alcedo, where they were both leading tour groups. Bico's guests happened to be German—one of three languages he speaks almost fluently—and Petra perked up at the sound of her native tongue. She herself was from Cologne, had an Ecuadorian ex-husband—"a *lawyer*," she says, spitting the word out as if it were dirt—whom she left back in Quito when she came to the islands six years ago. She's been here ever since, hooking up with Bico soon after that Alcedo trip. They've done it all together: the finances, the crewing, the guiding. In the most pervasive sense, brought together both by what they desire and what they can't stomach, Bico and Petra are a Galápagos couple.

As they unload the dinghy, passing supplies and surfboards up to Andrew and Sebas, a man and a woman emerge from the boat's cabin.

Jason smiles and shouts. "Hey, Lobo!"

The man turns, lets go the woman's hand, and reaches down to help with the loading. "Jason," he says, lifting two backpacks, "how you doing?"

Jason had heard Lobo and Mariana might be coming along, but he's surprised to see that they're actually here. It's been only two months since the accident. The shock, for many, has still not worn away. People pass Mariana on the streets of the village and sometimes they cross to the other side. Or they just look away, as if they don't see her, because they don't know what to say. What can be said after such a terrible thing?

There are some who blame Mariana, and Lobo as well, for leaving the baby at all. Yes, it was just for a few days, while they went to the mainland for a short vacation. And yes, Mariana's mother assured them not to worry, that her precious *nieta*, her little granddaughter, would be fine in her care. But couldn't that vacation have waited? Or couldn't they have brought the child along? After all, the little girl was two years old, certainly able to travel.

There are those on the island who say it was simply God's will, punishment for some sin Mariana must have committed. That's what the priest told Mariana when she went to see him after the death. It was God's will, the priest said, that Mariana's mother went to work that morning at the school where Mariana's father, Carlos, is the principal, and took the baby along and left it alone for just a few minutes in that room with the old piano. Who could guess that the child would go to that instrument, move it in some small unseen way, and that the old awkward upright would fall over, the baby beneath it?

The baby was not Lobo's; Mariana had been married before. But Lobo loved the little girl as his own because he loved Mariana so much. It tore at his soul as deeply as it did at hers to come home to the child in that coffin. But Lobo was the one who had to be strong because Mariana was falling apart. She could not take it, the guilt that the priest made her feel, the urgings from her mother to have another child, quickly, and her father berating her because she was acting so weak.

No, Jason did not expect to see the two of them here. But somehow Lobo had swung a few days off from his guiding. And Mariana agreed that this might be a good thing, to just get away. And so they have come, stowing their gear in a berth down below, next to Bico and Petra's.

Now they are ready, the sun just past one, the harbor sparkling as it does almost every day at this time. Robert and Sebas hoist the anchor, lifting the slick, heavy chain hand over hand. Bico kneels over the boat's stubborn engine, adjusting some screws until the motor sputters to life. Lobo and Mariana have gone back below. Petra is down in the galley, putting away groceries, and Jason and Andrew are setting the sails.

Before they have even reached Punta Nuñez, past which lies open sea, Bico has cut the engine to near-idle, and the sails are filled with a following breeze. The teens, Robert and Sebas, and twenty-year-old Andrew are sprawled on the foredeck, wearing nothing but swim trunks, the sun beating down on their darkly tanned skin, floppy hats shading their eyes as each lies back and opens a book. Jason is camped near the mast, the spray from the sea sprinkling his legs as he leafs through an old musty volume—*A Little Treasury of Modern Poetry*—from his mother's home library.

The ocean, so translucently turquoise in the still of the harbor, is now deep, dark, and inky beneath them. White puffs of cumulus clouds billow on the bright blue edge of the distant horizon. To the port side, a sea lion surfaces with a fish in its mouth. Off the bow, hardly a foot above the ocean's swells, skims a red-billed tropic bird, its tail feathers trailing behind like white ribbons of lace.

"Now that's something you don't see every day," says Petra, watching the creature sail past. "You'll see them nesting on South Plaza and flying around there, but feeding out this far, you don't see that too often."

As Santa Cruz recedes to the stern, the craggy outline of Santa Fé takes shape ahead. In the most recent El Niño, only one year ago, the cliffs of Santa Fé, normally gray, brown, and barren, were awash with cascades of tumbling water. The entire island was nothing but sheets of white rapids, spilling down to the shore with a roar that could be heard by ships miles away. The ocean surrounding that island, normally crystalline blue, turned concentric circles of dark red and brown as the washed-away mud made its way out to sea. With a strong pair of binoculars, you could stand on the back patio of the Hotel Galápagos and peer toward the southern horizon at what looked like Niagara Falls.

It was this way on Isabela Island as well, where more than two dozen full-grown tortoises tumbled to their deaths down steep, flood-swept ravines and cliffs carved by the rain. But as bad as that was, those rains were nothing compared with El Niño of '82. That's the one etched in everyone's memory, a deluge of biblical proportions. The water fell in sheets that entire spring and summer and fall—not a figure of speech, but literal sheets, sheer curtains of water. And when it subsided, after nine months of downpours, the flora burst forth with a lushness like never before.

"The *palo santos*," says Petra, watching a bottle-nosed dolphin surface to the starboard side before sliding back into the sea. "You could smell them wherever you went, even out here, out at sea.

They were everywhere. *Everything* was green, bright, bright green."

Which was not a good thing, not in a place with such an anciently delicate balance of moisture and sunlight and the myriad forces that foster the rhythm of life on an island. The epic deluge and the subsequent drought, La Niña, drove the birds and the animals mad with confusion. Reports abounded during that climactic year of Galápagos finches gorging and overbreeding among vegetation run rampant and insects run amok. The birds reproduced manically, then stopped altogether the next mating season. Fire ants flourished, swarming and devouring young tortoise hatchlings in obscene numbers. Wild pigs and goats, protected from hunters by the mud and dense undergrowth, multiplied at a frightening rate.

Meanwhile, at sea, the rise of just one or two degrees in the temperature of the ocean was enough to wreak havoc. The carcasses of marine iguanas, starved by the sudden absence of the precious green algae on the sea-bottom rocks where they normally feed, littered the beaches and warm shoreline pools. The warmth of the water was astounding—disgusting, say those who compared it to swimming in urine.

The fragile coral that grow in the shallows were bleached by the warmth of those El Niño seas to a point where they could not recover. The mud carried down from the highlands and into the surf so clouded the shallows that the fish could not breathe. Driven to clearer and much cooler depths by the rising sea temperatures and tumbling mud, the fish left the sea lions with nothing to eat, and so the sea lion mothers left their babies to die on the sand. The sounds of those pups bleating for food could be heard by the tour boats passing at night.

Of course, it's all part of nature, the cycle of life and death. That's something Petra and all the guides make a point of showing their tour groups. Carcasses, casualties, the bones and flesh of dead boobies and seals are not tidied up in the Galápagos. They are left as they lie, a part of the landscape. This is the nature of things, the guides all point out. This is no Disneyland here, they say with tight smiles. It is not antiseptic. It is not manufactured. This is a place to ponder the awe of existence, the wonder of the creatures all over this planet, including ourselves, that have so far survived, and the lessons we can learn from the ones that have not.

Santa Fé is now near, its barren slopes glowing orange in the late afternoon sun. A heavy surf pounds at the jagged shoreline, spraying the guano-stained cliffs with geysers of seawater. At the top of those beige, sun-baked ridges, studded with *opuntia* cacti, the ground levels off, flat as a tabletop, like a New Mexican mesa. Up there live the last of a primitive species, the dull land iguanas, chewing on cactus pads, dragging their thick, yard-long bodies over the sun-hardened earth. "Like their brothers the sea-kind," wrote young Charles Darwin in his seagoing journal, "they are ugly animals, of a yellowish-orange beneath, and of a brownish-red colour above: from their low facial angle they have a singularly stupid appearance."

The shadows have lengthened as Jason and Robert haul down the sails and Bico restarts the motor and the *Symbol* glides into a small, half-moon cove. Two boats rest at anchor in the emerald water, one a small private ketch and the other a small cruise ship, its crew busy on deck as a *panga* approaches. Two rows of tourists—elderly, white, each wearing a bright orange life jacket—sit and face one another in the motorized dinghy as their guide stands at the stern, noting a booby diving nearby for anchovies. The group has been on the beach, a small spit of sand where a large, angry sea lion is now barking and bellowing, protecting his brood as all bull lions do. Sebas barks back, mocking the animal as he lowers the anchor.

The sky is pitch-black now, speckled with stars. The lights of the cruise ship dance on the water as faint music floats from its lounge. Petra uncorks a bottle of wine as the *Symbol*'s dinner is served—Bico's signature chicken and rice. The group huddles around a small makeshift table—a hatch door laid over the steps to the galley. The wine is sipped from a hodgepodge of cups, and the chicken is eaten with fingers.

When dinner is done and the dishes are washed, Jason settles back down at his spot by the mast, looking up at the stars as he opens his book. Robert and Sebas nestle alongside him, inside sleeping bags zipped up to keep off the chill. Andrew has gone down below, as have Bico and Petra and Mariana and Lobo.

The boat gently sways as the surf washes the shore. Jason's soft voice drifts out over the cove as he reads from a page:

> *Some say the world will end in fire,*
> *Some say in ice.*
> *From what I've tasted of desire*
> *I hold with those who favour fire.*
> *But if it had to perish twice,*
> *I think I know enough of hate*
> *To say that for destruction ice*
> *Is also great*
> *And would suffice.*

And the sea lions sleep on the sand.

FIVE

San Cristobal

Isla
San Cristobal

Puerto
Baquerizo Moreno

JANUARY 2, 2000

Norwegian settlers, 1920s

It's an hour before dawn and the cove lies in blackness, shielded from the moon by a bank of low-lying clouds. The two tour boats are silent—still and dark. But on the *Symbol* there is movement, a single figure, Bico, choking the throttle to start the engine. Robert and Sebas stir in their sleeping bags out on the deck alongside the surfboards, regretting now that they chose to sleep under the stars rather than squeezed down below with the others. The night air is so cold they can see their own breaths.

As the inboard coughs to life, the boys do their duty, lifting the anchor while Petra brews coffee on the small galley stove. By the time streaks of pink pierce the sky to the east, the *Symbol* has left Santa Fé, slicing full sail through a gray, choppy sea, bearing southeast toward San Cristobal. The island is hardly in sight, a smudge on the horizon, but Jason is already worried that they may find no waves. The clouds, the breeze, the feel of the ocean—it just doesn't look good, not to a surfer.

He peers off toward the sunrise, where the sky now glows tangerine. A flock of storm petrels sweeps past like a cloud of mosquitoes. But Jason hardly notices. He's thinking about waves, and their fecklessness. With all the technology wrapping the planet today, with satellites downbeaming data on wind speeds and directions all over the world, with ocean buoys hundreds of miles at sea rigged to record passing swells, with surf-forecasting Web sites like "Bluetorch" and "Swell.com" broadcasting on-line reports from all over the globe, it would seem that wave hunting is no longer an art but a science.

But Jason knows better. No matter that the forecast looked good when they set sail yesterday. The surf gods are fickle; they'll turn on a dime, and Jason is nervous about what lies ahead. This trip took some planning, and money to boot, and his parents weren't happy with him leaving the store for four days. If the waves are as hoped for, it will all be worthwhile. If they're breaking the way they so often do, at Corolla and Tonga, where the shaped thirteen-footers have become legend as word has crept out during the past couple of years, and the Galápagos have become the latest frontier among the "surferati," the way Bali became just a decade ago, then everything will be fine.

The boys are excited, Sebas and Robert, chattering about the crew from *Surfer* magazine who came down not long ago, bringing cameras and writers and four world-class champions to see if the buzz about these islands is deserved. Joel Tudor, Brad Gerlach, Kahea Hart, Chris Malloy—Sebas pronounces the pro surfers' names as if they are holy. He still can't believe these guys actually stayed at the Hotel Galápagos for a couple of days before heading out to Seymour and Baltra and Las Palmas, where they found green, crystalline tubes that they surfed with the sea lions, the animals riding beside them as they shredded the waves for the cameras on shore. It was all that the big shots at *Surfer* had hoped for. The piece was published in the slick magazine, and the video was broadcast on cable TV in the States and Australia and all over the world, building the buzz even louder, which is a worry to those who'd like to keep this Galápagos surfing a secret. But right now, thank God, at least as far as Jason and his friends are concerned, these waters remain largely unpeopled, pure and pristine.

And, also, unfortunately, flat at the moment, as San Cristobal comes into clear sight.

To the left, about four miles north, looms the outline of *León Dormido,* or "Kicker Rock," as it's called in most tour guides. If there is one image of the Galápagos Islands recognized by the rest of the world—besides the iguanas and tortoises and Bartolomé Island's breathtaking "Pinnacle Rock"—it's this volcanic spire. A steep, sheer slab of stone, it juts five hundred feet from the surface of the sea, like the fin of a herculean shark. Eons of waves and wind have split the formation top to bottom, creating a channel—no more than a crack, really—barely fifty feet wide, through which a tour *panga* can pass when the ocean is calm. Tourists love to shout and delight in their voices echoing eerily off the vertical faces of the soaring stone walls that flank them. It's called "Kicker Rock" because, to some, the split stone has the look of a boot. But to

Galápagueños like Sebas, who points toward the formation and shouts out its name, it is *León Dormido*, "the Sleeping Lion."

Sebas' excitement is not shared by the others, who stare ahead toward the island, where the sea gently laps at the black lava coastline. There are typically waves here of ten to twelve feet; strong, muscular breaks that curl then explode off those rocks at Corolla. Or off to the right, at the spot called "Canon," because of the old gun emplacement that sits on that point. The weapon has never been fired, but the Ecuadorian Navy, which maintains a small base here (for God knows what reason, laugh some of the townsfolk) insists that the rusted old cannon remain. So it does, and right now it is aimed at an ocean as smooth and flat as a mirror.

"*Vamos, Corolla!*" Andrew shouts at the motionless sea.

"We are looking," says Robert, running a hand through the ringlets that cover his head, "at shit."

As they enter the harbor—Bico carefully weaving his way through the razor-edged reefs—they see flags of all nations on the masts of the yachts and sailboats at anchor. Greek, Italian, French—the pennants hang limp in the still morning air. It is not yet nine A.M. and already the temperature is edging into the nineties. The sun, hardly higher than the brush-covered hills that slope down to this sleepy port village, is relentless, baking the air, the sea, and the ground.

The town is called Puerto Baquerizo Moreno, and, on paper, at least, it's the hub of these islands, the provincial capital of the Galápagos, which sounds fairly important. But in reality the place is no more than a small, dusty village, home to perhaps five thousand people. The houses and small businesses that rim the brief waterfront are dreary and sad, painted in muted hues of sea green, blue, and beige. The palm trees that bend over the seawall and wharf are sun-beaten and brown. As Bico settles the *Symbol* in place to drop anchor, not a soul is in sight on the shore.

"It's always like this," Robert says as a dog's bark breaks the silence from somewhere in the village. "This place is creepy."

Darwin felt much the same way when he first set foot on San Cristobal on the morning of September 17, 1835. He was twenty-six years old. It had been four years since the HMS *Beagle* set sail from England for what was intended to be a two-year expedition to survey the South American coastline. The *Beagle* would not return home for yet another year after this.

San Cristobal was the first island Darwin explored during the five weeks he spent in the Galápagos. And he was less than impressed, as he wrote in his journal:

> *Nothing could be less inviting than the first appearance. A broken field of black basaltic lava . . . is everywhere covered by a stunted, sunburnt brushwood, which shows little signs of life. The dry and parched surface, being heated by the noon-day sun, gave the air a close and sultry feeling, like that from a stove: we fancied even the bushes smelt unpleasantly.*

There were no people living on San Cristobal at that time, at least none who were mentioned in the diary Darwin kept during the six days he spent roaming this island. In fact, the only humans who had lived anywhere in the Galápagos up to that point had arrived here by accident or had been brought against their will.

The very discovery of the Galápagos was sheer happenstance. There is evidence that ancient Incans encountered the islands while riding rafts made of balsa in pre-Colombian times. Author and archaeologist Thor Heyerdahl concluded as much after studying pottery shards on the beaches of Santiago, Floreana, and Santa Cruz in the summer of 1953, on the heels of his fabled *Kon-Tiki* voyage.

The Incans were most likely first. But the man who is credited with "discovering" the Galápagos is a Spanish priest and Panama's first bishop, a man named Tomás de Berlanga, whose ship was becalmed then swept away from the west coast of South America in the winter of 1535 by a current that carried it into an uncharted part of the Pacific, where it drifted for six days before encountering land. Actually, "land" is a generous term, considering de Berlanga's own account of first seeing these islands. "It seems," wrote the bishop in a letter addressed to his lord, the king of Spain, "as though some time God had showered stones."

Before the end of that century, this shower of stones had a name, *galápago* (from the Spanish term for a cleated saddle, which the shells of the giant tortoises resembled), and it now had a place on navigational maps as well. Over the next two hundred years, those maps became a bit confusing as British buccaneers, prowling the South American coast for slow-sailing Spanish ships heavy with treasure, turned the Galápagos into a home base of sorts: a place to rest, heal their wounds, and stock their holds with live tortoises before setting sail for more plunder.

An odd sense of patriotism compelled these pirates to give British names to the islands. To this day, Floreana is also called "Charles" by some, San Cristobal is sometimes called "Chatham," and Santa Cruz is occasionally called "Indefatigable" by those who are able to pronounce the word.

Although the buccaneers spent a good deal of time searching these islands for food and hiding from pursuers in hundreds of small coves and inlets, the only people who actually lived here were castaways, mutineers, and other miscreants whose punishment by their brethren was to be left alone on these godforsaken, freshwaterless shores.

Some legends have it that Alexander Selkirk, the Scottish sailor upon whom Daniel Defoe based *Robinson Crusoe*, spent his four years in exile on a Galápagos island. In truth, Selkirk was actually marooned far to the south, on an atoll off the coast of Chile. But he did visit the Galápagos soon after being rescued by a shipload of British buccaneers in 1709, who carried him with them on a raid of Guayaquil's harbor. From there they retreated to the Galápagos, where Selkirk and his new shipmates regrouped, then moved on.

The Galápagos' own Robinson Crusoe was an unfortunate Irishman named Patrick Watkins, who was set ashore almost a century after Selkirk, in 1807, on the island of Floreana, where some quarrelsome shipmates left him to die. Watkins refused to oblige, surviving on meager crops of potatoes and—of all things—pumpkins, which he traded to passing ships in exchange chiefly for liquor. During the War of 1812, when the U.S. warship *Essex* arrived in the islands with orders to wreak havoc upon the British whaling fleet sailing these waters, its captain, David Porter, was so intrigued by the stories he heard of this man/beast named Watkins that he set down a detailed description in the *Essex*'s log:

> *The appearance of this man, from the accounts I have received of him, was the most dreadful that can be imagined; ragged clothes, scarce sufficient to cover his nakedness, and covered with vermin; his red hair and beard matted, his skin much burnt from constant exposure to the sun, and so wild and savage in his manner and appearance that he struck everyone with horror. For several years this wretched being lived by himself on this desolate spot, without any apparent desire other than that of procuring rum in sufficient quantities to keep himself intoxicated, and, at such times, after an absence from his hut of several days, he would be found in a state of perfect insensibility, rolling among the rocks of the mountains.*

This is what the Galápagos can do to a man. By the time Porter wrote these words, Watkins was four years gone from the islands. He hijacked a shore party of five sailors with their longboat and made his getaway to Guayaquil, where he arrived, noticeably alone, in the summer of 1809. Rumors persist today that Watkins' meals during that journey to the mainland consisted of his hostages' bodies.

That left those British whaling crews as the only humans who set foot on the islands during that time. And they—or more precisely, their ships—were what the *Essex* had come for.

The first whaling ships had arrived in the southeastern Pacific in the late 1700s, from Great Britain and New England. Sailors in this region had long known that large baleen whales—fins, sperms, and humpbacks—were abundant in these waters. The sailors were also familiar with a remarkably strong ocean current that swept up from Antarctica along the Peruvian coast before bending west at the equator—a swift, frigid stream of seawater that ran straight through the Galápagos. That current was eventually charted by a nineteenth-century oceanographer named Alexander von Humboldt. Scientists thereafter quickly made the connection between the Humboldt Current, which was cold enough to support rich swarms of plankton in the heat of the equator and the proliferation of plankton-devouring whales in this region. Some biologists, including Darwin, went on to make the further connection between that current and the odd sea and animal life found in and around the Galápagos, creatures that simply do not belong, such as the penguins that still roam the western islands of Fernandina and Isabela.

But those British and New England whalers had no interest in science or penguins. What lured them to this part of the Pacific was the oil to be found in those whales, which were hunted and harpooned with a fury. By the start of the War of 1812, dozens of American whaling boats roamed the eastern Pacific, with as many British and European vessels hunting alongside them. The crews of those ships, who were at sea for months, sometimes years, at a time with no refrigeration to preserve meat or produce, typically ate nothing but salt pork and biscuits. Once they learned of the tortoises that abounded on the Galápagos, many weighing as much as six hundred pounds—six hundred pounds of meat that would keep itself fresh inside an animal that could survive for a year without food or water in the hold of a ship—a slaughter began on the scale of that which would soon visit the American buffalo. By the end of the nineteenth century, entire populations of tortoises on several Galápagos islands were extinguished. When the whalers first arrived at the turn of the 1800s, several hundred thousand tortoises roamed the Galápagos. Today there remain perhaps 20,000.

In much the same way that the whaling crews preyed on the slow, witless tortoises, David Porter and the crew of the *Essex* had their way with the whalers. No sooner did Porter arrive in the Galápagos in April of 1813 than he headed straight for the island of Floreana's "Post Office Bay," so-called because of a crude mail system set up on its beach. It consisted of a box nailed to a pole, into which passing ships would deposit, as well as pick up and eventually deliver, letters addressed to all points on the globe.

Porter's plan was quite simple: Raid the box, study the letters, deduce which whaling ships were in the area, and attack them. It was not an intricate strategy, but it was effective beyond Porter's wildest hopes. Hoisting British colors, which allowed it to approach its targets without causing alarm, the *Essex* captured three British whalers within the first month without a shot being fired. In the four months that followed, nine more ships were as easily taken. So successful was Porter that he soon found himself as fabled back in the United States as John Paul Jones. He also soon found himself as the *Essex*'s only officer. The others had gone, each having been awarded the command of a British vessel the *Essex* had seized. Among those young officers was Porter's adopted son, a twelve-year-old midshipman named David Farragut, who would later become the young United States Navy's first admiral.

Porter eventually lost the *Essex* in a vicious battle with a British frigate off the coast of northern Chile in late 1814. He was returned to the United States as a "prisoner on parole," which somewhat dampened the glory of his Galápagos exploits and which might explain why his suggestion that the United States annex the unclaimed Galápagos Islands—a suggestion he urgently made both to his naval superiors and to Congress—was met with utter disinterest.

That left the door open for Ecuador to annex the islands some eighteen years later. It was three years after that that Darwin arrived on board the *Beagle.* When he stepped ashore here at San Cristobal, he encountered what he described in his journal as a "Cyclopian scene" of slaglike lava and odd little finches "so tame and unsuspecting," he wrote, "that they did not even understand what was meant by stones being thrown at them."

There were no people on this island at the time Darwin arrived, and, from what Jason and Lobo and the others can see as they lower themselves into the *Symbol*'s dinghy to paddle ashore on this still Sunday morning, there is no one here now.

The empty *pangas* they pass, bobbing in the bay's sparkling, green water, have coils of barbed wire or sharp, naillike spikes attached to their sides to keep out the sea lions, which infest this harbor like pests. The creatures have a habit of crawling up into unprotected dinghies and ransacking the contents, not to mention relieving themselves on the boats' interiors.

Onshore, a young girl appears, sucking a *bolo* (frozen fruit juice in a clear plastic bag) as she strolls past the wharf. A teen in a soccer shirt pedals by on an old beat-up bicycle. Four young boys appear at the far end of the bay, diving into the shimmering water without making a splash. Petra smiles and remarks on their Huck Finn–like innocence. Bico responds with a smile of his own. "They're probably diving for *pepinos*," he says.

Climbing ashore, the group splits apart. Jason and the boys head off to sniff out the surf conditions while Bico hikes uptown to locate some relatives. Lobo, Petra, and Mariana find a tiny, two-table café on a narrow sidestreet and sit down to order a late breakfast of three cold *cervezas* and three bowls of ceviche. There is only one item on the café's small chalkboard menu: ceviche. There is nothing, the trio agrees, like good, fresh ceviche—the raw octopus, shrimp, sea snails, and fish, all taken fresh from the ocean that morning, chopped up and sprinkled with fresh lime and vinegar. And there is no ceviche in the world, they insist, like that found in the Galápagos.

The seafood arrives, with a side basket of popcorn, for 8,000 *sucres* apiece—about forty cents each. Outside, the bright sun beats down on the sloped cobblestoned street. Across the way, a small, lightless shop displays sacks of rice, bottles of ketchup, and fresh mangoes and limes. The cracked, broken sidewalk is empty of tourists, empty of anyone. Block after block of half-finished buildings—concrete and cinder-block pillars and walls rising jaggedly like rows of bad teeth, corrugated asbestos roofing held up by long bamboo poles—lead to the north side of town, where a hard, red-clay road winds up a hill to an unlikely "visitor's center" overlooking the bay.

The center was built with money raised by a group based in Spain. There are buildings all over these islands built with money donated by nations beyond Ecuador. This one is modern, octagonal. With cathedral ceilings and walls made of fresh cedar, with broad, plate-glass windows, clay-tiled floors, and Park Service maps mounted behind panes of clear glass, the place would fit well in Yellowstone or Yosemite, where crowds of tour groups would line up at the door.

But there are no crowds here, not at the moment. And not in the past several days, according to the register that sits by the front entrance. A short list of signatures was entered on New Year's Eve: Janice Bonaparte from Milton, Massachusetts; The McGaughan Family from Washington, D.C.; the Nelsons from Manchester, Massachusetts. The first entry on January 1—the first official visitors of the new millennium to the island of San Cristobal—are Joan and Thomas Rice from Portsmouth, New Hampshire.

By the time the ceviche is finished, Jason and the boys have returned from their mission. The surf, they've been told by a couple of Brazilians at a bar down the way, is not bad up past the airport, at a spot called *La Lobería*—"the Place of the Sea Lions." And so they head in that direction, their boards under their arms, while Petra returns to the boat to join Bico for an afternoon nap, and Lobo and Mariana see about catching a truck for an afternoon drive into the highlands, where maybe they'll go take a look at the ruins of El Progreso.

El Progreso. Lyrical labels like this have been laid upon dozens of ill-fated ventures launched all over these islands during the past century or so. Ranches, farms, communes, resorts, plantations, mines—the litany of doomed enterprises in the Galápagos is as sad as it is long. In some cases, it is savage as well. Forced labor, torture, and killings without conscience were as common here in the nineteenth and early twentieth centuries as they were at other so-called frontiers on the planet. There are phantoms all over these islands, ghostly wisps of past pain and unspeakable suffering curling into the air like the smoky remains of burned-away memories. Nowhere is that smoke any thicker than at the nightmare they called El Progreso.

Soon after the Galápagos were annexed in 1832, Ecuador dispatched a renowned military officer, a general named José Villamil, to govern the archipelago's first colony, on the island of Floreana. The "colonists," such as they were, consisted of two hundred or so political prisoners and prostitutes shipped out from the mainland. Their purpose was to ostensibly harvest a wild moss called *orchilla*, used to make dye. But in reality the place was no more than a penal colony. It was christened Asilo de la Paz ("Haven of Peace") by the government, but within a matter of months it was better known as Reino Perro ("the Dog Kingdom") because its governor could go nowhere without the protection of a large pack of hounds.

Within thirty years that colony was abandoned, a pathetic failure. Not long thereafter, in the late 1870s, a new one took shape on the neighboring island of San Cristobal, with *orchilla* again to be grown, and sugarcane, and coffee as well, on a much larger scale than the previous effort. This time there was no pretense that the setup was anything other than slavery. A businessman named Manuel Cobos was given free rein over boatloads of conscripted workers shipped from the continent, who sweated in his fields under satanic conditions. Floggings were routine, as were shootings by firing squads. When Cobos was in one of his fouler moods, he would order a marooning on one of the surrounding small islets, where an unlucky soul would be left on the rocks to cook in the sun until he or she died.

The place was called El Progreso, and it actually prospered through the turn of the century, until the prisoners, who by then numbered more than four hundred, finally revolted on a January morning in 1904. Cobos, clad only in his underpants as he sat in a rocking chair on the porch of his villa, was confronted by a small group of convicts who had surprised his sentries and seized their weapons. They shot Cobos twice—in the stomach and chest. Staggering, still alive, he retreated into his bedroom, where he was struck twice in the head with a machete, and finally fell dead. A month after that, a ragged sloop with no papers and flying no nation's flag drifted into the port of Tumaco on the southwestern coast of Colombia. Eighty-five hollow-eyed men and women helped one another down the gangplank to shore, relating their horrific ordeal in bits and pieces. The story shocked all of Ecuador, as did the trial, where the cruelty of Cobos was revealed and all but two of the defendants were set free.

The remains of El Progreso are mentioned in most Galápagos guidebooks, which tell tourists to look for the ruins on their way up to a lake called El Junco, the only significant freshwater source in the entire archipelago. The lake sits atop the island, where over the eons a volcanic crater has turned into a rainfall-fed reservoir. That water was one reason Cobos chose this location to build his plantation, and it would seem a good reason—besides being the Galápagos' provincial capital—that Puerto Baquerizo and not Puerto Ayora should be the hub of these islands today.

But it's not. And the reason, the watershed moment, the single event that set the course for the future of San Cristobal—and for that matter, of the entire Galápagos—was the Japanese attack on Pearl Harbor.

As early as the mid-1930s, the U.S. Navy was nosing around the Galápagos, scouting the archipelago's coves and inlets, surveying suitable sites for an air base, preparing for possible war in the Pacific. Franklin Roosevelt stopped by to visit in 1938. But by late 1941 no ground had been broken and no troops yet deployed.

That all changed with December 7. Four days after that, several squads of U.S. troops, dispatched from the Canal Zone, arrived on the islands. The decision now had to be made, and quickly, where to build that air base.

It would have made sense, at least at first glance, for the base to be built at San Cristobal. There was fresh water. This was where most of the Galápagos' 800 or so residents lived at that time, centered around a fish-processing plant built at Wreck Bay in the late 1920s by a group of Norwegians.

But San Cristobal was simply in the wrong place. The base's primary purpose was to serve as a spotting station, a warning post against a possible Japanese invasion of the Panama Canal. If that attack came, it would arrive, of course, from the west. San Cristobal lies east, as far east as one can get in the Galápagos.

So the Americans decided on Baltra, more centrally located and conveniently flat. Construction began there in February 1942. Within two months a mile-long landing strip had been blasted out of the lava. Around it stood more than 200 structures, including barracks enough to house the roughly 1,000 U.S. soldiers and sailors assigned duty there.

For the ensuing four years, Baltra, the little lunarlike island just above Santa Cruz, became the heart of the Galápagos. It was called "the Rock" by the GIs who were stationed there, and their duty was dead serious. Indeed, if the Japanese had prevailed at Midway a mere seven months after those first U.S. troops arrived here, the Galápagos would have been the next battleground.

But that didn't happen. And so the soldiers and sailors who lived in this desolate compound of barracks and Quonset huts wound up with little to do but drink beer and shoot iguanas. So much beer was consumed by the GIs on Baltra that the Army sent down a team of investigators to see if their boys weren't selling the brew to the locals. The investigators found that while the troops occasionally did trade tins of Spam for fresh fruit and vegetables from their island neighbors, the soldiers kept the beer to themselves. To this day, if a visitor steps to the edge of one of the hundreds of cracks and crevasses that split the stony, brown-and-black fields flanking the airstrip at Baltra, he can peer down and see the sunlight glinting off the remains of broken beer bottles, tossed off more than half a century ago by bored U.S. GIs.

Those fields are still studded today with the cement foundations of what was once a small city. Besides its barracks, hangars, and office buildings, the Baltra base had an outdoor beer garden, a chapel, a cinema (which the troops dubbed the "Rock-Si"), a bowling alley (added after Eleanor Roosevelt visited the base and bemoaned the horrid conditions), and a mess hall, where the soldiers ate fresh local vegetables and fruit, including, apparently, watermelons. Now, as then, it rarely rains on Baltra, but when it does, small green melons sprout as if by magic from the spots in the rocky soil where those sailors and soldiers once spat their seeds.

Wild goats roamed the islands even then, left by the buccaneers a century before, and Baltra's communication system often went dead, the result of the goats chewing through the cables that snaked from one building to another. Despite a wealth of Army-issue fishing gear and free time to swim and sun, the men based on the Rock suffered from the same grim realities as the locals on surrounding islands. A dispatch cabled from a *Time* magazine editor covering the outpost's closing in July of 1946 described a vista as bleak as any battlefield:

Dysentery laid many low. Dead were buried in graves blasted out of the volcanic rock. Loneliness also took its toll. Stories abound about the way men called the rocks by name and greeted goats as friends.

No sooner did the Americans move out, formally leaving the base's stripped-down remains to the Ecuadorian government, than the *Galápagueños* on Santa Cruz began arriving by boat, peeling the precious wood from those buildings and carrying it back to build their own homes. There still stand rickety structures in the town of Puerto Ayora that were built with what the locals lovingly, laughingly, call "Baltra pine."

The air base at Baltra sounded the death knell for San Cristobal, though the bell didn't actually ring until thirteen years after the base was shut down. That's when the Galápagos National Park came into being, in the summer of 1959, with outlines for a purposeful tourist industry, a plan that included taking that abandoned runway at Baltra and turning it into a modern airport—modern, at least, by Ecuadorian standards. When the airport eventually opened for regular, once-a-week flights in 1970 and a roadway was put through five years after that, running twenty-five miles from Baltra south over the mountains of Santa Cruz to the village of Puerto Ayora, the fate of San Cristobal was sealed.

One last pathetic attempt to "colonize" Cristobal was made in 1959 by a group of Americans from Washington State lured by a newspaper ad that read:

> **Wanted: Swiss Family Robinson. Is your family one of the 50 adventurous families with the spirit of America's early pioneers needed to establish a model community on a beautiful Pacific island?**

The ad was placed by the founder of a sketchy utopian organization called *Filate Science Antrorse* ("Together with Science We Move Forward"). More than one hundred men, women, and children answered the ad, with plans to occupy the old fish-processing plant left by the Norwegians from the 1920s. They envisioned a lobster fishery there, and a working farm as well, on the land that was once El Progreso.

They didn't get far. Upon their arrival, they found the processing plant in ruins, virtually useless. Their feeble attempts at gardening were destroyed by wild pigs and burros. On the Ecuadorian mainland, where a national election was taking place, the Americans on San Cristobal became an issue. A Communist Party candidate warned in a campaign speech, "Ecuadorians awaken! The small band of Americans in the Galápagos is but a prelude to a major-scale invasion. Yankee imperialists are about to take our islands." One Ecuadorian newspaper editorial was headlined: "Don't Let the Same Thing Happen to the Galápagos That Happened to Texas." By January of 1961, all but one of the American "colonists" had returned to the States.

A few tourists today still arrive in the Galápagos at San Cristobal, but not many, not compared with the jetloads that land twice a day at Baltra. While dozens of cruise ships crowd the harbor at Puerto Ayora, only a small handful are anchored at Wreck Bay. And the one flight that arrives each morning at San Cristobal's airport, which was opened in 1987, is sometimes filled with no more than a couple of bureaucrats, come to take care of dreary government business.

A nicely paved, two-lane road runs from Wreck Bay up to that airport. The airport's terminal, like the one at Baltra, looks like a large picnic shelter, an open-air pavilion, where ocean breezes blow past passengers and baggage waiting to be processed.

There is no one in sight on this morning. But there is a faint noise, the soft sound of music drifting out from behind a closed door beyond the closed snack bar. Move closer to that door and the music takes shape—Frank Sinatra's "My Way."

There, in a small, wood-paneled office, a large, middle-aged man in a shirt with no tie, nice slacks, and shined shoes peers through spectacles at some documents stacked on his desk. An air conditioner hums in the room's only window, above a small CD player, which, when Sinatra is finished, shuts off. A woman sits alone at a desk by the door, answering the telephone when it rings, which is hardly at all.

The man's name, if you ask, is Abdon Guerrero, and this is his airport—or it may as well be. He's the architect who designed it. When it was done, he became its manager, running the place for Saeta Airlines, whose planes are the ones that land here once a day. Compared with TAME, Ecuador's only other air carrier, which is owned by the military and controls nearly all the nation's flights—including those lucrative, two-a-day loops from the mainland to Baltra and back—Saeta is but a speck, a wink at the concept of competition. Every morning, Guerrero arrives at his desk half-expecting to hear that Saeta's shut down and he's out of a job.

Don't get him wrong, he still has hope. This island might not be growing, he'll be the first to admit, but it's not dying either—at least not yet. He still believes, as he did when he moved here ten years ago with his wife and kids from their home in Guayaquil, that given the chance, San Cristobal could become something big, even if the tourism doesn't work out. In the time that Guerrero has been here, he's seen even the day tours dry up. The foreigners who land here are taken straight to their cruise ships anchored out in the bay. Those ships used to hang around for a day, maybe two, and their tourists would spend time in town, spending their money in the restaurants and bars and hiring taxis and drivers to take them up to the highlands. But in the last five or six years, those ships have gone straight out to circle the islands, taking the tourists and their money along with them. If they make a port call at all, it is over in Puerto Ayora.

But then, isn't it like that everyplace? Guerrero sighs. The rich get richer, while the poor—well, just look around at the half-finished buildings, the hotels with no guests, the harbor with hardly a tour boat in sight. If it weren't for the government and the navy base out on the point, there'd be no business at all here in Puerto Baquerizo, at least none you could count on.

What they really should do, if they had any sense at all, says Guerrero, is establish an institute here, a college of oceanography and biology and Galápagos culture, a *real* university with *real* professors and students, not a strange setup like the one they've got over on Santa

Cruz, that Research Station, or whatever they call it. Guerrero doesn't quite know how to say it, but the people who work over there, with their long hair and beards and their torn, dirty T-shirts, it's like they're . . . well . . . *hippies*, not scientists. What Guerrero would like to see, what would save San Cristobal and launch it headlong into the twenty-first century, he believes, would be an actual campus with buildings and classrooms to outshine that . . . that crude *camp* that they've got over there.

His wife says he's a dreamer. So okay, he's a dreamer. Is that, he asks, such a bad thing? The fact is, he feels lucky to live in this place, a place of such peace. But if, God forbid, he should ever lose this job, it would not be the end of the world. He'd go back to the mainland and find something else. It's an option he knows most of his neighbors on this island don't have, and he does not take this for granted. He's lucky, he knows, to have lived the life that he has, to have taken his wife and his children to the United States, to see New York City. That photograph on his desk of the four of them standing in front of the World Trade Center, that trip was like a dream, says Guerrero. Like visiting another planet.

How, he asks, could anyone not love the United States? Frank Sinatra. "My Way." Or how about that big band from the old days, from World War II, what was their name? Yes, the Glenn Miller Band, that's the one. Now listen to this, he says, and he puts on a disk, and the strains of a clarinet pour like sweet syrup from his small CD player. When the Americans were here at that base over in Baltra, he says, closing his eyes and leaning back in his chair, *this* was the music they played.

It continues to play as the door closes shut, and the taste of the sea hangs in the hot air, and the afternoon breeze blows bits of paper and dust across the black tarmac runway, and the faint sound of the surf carries up past the cactus and lizards and rocks.

The surfing is pathetic. There's no kinder way to put it. Eight people were here—four Venezuelans, three from Peru, one from New Zealand—when Jason, Robert, Andrew, and Sebas arrived late this morning at the clear turquoise cove that opens out to the breaks of

La Lobería, just below the San Cristobal airport. Only the Venezuelans are still out there, bobbing like corks as they sit on their
boards, peering toward the horizon and praying for something more
than the soft, three-foot swells undulating beneath them.

The Peruvians are playing tag with a sea lion in the cove's crystal
shallows, while the New Zealander lies on the white, powdery beach,
asleep on a towel with his girlfriend beside him. Jason tries staying
upbeat, but he can't hide his disgust. They could have stayed home
and found better waves in Puerto Ayora, at Tortuga, or even up by the
Research Station, at the break they call *La Ratanera*—"The
Rathole"—where Jason first learned to surf.

After a couple of hours, they call it a day and unzip their wet suits,
sling their packs on their shoulders, slide their boards under their
arms, and trudge back up toward town. As they reach the top of the
ridge, where the trail flattens out, Jason turns to take one last look
down at the surf.

"Don't," says Andrew, as he grabs Jason's arm and turns him
around. "It always starts breaking when you stop and look back."

The hike home is a long one, the sun beating down on the dusty
clay path. The boys pass a quarry, layers of red earth and black rock
formed over the ages, now laid open and stripped bare. There are no
men or machinery in sight, just a raw gaping crater, a violation somehow of a landscape where there still exist plateaus and slopes and
ravines on which man has never set foot.

By the time the group reaches the village, the sun's almost
down. Bico and Petra are uptown visiting friends. Mariana and
Lobo sit by the harbor, on a bench near a tree strung with bright
Christmas lights. Across the road, on a cracked concrete wall, the
words *"FELIZ MILLENNIUM"* are scribbled in paint.

Lobo shakes his head, smiling, as his defeated friends approach.
They don't know what they will do tomorrow, they say. Maybe
they'll stay here and hope to get lucky. Or maybe they'll leave,
who knows. Right now they're heading back to the *Symbol* to
change into some clothes. They'll spend the night on the boat later
on, after they've killed a few hours checking out a few bars. They
wouldn't mind a nice bed in one of those little hotels just up the

way, but they don't have the cash. No big deal, Robert says, shrugging, dancing away toward the wharf, singing aloud: "*If I were a rich man . . .*"

Lobo and Mariana didn't make that trip up to the highlands. They couldn't find a ride. Still, it's been a good day, just being here, together, alone. Mariana's even smiling a little, watching the villagers emerge to stroll the streets as the night coolness falls. She's in her late twenties, but she looks ten years younger, her shining, black hair cut short and straight like a boy's, her slim, shapely figure clothed in a tank top, gym shorts, and a pair of white sneakers. She's talking right now, in clipped broken English, about an American man she wishes she could meet. His name is Leo Buscaglia. She has read his books, about grief and loss and the paths back to joy. She wonders where this man lives. She wants so much to write him a letter.

Lobo just listens. He wishes there were more he could do, but what might that be? He's not a psychologist, and if he were, can a man be a therapist to the woman he loves? Can he answer the questions she has about the things that he does—or can't do—that are so much a part of the problems she feels?

Mariana knows Lobo loves her. She knows he's a good man, doing the best he can. But there's no question this thing—the death of her daughter—is taking its toll on everything in their lives, including their marriage. It doesn't help that Lobo's job takes him away for weeks at a time, on those boats with those tourists, while Mariana stays home with the walls closing in. When they get back tomorrow, or maybe the day after that, he will leave right away on a six-week tour aboard the *Santa Cruz*. It's as if Lobo's a soldier, always going to war while Mariana stays behind to deal with the grief and the guilt by herself.

It's been two months since they buried the baby, and Mariana hasn't once been to the cemetery, though it's only a few blocks from her home. She's emptied the room where her little girl slept, thrown away everything, as if the child never existed. Her parents said that would help, but it hasn't. Nothing has helped. Her friends tell her to confront what has happened, then move on. But she's afraid to do that. If she faced this thing fully, gave herself to her feelings, she's afraid she'd fall into those feelings forever. Just keep falling and falling.

She loves Lobo, there's no question about that. But she doesn't know if she can take this anymore. She doesn't know what she will do.

Lobo sits quietly, sipping a beer, the evening breeze at his back. Mariana asks for a tequila, which he brings her with lime and some salt.

"*Caliente,*" she says softly, wincing and smiling after downing the shot. It makes her feel, how you say . . . *dicha*? Happy?

"*Borracho,*" laughs Lobo. "Drunk."

Mariana lights a cigarette, but Lobo demurs. He quit not long ago. When he was a kid, no older than six, living up in New York, he and his friends used to scour the sidewalks and gutters, hunting for half-finished smokes. When they found one, they'd cross themselves, like good Catholic boys, before lighting it up. "Blessing the butts," Lobo laughs. That's what they called it.

By midnight everyone is back on the *Symbol,* asleep as the sea lions glide past the hull. In the morning, the boys give the surf one more chance, at the spot they call Tonga, up by the naval base. But the waves just aren't there, and by midafternoon they've set sail in the direction home. It will be dark when they get there, but that's not a problem. The reefs and currents off Puerto Ayora are nothing like those at Wreck Bay.

By dusk they're beyond Santa Fé. For dinner Petra boils some shrimp and *pulpo* (octopus) and serves it with rice. Then they each find a spot on the deck and gaze up at the stars as the outline of Santa Cruz takes shape ahead. Less than two hours later they are there, the harbor aglitter with the lights of the tour boats, the sounds of traffic and music and laughter drifting down from the length of Darwin Avenue. The tourists strolling past the night-shadowed wharf hardly give them a glance as the ragged crew unload their surfboards and gear, hug one another goodbye, and head home to their beds.

SIX

Four and a Half

Isla Genovesa

JANUARY 5, 2000

"Mary" and "Miriam" of Quatro y Media

It's been only four days since Jason and his friends left for their surf trip, but the *sucre* has plunged in that time from 20,000 per U.S. dollar to 25,000. The experts in Quito are talking of hyperinflation, an economy spun out of control. The government is tottering on the brink of collapse. There is talk among Mahuad and his staff of scrapping the *sucre* entirely, dumping those near-worthless coins and deflated bills and adopting instead the same dollars the United States uses. An old Ecuadorian proverb—"To cure rabies, kill the dog"—has been quoted to justify the plan. But not all dogs die quietly.

Even as Mahuad's advisors debate this so-called "dollarization," they can hear shouts and chants rising up from the street outside the presidential palace in Quito, where thousands of demonstrators—students, laborers, Indians—have been massing for days now. The smell of the tear gas fired each afternoon to disperse the mobs still lingers the next morning as the crowds reappear to face the helmeted troops yet again.

This is the world Jason and his friends had tried to escape, if only for a few days. But there is no getting away from it, not even here, on this island, in the middle of the ocean. When he shows up at the store this Tuesday morning, Jason finds Christy there, and José-Luis too, but the front door is locked, and a sign says CERRADO—"Closed."

Christy's upstairs in the small attic office, counting tall stacks of twenties and fifties and hundred-dollar U.S. bills. Some of that money is hers and José's, but most belongs to friends, who trust Christy to take care of their cash and send it on to an account she keeps in Miami. It's been years since she had to do this, to act as a private bank—there was no bank in town when she last brokered money like this—but the sky is falling right now, and so she's at it again.

As for the store being closed, the *sucre* is sinking so fast that the price tags on the shop's products mean nothing. Beyond that, the suppliers on the mainland have been shut down for days, so the store's shelves are half empty. It's a good time to take inventory, which Jason now begins and will continue to do for the next several days.

No one's taking inventory up at the Quatro y Media. No one there seems to care about news from the mainland. No matter which way the wind blows, the Quatro y Media is open for business at five each afternoon. Its women are ready and waiting at the bar or along the bench by the dance floor, where the disco ball glitters and the wall-to-wall mirror shines, or out on the concrete front porch, which looks down on a sloping landscape of *opuntia* cactus and bleak brush-covered fields, four and a half kilometers north of Puerto Ayora in the middle of nowhere.

"Four and a Half." That's what the townspeople call this place, though its proprietor, Mary Rodriguez, wrinkles her nose at that name. The actual name of her business, she insists, is Amazonas. That's what she's got printed on the cards she hands out to the people who ask, though few of her customers have reason to ask. They've been coming here for years, most of them. And for the newcomers, well, it's easy enough to find the way. Just flag down a taxi, or if it's a weekend, look for the bus with the colored lights strung on its roof. Mary's got a deal with the vehicle's owners, and every Friday and Saturday night they drape those lights on the bus, like it's Christmas, and it winds through the town, stopping at the outdoor restaurants and bars, picking up anyone who wants to climb aboard and carrying them for free up to Mary's place. The bus brings them back, too, as long as they're finished by, say, three A.M. That's when the driver goes home. If the customers aren't done by then, they can pay for a taxi, or—and many do this—they can just walk back to town, the stars showing the way as they stumble downhill toward the ocean.

There are those who are upset that such a business is here. On the mainland, okay, but not here on these islands. Most of the tourists have no idea this place even exists, but the townspeople know, and there are those who all but spit upon Mary and her girls when they come down to the village to shop or have some lunch at a café on the water. The priest on the radio has a field day with Mary, as if she gives a damn. She's seen so many priests come and go over the years she can hardly remember their faces. As for the town's women, who huddle and whisper when Mary comes into view: Well, let's see now, how many of their husbands and boyfriends were up at her place just last weekend?

No, Mary doesn't give a damn what any of them think. She makes a good living, depends on no one to support her, and does nothing illegal—well, okay, maybe she's spent a night here and there in the jail. But that's politics more than anything else, Mary explains. Morality? She just laughs. The same men who have put her behind bars are customers at her club. She doesn't hold it against them. It comes with the territory.

Mary understood this when she first opened this business in the spring of 1992. It kind of surprised her husband, to come home from a trip to Spain and discover his wife had taken their house on the farm up near Bellavista and moved three young women into it, who charged by the hour for the pleasure of their company. This, in the same bedrooms where Mary and he and their two children had once slept. But Mary's husband adjusted, and though they soon divorced, the two remain friends and partners. The property the place sits on is half his, though he has nothing to do with the business itself.

It was tough getting started, Mary will tell you, her thick, little legs crossed as she leans back in a chair by the door of her "cabaret," as she calls it. A nest of orange hair tumbles down from her head, and it quivers when she laughs, which is often. She wasn't open three days, she recalls, when the police came and shut her place down. "These islands," the mayor and his lot told her, "are for the plants and the animals." Mary remembers their words exactly. This thing she was doing, they said, this is not "the morality of the Galápagos."

Mary lights up a Belmont and blows the smoke out between thin, hard-set lips. "The morality of the Galápagos." She smiles, repeating the phrase. The same men who told her these words collected bribes every day for the decisions they made. They were businessmen, right? Fine. This was a business as well, she told them, pure and simple. Her friends, she admits, did not quite agree. Actually, she says, they were neighbors, not friends. Would friends have so swiftly shunned her? "Who needs them?" she says, taking another drag from her cigarette.

Her children, however, now that was a problem. Her daughter was ten when Mary started this place, her son only six, and their classmates at school made fun of them both. The priest mentioned her children by name on the radio, as he railed against Mary, and that was simply too much. She didn't care what the priest said about her, but to do this to her children was going too far.

Her children were affected, Mary admits, nodding her head. They begged her to please leave this job, leave this profession. But Mary said no, she would not. Instead she sent them both to the mainland, where her son is now finishing school and her daughter is married.

The townspeople think this is easy work. Mary smiles. They have no idea how hard it can be running a business like this. *She* had no idea, not when she started. Those three girls she began with arrived from the mainland by word of mouth. They heard someone was trying to get this thing going out in the Galápagos, and they came on their own. When the police shut the place down, Mary moved the girls down into town, where she and her husband owned a small pharmacy. The girls worked the front counter, and there were rooms in the back. Business was so good the girls sent word to Guayaquil, and two friends came out to join them. For a while no one asked why five women were needed to fill prescriptions at such a small *farmacia.*

The police finally caught on, throwing Mary and her *chicas* in jail. Twenty-four hours for the girls, Mary says with a smile, eight days for her. When she was released, it was business as usual, only now her girls simply worked on the streets: in the park, down by the wharf, in front of the priest's chapel itself. Eventually, Mary flew to the mainland, where a friend up in Quito arranged a meeting with a government minister. When Mary returned from that trip, she had a permit in hand. On the continent, she explains, this kind of business is not only an accepted thing, it is actually required in some communities, where laws have been written stipulating that for every so many hundreds of people, a bordello must be provided; the same as a hospital, or a library, or any other public service. Or so Mary says.

In any event, when she returned from that 1993 trip to Quito, Mary's business was legal, and it's been so ever since. She's got a staff of ten women now, rotated each month from the continent, where some live respectable lives, Mary explains, with only their close friends and families having any idea what they do when they visit the Galápagos.

A young woman named Miriam takes a seat beside Mary and says that it's true, that her life is like that. She and her husband own a home in Guayaquil, Miriam says, where nobody knows what she does for a living. Mary buys her a plane ticket—four million *sucres* round trip—and takes it out of her pay, which is par for the course. At the end of the month, Miriam says, she still clears ten million *sucres* (about four hundred dollars), which is three times what she would make on the mainland for the same work.

Miriam says she is twenty-five, that she was born to a poor farming family in the east Ecuadorian region they call the *Oriente*. She says she was sold as an infant to a rich husband and wife who wanted a daughter. The family threw her out on the street, she says, when a daughter of their own was born. Miriam was forced to have sex to survive. She became pregnant and gave birth to a severely deformed baby boy, which she gave up for adoption because she could not afford his medical care. There's no telling how much of Miriam's story is true, but the tears washing down her face when she's finished are real.

As Miriam sits beside Mary, half-dressed women come and go down the hall, getting ready for work. The barman is stocking the cooler with cases of beer as a mutt curls beside him asleep. Outside, the sun bakes the gray gravel parking lot, which by nightfall will be crowded with pickups and taxis, as the deejay spins Prince and Kiss on the sound system and the disco ball twirls, and the girls work the crowd, luring the shy ones away from their friends.

Mary's rates are fair, say the men who come here routinely. For 90,000 *sucres* you get fifteen minutes, which is cheaper, they say, than the rates on the mainland. If you want—and if Mary's business is slow—you can have a woman all night for only 260,000 *sucres* . . . just over ten dollars. You can't keep her here, though. Mary doesn't allow it. If you buy a woman for the night, you've got to take her away and bring her back in the morning. Some guys do it right, say the regulars. They take the girl down into town, treat her to dinner, maybe go to a disco, then rent a hotel room. The whole nine yards. Others, well, they simply hire a taxi and tell the driver to take them someplace and park. Then there are those who don't even bother with that. They just take the girls out into the fields around Mary's property and spend the night there.

To Mary it's all the same, it's all business. The question of health has come up in the past several years, but Mary claims her girls are all clean, that not one case of AIDS has come out of the Quatro y Media. The fact is, it's hard to tell how many cases of AIDS there have been on the islands at all. Max Parédes, who's in charge of the hospital in Puerto Ayora, which is really no more than a clinic, stated not long ago that you could count on one hand the number of AIDS cases they've had in the Galápagos. But there are plenty more locals than that who will tell you of a friend or a relative who has contracted the virus. Most of them had to move to the mainland to find adequate care. That's where some of them are still living and where some have died. Maybe that's why Max Parédes' numbers don't quite add up.

Who knows if Paredes is counting the guide from San Cristobal, the one everybody called George—just "George." He had HIV, only he didn't tell anyone, and he slept with a good number of women, as some tour guides do. That's one of the perks of the job, the guides will tell you. "The pussy, man," they say, tossing back drinks at the Galápason, pursing their lips and shaking their heads. "It's *amazing.*"

It makes perfect sense, they explain. Here are these tourist women in this exotic place, far away from their jobs, their homes, their friends, their *identities*. They can do anything they like here. No one back home will know about it. And what a lot of the tourist women like, the male guides will tell you, is a fling with a Latin man. As for the guides themselves, quite a few are more than happy to oblige.

George was one such guide. The word is, he wound up infecting several women, including his wife, who was pregnant at the time. Their baby was born healthy, but at least two of the women George slept with were not so lucky. They contracted the virus, as did an untold number of men George's wife subsequently had sex with (she was no more faithful than George). Between them, the couple had quite a few islanders, as one puts it, "shit scared." Because of George and his wife, the village's schools began teaching about AIDS, and free testing was offered, and it still is today.

One of José-Luis's nephews died of the disease back in 1994. The best the family could figure was that he contracted the virus from a blood transfusion, during an operation he'd had six years earlier. But there's no way to be sure. When the young man got sick, his family went down to the hospital to check on his records and found that the hospital had been sold to new owners, who burned all the previous records.

Christy thinks it was in 1994 when José-Luis's nephew died. No, she's sure of it, because the young guy was determined to stay alive long enough to watch the World Cup that year. And he did.

Then he died. Which, for some reason, makes Christy think of that basketball player. You know, she says, the big, red-headed guy, vegetarian, tall, tall, *tall*, really into the Grateful Dead, had a career in the NBA . . . what's his name? Yeah, Bill Walton, that's the one. There was that time he showed up in Puerto Ayora with some friends—his brother and a couple of other guys, all Americans—and they wound up in a game against some of the village fellows, Pepé Villa and his buddies, on the outdoor court up at the school. A huge crowd gathered and watched, and it was hilarious. None of the Ecuadorians was over 5'4", but they had a blast. And when they were done, Walton gave Pepé his jersey as a gift, right there on the court. Pepé put the thing on, and it hung all the way down past his knees, like a dress.

Now how, Christy wonders, did she get off on Bill Walton? Oh yeah, the World Cup. Soccer. Sports. That's it. After that basketball game, Jack had Walton and his friends over to the hotel, fixed them all up with some food, which they really enjoyed. Walton and Jack had that Grateful Dead thing in common, what with Jack's old San Francisco days and Walton's well-known friendship with the band, so you might have thought they'd hit it off right away. But Walton kept to himself, didn't say much, and that was okay with Jack. He's never been one to to be dazzled by influence or fame, and he's certainly never sought it out.

Plenty of powerful people, the rich and the famous, have checked into Jack's hotel over the years, but by the time they get here, all the trappings they might wear in the world—wealth, status, celebrity—are dropped like unneeded clothing. Indeed, there is a kind of social nakedness on these islands, a bareness to the way in which people connect. The demographics of one's life—your job, family, even the country you come from—these things hardly matter here. What counts is the kind of person you are at the moment, right here, right now. If a chord of friendship is struck, this is how it is played, human-to-human in completely present-tense terms. That's how it happens with Jack and the hundreds of people who pass through his hotel each year. That's how it went when, a few years after Bill Walton's visit, Bill Kreutzmann, the Dead's longtime drummer, stayed at the hotel. He and Jack connected in a way that simply didn't happen with Walton, and they talked late into the evening about, well, about everything.

Jack's up at the hotel on this bright Tuesday morning, out in the open-air shed behind the laundry, rigging up one of the pieces of art he likes to cobble together from the wood, rocks, and bones he's collected over the years. This is a big one: heavy chunks of sun-bleached coral bound with thick copper tubing. The assemblage is dangling from the shed's wooden rafters while Jack goes at it with a glue gun and pliers. When it's finished, he plans to mount it in the lobby, which is like no hotel lobby his guests have seen anywhere else.

The lobby's cement floors are laid with reed mats. The chairs are pegged-wood and leather, built by a carpenters' cooperative on the mainland, in Cuenca. The co-op was started by a U.S. Peace Corps volunteer back in the mid-1960s. Jack's dad took a trip there in 1969 to pick up that furniture, and the stuff's still in the lobby today.

On the walls are hung paintings and collages created by Jack, and by Romy and Christy as well. The pieces are not quite what you'd find in a Holiday Inn. One is a pastel of a football-sized cockroach. Another is an acrylic, a bright Day-Glo image of Christ on the cross. A portrait of Darwin (the face of the bearded old man he became back in England decades after his trip to the Galápagos, not the clean-shaven, young ex-divinity student he was when he sailed through these islands) glares from behind a latched window frame. From the rafters hang a pelican skeleton and the bleached bones of whales suspended by wires, bones Jack has scavenged from beaches all over the islands. They are here now, reassembled, as if the creatures have come back to life.

Beneath the hovering bones is the bar, which is fashioned from the corks of hundreds of long-emptied bottles of liquor and wine and from old life preservers as well. No bartender is in sight, and none ever will be, not as long as Jack Nelson runs this place. His system is the same as it was when his father first set out a couple of fifths of whiskey and gin almost forty years ago. Pour your own. Jot your tab on a pad by the sink. The total becomes part of your bill, which begins at $60 a night for your room ($100 for two people), plus your meals (which are marked on a chalkboard), plus the bar bill, which you keep for yourself. Such a system of honor might not work at an Econo Lodge back in the States, but here, somehow it seems perfectly natural.

The shed in which Jack is working is dusty and hot. An owl chortles up in the cobwebbed rafters. Tiny gray geckos skitter across the rough concrete floor. Forrest and Jack built this shed in the summer of 1969. The table saw against the back wall, dust-coated and flaking with rust, was built by José-Luis for Forrest forty years ago, out of red mangrove shipped from the mainland, from the province of Esmeraldas. Red mangrove is almost extinct in Esmeraldas today, logged out like so much of the timber in Ecuador. But the saw is still standing, and though it looks like a ruined antique, it still works, as does the weathered block-and-tackle rig holding Jack's sculpture aloft.

His dad built that rig with pulleys that came off his sailboat, the *Nellie Brush*, the sloop that first brought Forrest down to these islands in the 1950s. Jack's father's hands are all over this place, though Forrest himself is no longer around. He took off to Thailand back in 1986 with a friend from Miami, a fellow named Ken Calfee.

Forrest said the islands had just changed too damned much. Too much bureaucracy, too many hangers-on, too much noise. There was a time when Forrest had known exactly what he wanted Jack to do with his corpse when he died.

"Wrap me in some chicken wire," he'd once said, sitting out behind the hotel, looking over the bay. "Attach some stones, take me out deep, and dump me." But that was before Forrest decided to leave, and now he's living in a place called Chiang Mai, up in the north part of Thailand, with his buddy Ken. That's where Forrest Nelson now wants to be buried, in Southeast Asia, not the Galápagos.

Actually, Jack's kind of worried about his dad at the moment. The old man's eighty-four; his knees are just about shot. There's been talk of a wheelchair, and not long ago he had to spend some time in an oxygen tent.

"He hates it," Jack says, dabbing glue on the coral. "It really pisses him off." The fact is, Forrest needs someone to care for him now, and that's too much to ask of Ken Calfee. So Jack's thinking about flying to Chiang Mai and bringing his father back home to the islands.

It would be a hell of a journey, no question. And there's no way Forrest would even agree. In terms of the bullshit that drove him away, the Galápagos is far worse now than it was when he took off fourteen years ago. Overpopulation, pollution, crime, corruption: Puerto Ayora now stinks with the very problems the old-timers who first moved to these islands were trying to escape. And some of the people who are supposed to be solving these problems stink even worse.

Look at the mayor. It's nice that the main streets in town have been paved since he was elected to office. But back up in the village, where the poor people live, the roads are still dirt, rocks, and dust. Why is it, some of them ask, that the pathway from town to the beach at Tortuga, a splendid mile-and-a-half walk through an Eden-like forest, was paved over just last year? Ask almost anyone in town, and they'll tell you that pathway was prettier and far more appropriate in its natural condition. The tourists seemed to enjoy it the way that it was, and those tens of thousands of cobblestones that were laid down to pave it surely could have been put to far better use up in the village.

Beyond the issue of where all these cobblestones ought to be laid, a more troubling question, say some of the locals, is why the town is spending so much money on street-paving at all, when so many people here are without electricity, decent medical care, a sound education for their children, or even fresh water. Puerto Ayora's desalinization plant, the only one on the islands, was a huge breakthrough when it was built in the late 1980s. But that water gets to only a small number of customers, with the vast majority of households still depending, as they always have, on roof-mounted tubs and rainfall, or on water trucked down from the hills (for which they pay by the barrel).

Could the fact that the mayor's brother-in-law owns the company that manufactures the cobblestones have anything to do with street-paving becoming such a priority?

When the mayor showed up with his wife not long ago at the Panga Discoteca and found his mistress dancing with the port captain, he dragged the woman out in the street and began beating her until he was finally stopped by some men who began beating *him* (hey, the mayor had brought his wife with him, they said, so he had no business attacking his mistress like that). Was it just a coincidence that immediately after, the paving of a certain roadway was suddenly halted, the roadway that ran past the mayor's mistress' house?

Or how about Fanny Uribe, one of the Galápagos' two representatives to the Ecuadorian Congress in Quito? Her face is on T-shirts worn by men, women, and children all over Puerto Ayora, shirts Fanny passed out like candy when she was running for office. People say it doesn't take much to get elected in Ecuador, and they seem to be right. That's how Bucaram became president, going through the poor sections of Ecuador's cities and into the countryside, passing out free bags of rice—something the people could hold in their hands, something they could eat. Bucaram knew. The people have heard so many promises from so many politicians for so many years that words mean next to nothing to them. They want something tangible, and they want it now. And who can blame them? Such thinking, of course, completely forfeits the future, which is one reason, say many, why Ecuador seems to get nowhere, why such concepts as long-term planning, long-term *anything*, are foreign to so many of its people. Again, who can blame them? A bird in the hand is a persuasive gift when those birds in the bush never seem to appear.

No one seemed to care much when it was discovered that the flat roof of Fanny Uribe's home in town was covered with *pepinos*, laid out to dry in the sun. A congresswoman dealing *pepinos!* Jack Nelson's friend, Mathias Espinosa—the two run the Hotel Galápagos' dive shop together—rounded up a group of protesters and a video camera and marched over to Fanny's house to shoot footage. Those cucumbers wound up on national television once the mainland stations got hold of it. But Fanny didn't budge. Her only response was to spit at her accusers: *"Usted esta denigrando mi personalidad!"* ("You are denigrating my personality!") and that was that. Case closed. Fanny Uribe still sits in Congress today.

Sure, it's funny, says Jack. It's hilarious in a sick, tragic way, especially if you don't live here. But for the people who do, he says, these absurdities are real. People are left suffering, these islands are left exposed and endangered, and it's getting worse all the time.

"Facade," Jack says, peering through spectacles at the bead of glue he's just laid on some coral. "So much of what you see in this town is facade.

"Take the restaurants," he says. "From the street they look fine, with drinking glasses and tablecloths and silverware. But take a look in the back, in the kitchen. Some of them don't even have running water. Some have no plumbing.

"And those boats," he continues, nodding toward the harbor. "They're each required by law to have a first-aid box. The law specifically states that the box must be mounted on a wall, painted white with a red cross outside. What's *inside* makes no difference. There might be nothing in there but a bottle of rum, three cockroaches, and a Band-Aid. But if it's white and it's got that red cross, it passes inspection.

"On the other hand, if you have a box filled with tourniquets, splints, antibiotics, an airway tube, a manual of operation, every conceivable kind of medical supply, and that box is stained cedar and varnished on the outside—no white paint, no red cross—you don't pass. That," he says, biting his lip as he bends a section of copper, "is what I mean by facade."

Ask Jason and José-Luis up at their hardware store and they say the same thing. They see it firsthand, selling the supplies these boat owners use to make their repairs. Some of those boats out in that harbor are held together by nothing but tape. A navy inspector arrives, they paint over the tape. If they own two boats but just one fire extinguisher, they don't buy another extinguisher; they just move the one they have from one boat to the other whenever the inspector arrives. The inspectors wised up to this not long ago and began asking to see receipts for the individual extinguishers. No problem. The boat owners promptly came into the store asking for receipts; not extinguishers, but receipts. If Jason or the guys working the counter beside him refused to sell the boat owners the false stubs, that was no problem. There are other hardware stores in town.

One of Jack's hotel staff, a young Ecuadorian man, appears with a quick, hurried question. Jack responds in smooth, fluid Spanish, not taking his eyes off his work. His manner is unhurried, controlled. There is nothing animated in the way that he speaks, showing few traces of emotion other than the occasional sign of bemusement. Jack's face is rock-jawed and craggy, but still he looks young, younger than he should after the fifty-two years he has lived. His coppery hair, which once trailed down his back, is now graying and cropped short. The beard he wore in his twenties and thirties is gone. So, too, are the ropy muscles of his youth, though he's still lean and strong enough to tend to the carpentry, plumbing, and masonry work required each day to maintain a hotel in a place where materials and labor are often impossible to find.

This shed itself is a testament to resourcefulness and ingenuity, the ability to recycle and reinvent odd scraps of wood, plastic, and metal that would be tossed on a trash heap in more "developed" environments. Metal springs, PVC piping, loose planks of wood, pieces of rubber—Jack's got this stuff piled all over his property. Nothing is thrown away here. Everything eventually finds a purpose, which is fitting in a place like the Galápagos, where the concept of purpose—of use, of need—is at the root of the process of natural selection, of evolution, of survival.

The worn, mildewy books lining a shelf in Jack's office just off the lobby are bibles of the hands-on kind of knowledge it takes to have lived here all these years. One is a hardcover titled *The Way Things Work*. Its do-it-yourself chapters range from instructions on building a steam boiler to wiring a radio receiver to fixing a sewing machine and finally to a section titled "Why Does a Ship Float?"

Beside that book sits a heavy tome titled *Henley's Twentieth Century Formulas, Recipes and Processes*. This one was published in 1927. Jack's dad picked it up in a used bookstore before making his first trip to the islands in the '50s. Its subtitle reads *Ten Thousand Selected Household Workshop and Scientific Formulas, Trade Secrets, Chemical Recipes, Processes and Money Saving Ideas.* Among these are an ingredient list for homemade glue, instructions for treating hemlock poisoning, a recipe for imitation roquefort cheese, and an entry titled "To Protect Papered Walls from Vermin."

Finally, fittingly, there is a crumbling 1968 first edition of the *Whole Earth Catalog*, which Jack acquired when he first joined his father. The pages are sprinkled with Jack's hand-scribbled notes written decades ago: references to weaving, paper fasteners, wart cures.

Jack himself will be the first to tell you he's a jack-of-all-trades, master of . . . well, maybe a few. Just like his dad. They've always been able to take care of themselves, do whatever needs doing, which is what this hotel is all about. It may not have the luster of, say, the Red Mangrove Inn, Polo and Monica Navarro's place, which sits right next door in all of its splendor. Its mosquelike architecture, bright pink paint job, blue-cushioned deck furniture, four-person hot tub, and open-air bar with its hop-to-it bartender, all overlooking the bay. But then there are those who wonder whether a place like that belongs in the Galápagos. It's so . . . Club Med. That's the image a lot of the locals, the ones disgusted by all this development, use to describe the

Red Mangrove. But you won't hear Jack Nelson say it. He's far too cir-
cumspect to go bad-mouthing his competition. But it's clear by the
way he runs his place that the world of the Red Mangrove is a universe away.

As far as Jack is concerned, true traveling—and he's done his fair
share of it, from Tahiti to the Arctic—is about stepping outside
your comfort zone, leaving behind the world that you know, the
life you control, and putting yourself in a different environment,
where the fundamental requirement is that you go with the flow.
This is what too many travelers Jack has seen over the years—
mostly Americans and Europeans—don't know how to do. They
just can't bring themselves to give up that viselike grip on their
lives as they know them. They come here, to the end of the world,
and they want to know where the ice machine is, if their room has
a phone, and why the showers don't get hot right away.

The problem, as Jack sees it, is that these people are simply
unable to adapt! Ironic, isn't it? He smiles. They come to this near-
holy place, where every rock and every creature resonates with the
passage of eons, where the very air vibrates with the ageless magni-
tude of life on this planet, and all they can think about is their six
o'clock dinner reservation down at the Garrapata and whether the
limes with their gin-and-tonics are fresh.

As far as Jack can figure it—and God knows he's given this
plenty of thought—these people are rarely required to adapt in the
environment that breeds them. If something breaks down, they call
someone to fix it. Something goes wrong, and there's someone who
will come make it right: a repairman, a doctor, a lawyer. The culture that's developed in America and societies like it, says Jack,
breeds dependency, liability, blame. He hates to say it, but the safer
you make a society, the softer the people become.

And more helpless as well. Make a place idiot-proof, he says with
a shrug, and you wind up with a large number of idiots. Who, he adds,
wind up in over their heads when they travel abroad. He's seen it so
many times over the years: tourists who run into trouble, say, in Peru
or Indonesia, and the first thing they do is call their embassy to come
bail them out. It doesn't occur to them that the point of journeying

into these places, the essence of true traveling, is to put yourself out there on your own, with no safety net, nobody to sue if you happen to step into an open manhole on a side street in Istanbul.

The same goes for the Galápagos tourists who sometimes forget that those animals they mingle with on these islands and beaches, for all of their innocence, are still animals. If your guide says beware of that sea lion bull raising up on his hindquarters to protect his harem, it's best that you listen. You've got to be on your toes to travel this way, says Jack. And when you stop and think about it, what's wrong with that? he asks. Being there, really *being* there—isn't that what a journey of any sort should be all about?

When Jack thinks of what it was like just to *get* to the Galápagos in the old days, well, the tourists who complain about the bad food on those TAME flights—and the food is pretty bad, he admits—have no idea how good they've got it. One of Jack's first boat trips out from the mainland, at the turn of the '70s, was on a recycled and refitted World War II American landing craft that was renamed *El Presidente* by the Ecuadorian entrepreneur who'd bought it. The thing was powered by eight diesel engines, four for each of the boat's two bent propeller shafts. Every three months or so, *El Presidente* would leave Guayaquil for the islands so overloaded with people and freight that it actually sagged at both ends and bowed up in the middle—a condition seen in tired, overloaded hulls called "hogging." It was hard to find qualified men willing to captain such a decrepit wreck. The boat's skipper for Jack's trip was a young Ecuadorian naval lieutenant who was dragooned for the job. The kid had done something wrong, and his punishment was to navigate this floating disaster out to the Galápagos.

The trip took five days, recalls Jack, and what he remembers most vividly is that those eight engines never worked all at once. You could hear the mechanics banging away night and day, pulling pieces off one to repair another and then *that* one would break down, and so on. At one point, all eight engines quit, and *El Presidente* sat dead in the Pacific for five hours, an experience Jack recalls as being not entirely unpleasant. It being March, the sea between Guayaquil and the islands was calm and flat, the sky cloudless and blue. Surrounding the ship were vast shoals of blue crabs, thousands of them sliding past just beneath the sea's smooth glassy surface. Every so often a slight ripple would appear—the fin of a sea turtle swimming lazily past the becalmed barge.

There were 140 passengers squeezed onto that boat. They slept in the hold, on the deck, on the cargo, on each other. But as bad as that was, the return trip to the continent was worse. Jack took that trip once, on a different ship, and he'd sooner swim the whole way than ever do it again. The humans were mixed in with large herds of livestock—cattle and goats sold by Galápagan farmers and bound for the mainland. The animals stood shoulder to shoulder from the bow to the deckhouse, more than one hundred cows tied to the rails, and more than four hundred goats rioting in the hold.

Jack was lucky enough on that trip to have a cabin. Unfortunately, he had several roommates. One was a British scientist named Ian Thornton, who later wrote one of the first guidebooks to the Galápagos. Thornton was delightful company, but Jack's other two cabinmates were a mainland Ecuadorian couple coming back from a honeymoon on the islands. With them were some of their wedding gifts, including two baby goats, which did nothing, as Jack puts it, but "shit, piss, and bleat" from the moment the ship lifted anchor. Jack soon evicted the kids—the goats, not the couple—and when the honeymooners tried bringing the animals back in the cabin, he threatened to fling the things overboard.

As bad as it was in that stinking cabin, it was worse up on deck, where the cattle were constantly seasick, as cattle on ships often are. When cattle get nauseous, Jack explains, they produce unending strings of slick, viscous drool, which hang from their snouts to the deck. Think of the worst seasickness you've ever experienced, then imagine what it must be like for a creature with five stomachs. By the time that ship reached Guayaquil, recalls Jack, its deck was coated with a thick, slippery layer of slime.

It's not just the tourists who have no idea what it was like back in those days. Most of today's locals weren't here at the time. But they do understand, most of them, the harsh realities of these islands.

And they respect those realities. They know that behind the spectacular allure of this breathtaking place are dangers, both natural and man-made. This is something else about traveling, says Jack, this matter of respect. A true traveler approaches a foreign place with humility, with the acknowledgment that he is in someone else's land, on someone else's turf, playing by someone else's rules. He displays this humility by being open and aware, by listening rather than speaking, by receiving rather than delivering, and by accepting and responding rather than controlling and demanding. Nowhere is such humility more necessary than in a place where Mother Nature is in charge. She can be a seductive temptress, easily underestimated and brutally cruel when taken too lightly. There are few places on Earth where this is more true than in the Galápagos.

Jack Nelson has seen it firsthand, more times than he can count. A few years back, a guest checked into the hotel, a philosophy professor from Dartmouth who was spending his summer knocking around South America. The forty-year-old man was a long-distance runner. One morning he decided to take a jaunt into the hills to a tortoise reserve up near Steve Divine's place, just below the hamlet of Santa Rosa, a distance of about twenty kilometers.

The man told no one where he was going. Two days later, his bed was still unslept in, a fact reported to Jack by one of his staff. After confirming that his guest was indeed missing—that he was not simply sleeping off a bad hangover someplace up in town, which is not rare among vacationers here—Jack phoned the U.S. Consulate's office in Guayaquil. Search parties were sent up to the highlands and out along the coast. They found nothing that day, or the next. A week went by, and by then they knew they were hunting for a corpse, just as they had been when an Israeli photographer, a former commando trained in desert survival, wandered into this same jungle a few years earlier. (The latter's body was finally found six months later by some lobster divers on a small beach at the southwest edge of the island. The fishermen noticed a skull in the sand, dug away the dirt, and found an entire skeleton buried up to its neck. "Possibly in an attempt to keep mosquitoes off," says

Jack, "or maybe in a dying effort to conserve moisture." In any event, the Israeli was long dead, cooked by the sun and eaten by insects.)

This was what Jack and the search party expected to find when, ten days after the professor disappeared, he was discovered, curled by a rock in the highland jungle, a sliver of life still left in his dehydrated bones.

"He looked and felt dead," recalls Jack, who, after the man was carried down from the mountain, nursed him to life in one of the Hotel Galápagos' beds by feeding him teaspoons of orange juice. The man would have died, Jack is sure, if he hadn't been a long-distance runner.

Injuries and deaths among visitors to these islands are more frequent than might be imagined, though Jack would rather not talk too much about it. Again, bad for business. To the outside world, through the portraits painted by the tourism industry and by those ubiquitous television documentaries, the Galápagos seem so benign, just a natural stage upon which innocent animals, birds, and fish perform for the pleasure of their human audience. But these islands can kill.

Jack himself underestimated the heat when he first came here that summer of '67. His dad put him to work the day he arrived. They were building a dock. Jack wore a hat but no shirt. He wound up with third-degree burns on his back and his neck.

It's not only *gringos* who misjudge this place terribly. In the early 1980s, a battalion of Ecuadorian marines came to the Galápagos for their final exam, as it were, in survival training. Three hundred of them, with one day's worth of water and rations, were dropped off on the west coast of Isabela. Their challenge was to cross to the island's east side, a distance of about fifteen miles as a bird flies, but closer to twice that for a man on foot, who must traverse steep, stone-covered hillsides and vine-clogged ravines.

These marines were tough, and they knew it. Before even beginning their trek, many of them didn't think twice about chugging one of the two canteens of water they'd each been allotted. They knew they'd be finished long before the eight hours they'd been given to make this crossing.

They were wrong. The hills they encountered were covered with razor-sharp *'a'a* lava, the worst kind there is. The photos shown of smooth, syrupy, hardened lava here and in spots like Hawaii are of *pahoehoe* lava. *'A'a,* on the other hand, is like broken glass, fragile enough to crush underfoot and sharp enough to slice through the highest-grade combat boot—like the ones those Ecuadorian marines were wearing that day.

The thing about *'a'a,* say locals, is that it gets you both ways—in the feet and the hands. Imagine climbing a mountain of broken beer bottles, they say. It offers no footing, crumbling and breaking away with each step as it slices into your shoes. When you reach for a grip, it's like grabbing a fistful of razor blades.

Before the marines had gone two miles, their boots were shredded and useless, their hands bloody and raw. A sergeant who survived the ordeal later told Jack he could see a disaster in the making by the time the group had gone five miles. He ordered the soldiers within earshot to turn back, which they eagerly did. But the expedition had spread out so far by then that some men were separated, pushing on on their own. Three days later, ten men were rescued on the island's eastern shore. Nine others were never found.

The sea here can be as seductively deadly as the land. The scuba diving in the waters around the Galápagos is some of the most breathtaking in the world. Six-hundred-pound sea lions. Fifteen-foot hammerheads. Manta rays the size of dining room tables. And a technicolor array of every conceivable species of fish. That's what makes the Galápagos different from anywhere else, Jack says, but it's not for beginners. This is big-league diving, he warns. That's the term Jack uses, big league. What makes it so are the currents, the same unpredictably strong swirls that have played havoc with ship captains since Darwin's day. It's common for the most seasoned sport divers to misjudge those currents and wind up surfacing in a near-panic, far from their dive site. Dive boat pilots among these islands pride themselves on retrieving lost, disoriented clients.

But they're not always successful. Not long ago, a Brazilian couple was diving with a group off Wolf Island, at the far northern tip of the archipelago. Their dive master instructed them to swim on the surface from their boat to a rock ledge some thirty feet away. From there they would begin their descent. But the couple couldn't wait. Halfway to the rock, they went down.

When the rest of the group reached the ledge, they understood why the dive master was being so cautious. The rushing current was so strong it was all they could do to keep a grip on the wet rocks. They also realized, when they looked around, that the Brazilians were nowhere in sight.

Four minutes later, the husband burst to the surface. His dive computer depth gauge showed 364 feet. He was distraught, confused, drunk with nitrogen narcosis from those few minutes of breathing compressed air at that depth. It turned out that he and his wife had hardly begun their descent when they were swept into a downward-bound current. The man lost sight of his wife almost immediately. He dove deeper, hoping to find her, until he realized he was beginning to pass out.

The woman's body was never found. As for the man, says Jack, "Other than losing his wife, he was okay."

News like this from the Galápagos often goes unreported. There is no newspaper on the islands, no bona fide journalism of any sort. The nearest professional reporters are on the continent, and by the time they get word of events way out here, it's often too late for more than cursory coverage at best. Natural disasters of epic proportions, on the other hand, attract swarms of international news crews: the 1995 eruption of Fernandina's La Cumbre volcano, for example, where rivers of molten magma poured into the ocean for months on end, boiling the fish, scalding the seabirds, and superheating the shoreline rocks, upon which frightened marine iguanas scrambled only to burst into flames; and the explosion three years after that of the Cerro Azul volcano on Isabela, which prompted an airlift evacuation of a colony of some seventeen tortoises that sat in the path of an oncoming lava flow; and of course, the press come with the El Niños, with all their disruption. Descending on the islands like locusts, the reporters fill every hotel room and bar they can find, gathering the requisite press packets from the Research Station and the Park Service. They file their stories, then, once the crisis has passed, they fly out, leaving the Galápagos as it always has been: a world apart, unto itself.

Not long ago, in the summer of 1998, there were two disasters on the islands that would have made national headlines had they occurred in the States. One was the crash of an ultralight glider carrying a two-man film crew who were shooting footage for an IMAX movie about the Galápagos. The men—one an American, the other a Canadian, the very man who invented the IMAX camera—were killed when their aircraft nosedived into the slopes of Cerro Azul during a sunrise shooting. That tragedy occurred just three weeks after a tour boat carrying sixteen passengers, all members of an Elderhostel group, capsized near Santa Fé. The group had gathered on the foredeck of a boat called the *Moby Dick* to photograph the sunset. The sea was calm, with soft, velvety swells. But one swell rolled through, larger than the others, so slowly, smoothly, and gently that neither the passengers nor the crew realized it was happening. The boat, which had been recently renovated (an extra deck added) to create more cabin space with no regard for the vessel's stability, turned over. Four of the passengers, all Americans, died, and it was Jack Nelson who had to relay the news to their families.

"Stupidity, sheer stubborn stupidity," he says of such accidents, which have happened in these waters more times than he can count, and certainly more times than have been reported beyond the borders of Ecuador. "It's always the same story," says Jack. "Negligence, ignorance, greed, laziness. They don't learn anything from what's happened before. Sometimes it seems this is a nation of amnesiacs."

Still, he cautions, it's a mistake to conclude, as some people do, that every boat in that harbor is unsafe, every tour operator corrupt. There are coalitions of responsible tour operators in the Galápagos whose concerns extend beyond their mere profit margins. These people realize, says Jack, that the future of their industry depends on the future of these islands. They set and maintain standards not just of safety but of the caliber of tours that they offer. They are intent upon educating their guests about the fragility of this archipelago, the threats that it faces, and what outsiders can do to help. (What they can do in most cases is join one of the many organizations created to protect the Galápagos and contribute resources—in most cases, money—to help those groups do their work.)

Too many people, says Jack, see the problems confronting these islands and assume that tourism is the culprit. It's just not that simple, he says. As he sees it, when it comes to a place such as this, there is simply no way to keep people away. No place is a vacuum, he says. No place on this planet can remain unchanged. Not Antarctica. Not the Amazon jungle. Not the Galápagos Islands. People are going to come, Jack says, and they're going to cause changes.

If that's so, he continues, it's probably best that those people come as tourists. Jack would prefer a gentler term than "rape" to refer to the history of man's hand on such places as the Galápagos. But accepting that term, which is often used by critics of tourism here, he considers the industry—and he smiles as he says this—a "kinder, gentler form of rape."

Far from hurting the Galápagos, tourism, Jack maintains, has actually helped. It's brought attention as well as funding. Those sixty thousand people a year who visit these islands, he points out, become lifelong ambassadors for the Galápagos; crusaders, as it were, for the cause.

No, it's not the tourists who are the problem, says Jack. It's the people in the culture and industry that have grown up around that tourism. The people and businesses that have flocked to the islands in pursuit of the dollars washing off those tour boats are the agents of destruction, says Jack. Most of the tour boats in these waters are safe, he points out again. But the ones that are not . . . well, they're like the proverbial bad apples, spreading their rot beyond their own skins.

Take, for example, the *Galápagos Explorer*. Actually, it's the *Galápagos Explorer II*. The first one, alas, ran aground a couple of years ago on the reefs off Wreck Bay, with a drunken first mate at the helm. That ship was owned by a Guayaquil-based corporation called Canodros. So is the *Explorer II*, which was built in Italy in 1990 before it was bought by Canodros and brought to the Galápagos just last year. It's the largest among the ninety ships currently licensed to tour the islands, and at first glance it's first-class. Each of the *Explorer*'s 100 passengers enjoys an air-conditioned suite with a television, VCR, refrigerator, bar, and bath/shower. The freshwater swimming pool goes without saying, as does the carpeted dining room, where dinner, served by tuxedoed waiters on a typical evening, goes something like this:

Marinated Sea Bass with Chef's Sauce
Broccoli Cream Soup with Quail Egg
Veal Enince with Roasted Potatoes
Salad of Belgian Endive
Peach Pie or Chocolate Mousse

The *Explorer*'s brochure makes much of the fact that the ship "is equipped with special systems to minimize the impact on the Archipelago. All soaps, detergents and shampoo used on board are biodegradable." Which is fine, as far as that goes, Jack says. But what about that thick oily smoke billowing out of the ship's stacks when she starts her engines? Does anyone care that this ship runs on bunker fuel? That's practically raw petroleum, for those who don't know, Jack points out. Crude oil. Sinks to the bottom like lead. Virtually impossible to clean up. Nasty shit.

A vessel running on bunker fuel shouldn't be allowed *near* the Galápagos, says Jack. But there it is, anchored right out in the bay. And even more alarming than the *Explorer* are the tankers that transport its fuel from the mainland. Some of these ships are as battered and rusty as those landing crafts Jack rode here in the '70s. They're pieces of junk, if the truth be told, and they're typically captained by men whose credentials are suspect at best. Hell, just last summer one of those ships loaded with sacks of cement ran aground while entering Puerto Villamil, over on Isabela. Its fuel tank, thank God, didn't break open. All that was spilled that day was waste water. But it could have been a major disaster. *That* would have brought out the reporters.

The fact that such boats are in the ocean at all is a crime, says Jack. That they are allowed to even approach waters as pure and precious as the Galápagos' is an abomination. But it's not surprising. If there were such things as true journalists on the islands, they'd have a field day tracing the ownership of those junk ships. Jack (and others who keep their ears to the ground on these islands) have no doubt the trail would lead directly to Quito and Guayaquil, into government offices where the very people who ought to be regulating these vessels refuse to do so because, directly or indirectly, they own them.

And so the supply ships continue to come and go, fleets of Third World freighters and barges casting their shadows on the animals and the birds and the beaches of the *Encantadas.*

"They shouldn't be here," Jack says with a sigh, turning back to his artwork. "Any accident at all with any one of them could be an unimaginable disaster."

He nudges the sculpture and watches it twirl. The coral and copper twist slowly in the afternoon light as a small finch flits in and alights on an old wooden barrel.

"Perfect," Jack says softly, surveying his piece. "Perfect."

SEVEN

The Station

*Volcán
La Cumbre*

*Isla
Fernandina*

JANUARY 6, 2000

Godfrey Merlen

It's been a bad morning for Roz Cameron. Never mind the two-man film team from England who dropped in first thing, looking for permits to visit Española, where they want to shoot footage of some relocated saddlebacks. Or the Korean TV crew that "just popped up," as Roz puts it, last week and has been camped at her door ever since, hoping to get out to the westernmost islands. Or "some blokes from Canada" who have also appeared without notice, and she's not even certain what they want. Then there's that frigging e-mail complaint that arrived sometime last night from someone in Germany who's upset about not getting credit in that IMAX film.

None of this niggling nonsense is what's bothering Roz. It's all part of her job. As the Darwin Station's director of public relations, her role every day is to act as a traffic cop at an insanely congested intersection of scientists, tourists, and reporters. Besides steering and shepherding the hordes of writers, photographers, and film crews who ceaselessly descend on the Galápagos from around the globe, Cameron must also keep track of the work of the researchers—the students, professors, and field scientists who shuttle in and out of their stints at this Station like foot soldiers in Vietnam.

At any one time, there are roughly two hundred Research Station personnel at this compound or out among the islands. More than two thirds are staff and volunteers; the rest come and go through grants, fellowships, and salaries paid by universities and research labs all over the world. Wherever they come from, for whatever reason, before they head out to the hinterlands of the archipelago, every one of these men and women must first check in at the Station. If the Galápagos Islands are a field scientist's Vietnam, then the Charles Darwin Research Station is its Da Nang. And Roz Cameron is the one with the clipboard, waiting on the tarmac to deal with the press and the public and anyone else who wants to know what these scientists are doing.

But that's not what's driven her out to the porch of her barrack-like office this morning for her third—or is it her fourth?—cigarette of the day. It's that shitstorm on the continent: the rioting in Quito, the tear gas, the arrests. Not that Roz gives a rap about politics per se. She couldn't care less about Jamil Mahuad or anyone else in that presidential palace. Don't get her wrong, Mahuad seems like a good enough fellow, better than any other leader Ecuador's had since Roz got here. And God, she says, taking a deep drag on her Marlboro, there have been so many "leaders." Four in one day, wasn't it? Yes, she nods, that's right. Four presidents in one bleeding day, back when Bucaram was tossed out.

She stubs out her butt on the porch railing and surveys the vista around her—the dry brush and cactus in every direction, the ocean spread below like a bright-blue carpet, and the road, one of the busiest thoroughfares in the entire Galápagos, a narrow mile-or-so stretch of dirt and gravel winding from the east edge of town (where the cobblestones of Darwin Avenue end), past Roz's office near the ocean, to that dusty encampment of cinderblock lodges, classrooms, and office buildings just down the way, ground zero for the world's students of natural selection.

It's not just the scientists themselves, pedaling back and forth on their beat-up bicycles from here into town, who make that dirt road so busy. There are the Park Service trucks as well, grinding their gears as they come and go from their own headquarters back up in brush to the west. Eliecer Cruz and his people have got 150 or so staff and wardens up there, plus 250-some guides who are constantly checking in at that Park Service compound of buildings and garages.

Then there are the tour groups, on port call from their boats, trudging past one another in packs of a dozen or so, each led by a guide who, once they arrive here at the Station, invariably steers the flock directly to Lonesome George's pen, where the tourists set up their cameras and tripods while the guide tells them about efforts to coax George to reproduce. For years now, the scientists here at the Station have been trying to find George a mate, but so far the seventy-some-year-old "bachelor," as the tour guides describe him, has not been responsive. At this point in the lecture, someone invariably makes a crack about Viagra, and the guide laughs politely. How many times has he heard that joke? He points out that George still has quite a few years left to become a father. This species, the guide explains, can live to 170 or even older, the longest lifespan of any creature on Earth. And George should be able to procreate until the day that he dies.

The reporters all want to know about George, just like the tourists. And Roz doesn't mind fielding their questions, the same questions, over and over. She loves this job. She believes in this place, the Station, and its purpose. As for the islands themselves, she's lost none of the awe that compelled her to sink her roots here eight years ago. That's something Roz wants to make perfectly clear before she even begins to discuss the downside of what's been happening lately, both in her own life and to the life of these islands.

"Look," she says, sweeping her blond bangs out of her eyes. "I adore this place. The power of it. The enormity of that visceral feeling you get sitting alone out on one of those beaches or up in the highlands with the tortoises. Connecting with a place on a plane that has nothing to do with being a human, feeling that vivid sense of just *being*, that's the essence of these islands, at least for me."

She pauses to answer a call on the two-way radio she keeps clipped to the pocket of her shorts. Her hair is pulled back in a tight, no-nonsense braid. Her tanned face is freckled. Her Station-issued sportshirt and shorts are a dark navy blue. "Ruddy" is a word that would aptly describe her. But don't make the mistake of asking if that accent of hers might be British.

"Australian," she snaps, with a mixture of disdain and delight.

She pulls out another cigarette and apologizes. She doesn't mean to be brusque, but this is a bad time right now, the worst she's been through since she first came to the islands. And she's been through a lot. There was, of course, her former husband, who couldn't shirk what Roz calls his "Latin ways"—his drinking, his visits to Quatro y Media, his trysts with other women—and so she finally threw him out of her life. But he still comes around almost every day to visit their son, Mason, who's now nearly seven. The locals look at Roz like she's some sort of freak, this *gringa* who has actually dug in and stayed, rather than fled like the rest of the foreign women who have their fling with an island man, find themselves pregnant, then go back where they came from once the relationship fails. And who could blame them? Why in the world would anyone want to stay here in such circumstances?

But Roz has stayed. She even bought her own piece of land, back up in the village, where she had planned to build a nice cozy cottage for Mason and herself. But that was before the economy went down the sewer. The estimate she got from the builder just two months ago to begin construction has now doubled. That's how crazy it's gotten, and what's worse is Roz couldn't cash in her chips even if she wanted. Her life savings are stuck in an Ecuadorian bank, which has frozen all assets and denied access to depositors. She doesn't even have the *sucres* to pay for her bleeding divorce, which is a moot point at the moment because there's no judge on the island to finalize it. There's been no judge for almost a year now, ever since Avellan was tossed off. But then that doesn't surprise Roz either. The Ecuadorian bureaucracy on the mainland has more pressing concerns at the moment than replacing a provincial judge in the Galápagos—concerns such as saving its own skin.

Roz would laugh if it all didn't hurt quite so much. Still, she's not about to bail out. For all that's gone wrong here, there's no place on the planet she'd rather be. She felt it the first time she set foot on these islands, late in 1991. She'd arrived out of sheer curiosity, just a side trip while traveling across South America. She was thirty-two at the time, restless and searching, though she was not sure for what.

Her whole life had been like that, from the time she turned nineteen and took off with a girlfriend from her home in southern Australia. Just the two of them, with all that they owned jammed in Roz's light green sedan—"a Datsun, belonged to my mum"— headed east across something called the Nullarbor Plain. It was a wasteland; a dry, treeless extension of the Great Victoria Desert. Roz and her buddy drove four days straight through, hardly a human in sight, nothing to get them across but a bucket of cookies crammed between the front seats, and Santana and the Sex Pistols screaming out of the stereo.

That was the beginning, says Roz. By the time she turned thirty, she'd been all over the Australian continent, from the small mining town of Karratha on the northwestern coast—where she worked as a barmaid, then spent three years driving salt trucks—to the village of Kempsey on the coast north of Sydney. There, she built her own house, busted her bum at a small local hospital, grew her own food, and, toward the end, learned how to surf. She took side trips to Nepal and Egypt and such, but it was not till she came to the Galápagos, on no more than a whim, that she realized she'd finally found what she was searching for. Which, even today, is a hard thing for Roz to put into words.

"I can only describe it as the culmination of twenty years of inner exploring," she says. "Something touched me here. It wasn't a person. It wasn't a thing. It was just this *energy*. Something resonant and real. Something raw, crude, and timeless.

"It wasn't what's here that did it," she says, looking out at the road and the Station and the town to the west. "It was out *there*, in those places where you can be all by yourself, in the highlands, on those islands."

What struck Roz as strongly as the sense of this place, she says, were the people she found here, men and women from all over the world who shared feelings like hers, who were expatriates in the same sense that she was. They were people for whom the term "counterculture" meant just that: They had fled from, for whatever reasons, the cultures they lived in, and had come here to live on their own terms, not unlike those Norwegians who first settled these islands in the 1920s.

"I've always tended to gravitate toward hard places with a mishmash of interesting people whose real story you'll never ever know," says Roz. "Those kinds of people can be a mess, but they can also be so incredible. And this is a place where you find them. This is a place that tests limits, and a lot of people like it that way. Those are the kinds of people who pass through a place like this, who *really* pass through. They're not your typical travelers."

Money was the last thing on Roz's mind when she decided to settle in Puerto Ayora. Money, in fact, was one thing she was trying to get away from. She'd had money before, more than she knew what to do with, back when she worked in the salt mines in the boomtown of Karratha. *"Phenomenal* money," she says—$30,000 a year with no expenses, which in 1979 in rural Australia was no small amount. It was like the early days on the pipeline in Alaska, Roz says, spigots of cash flowing like oil. That's what finally drove Roz away from that place, she says, all that money. It made her feel like a glutton, fat with excess and waste. "When I started buying color TVs for friends and flying a thousand kilometers to Perth every couple of months for a weekend break, just blowing away money because it was there, it began to feel wrong. It does *not* feel fulfilling."

It bothers Roz that she has to worry about money now. But she does, if for no other reason than Mason's well-being. She doesn't need much, just enough to feel safe. But she doesn't feel safe, not with the banks shutting down and the uproar in Quito, and the possibility that the talk of a coup might be more than a rumor. If that is so, then everything's up for grabs, including the Special Law passed just two years ago, the fate of this Station, and the future of the Galápagos Islands themselves. Roz would never share such fears with the press—her job, after all, is public relations—but she's not the only one here at the Station who's worried.

"People are shaky, nervous, terrified," she says of her colleagues and the stream of upsetting news from the mainland. "With the masses out in the streets there in Quito, and the military prepared to step in and take over, it's the French Revolution all over again."

For the time being, however, it's business as usual, and right now Roz has to run. But a good person to talk to, she says, would be Godfrey Merlen, if you can catch him. He might well be at the library, she says, down by the Station dock, just a short stroll from here.

It's not much to look at, the Darwin Research Station library, but it's the repository for the world's most complete collection of all that has ever been written about the Galápagos Islands. Thousands of research studies, periodicals, theses, and dissertations dating back more than a half century are squeezed onto the shelves

that line the walls of this small, cellarlike room. The buzz of fluorescent lights and the hum of an air conditioner are the only sounds
to be heard as one steps inside. On this particular morning, a young
pigtailed woman sits at one of the room's bare wooden tables. She
is bent over a laptop. Across from her sits an older, Asian man,
chewing the tip of his pen as he studies an unfolded map. Near the
door, at a desk by a bin where visitors stow their backpacks and
belongings, sits a slim bird of a woman who looks not unlike the
finches perched on the fence just outside. She is Gayle Davis, the
Station librarian, who also happens to be Godfrey Merlen's wife.

In *The Beak of the Finch,* which won a Pulitzer Prize for author
Jonathan Weiner in 1995, biologists Peter and Rosemary Grant are followed as they study finch behavior on the Galápagan island of
Daphne Major. Weiner's account includes a brief stop in Puerto Ayora,
during which he spends several paragraphs describing Gayle Davis
feeding rice to the finches, both here at the library and outside the
house in town that she shares with her husband. Weiner describes
Davis' hair as "pulled back in a bun, tropical-librarian-fashion," which
is the same way she's wearing it this morning. Weiner's book now sits
on a shelf behind Davis' desk, where at the moment she's logging
off her computer before going to lunch. Beside the computer are
stacked papers to be processed and filed—ongoing studies of four-eyed
blennies and great blue herons, the mating behavior of marine iguanas, and the morphology of lava flows on the Volcán Alcedo.

Some 9,000 species of birds, animals, and plants live in the
Galápagos, hundreds of which exist nowhere else on the planet,
most of which have been studied and written about in one way or
another by the scientists who pass through this Station. Oceanic
island systems, because of their isolation and self-containment,
have always provided ideal environments for the study of biology,
oceanography, climate, and geology. Such islands are, as the Galápagos are so often described, "living laboratories." There are precious few such systems left on Earth, certainly none with such an
astonishing range of biodiversity surviving in such relatively undisturbed conditions as that of these islands. Hawaii, the Solomons,
Guam, New Zealand, Micronesia—all these biosystems have been

disturbed beyond repair by the invasion of humans. Only the Galá-pagos remain as a keyhole through which scientists can continue to probe into and understand the evolutionary, ecologic, and geo-logic processes which shape all life on Earth. It's not just where we have come from that these scientists are studying, but where we are going.

This was what fascinated Gayle Davis when she first visited the Galápagos two dozen years ago as a Peace Corps volunteer, after earning her zoology degree from the University of Wisconsin. She was a Chicago girl, born and bred, but like so many long-timers at the Station today, she fell in love with this place at a time and under circumstances that made it easy to leave behind the world she knew. Rules and restrictions were almost nonexistent back then, largely because there was no need for them. Few people were living and working on these islands, and conditions were so diffi-cult for those few who were that there were no problems with over-crowding. Life for the scientists during the first couple of decades at the Station was much the same as it was for the people living in the village. If you could deal with the spartan conditions, the lack of amenities, the harshness of the setting and climate, and the near-absolute separation from the rest of mankind, well then, you were welcome to stay.

Now, there are rules at the Station just as there are rules—or the semblance of such—down in the town. Just getting on the list to secure a stint of study at the Station today—getting the green light, for example, to come down for three or four months to monitor the repro-duction of sea lions on the island of Marchena—is a formidable task. Finding a way to navigate the sticky web of immigration restrictions in order to actually stay and live on these islands is almost impossi-ble, for a scientist or anyone else.

Gayle Davis lives here. And she worries about the same issues that are on everyone's mind at the Station right now: the political unrest on the continent (where Davis is due to travel in just a few days to a clinic in Quito for an operation on one of her eyes), the collapse of the Ecuadorian economy, and the ongoing struggle between the Park Service and the local poachers. The *pepiñeros* continue to be a problem, and now some local lobstermen, unhappy with the Special Law's restrictions on shellfish, are starting to make threats against local authorities—the same kind of threats that led to the Station takeover four years ago.

Davis' eyes still narrow with outrage at that memory. When those jacked-up fishermen burst out of the brush with their machetes and Molotov cocktails, no one was more upset than she. Like her colleagues, she fled when the mob first arrived, but she could not stay away, not with her library in danger. Within a day, she and a small group of friends—scientists and students—sneaked back into the compound. "Just to make sure everything was all right," she says. "And in my case, to check my e-mail."

E-mail has changed everything about life on these islands, says Davis. It used to take days, sometimes weeks, to get news from the outside world. Now it arrives electronically in seconds, when the server's not down. Some of that news, frankly, is hard to believe. In a way it confirms Davis' choice so long ago to leave behind a culture that seemed to be going in some wrong, even crazy, directions. Like the decision—when was it, just four months ago?—by the Kansas Board of Education not to teach evolution in that state's public schools. Davis could hardly believe that one when she read it on the Web. None of the people at the Station could believe it. It flies in the face of all that they know, all they are doing. They can tell themselves, Okay, that's Kansas, but even right here, in the very crucible where the theory of evolution was inspired and continues to be explored every day, there are now Mormons walking the streets in their white shirts and ties, knocking on doors to rescue the unsaved. There are Jehovah's Witnesses doing the same. There is a Pentecostal church back up in the village, the Asamblea de Dios, where the congregation gathers three nights a week to garble in tongues and writhe on the floor and pray that the beast that their minister warned about, waiting to rise from the sea and swallow them whole, will stay away at least one more month.

Gayle is leaving for lunch now, but Godfrey's just up the road, she says, doing some work with some finches.

And so he is, right downtown on Darwin Avenue, just across from the Media Luna Café. Come this evening, he's quite likely to be out there on its porch sipping a pilsner.

Now, however, he's on task, standing motionless beside a head-high stone wall, staring up at a cactus plant a few feet away. He's wearing sandals, shorts, and a T-shirt—standard dress for a Galápagos day. His thick, sun-bronzed arms are crossed on his chest. A well-worn ballcap is pressed down on a head of wild hair. And those eyes—those Rasputin-like eyes—are fixed on that cactus.

A tripod-mounted video camera standing beside him is fixed on it, too. Over the camera is draped a neatly folded dish towel to shade the device from the sun. But the heat appears to mean nothing to Merlen, who shows no expression as he stands and stares. The minutes go past. Then hours. Nothing appears to be happening.

The tourists stop and look at this odd man. Then they glance up at the cactus; then they look back at the man and wonder what the hell's going on. Some even approach him and ask.

"Quite a lot, actually," he answers, his voice Britishly polite, his eyes still transfixed on the plant.

The tourists look back at the cactus for a second or two; then they shrug and move on. If they stayed a bit longer, a flit of movement would appear in a tree to the right of where Merlen now stands. A tiny black finch, the size of a canary, has darted in from the distance and now sits on a branch. Another flit and the finch is closer, its tiny head twitching from side to side as it hops down the tree toward the cactus.

"The longer you watch, the more you see," says Merlen. And it's true. There's a small hole in the cactus trunk, an opening the size of a softball. Look through the camera, and in the darkness of that hole small bits of twigs and slight shadowy movements can be seen. Look back at the finch, and in its beak is yet another twig. With one final dart, the bird is inside the hole, tending the nest for its babies.

The point of this study, explains Merlen, is to see just how closely a creature like this can coexist with the thrum of humanity: the pedestrians and traffic rushing past within a few feet of the nest, the restaurants and shops just across the avenue, the smells and sounds of a small city filling the air. To Merlen, the clamor is mere background, as it is to that finch. He and the bird are each focused on one thing at the moment, the nest.

"There you are," he whispers to himself as the finch hops into the hole. "There you are."

The tourists don't realize it, but this same man took most of the wildlife photographs featured in the Park Service calendars for sale in the souvenir shops down by the wharf. The pen-and-ink drawings of Darwin finches displayed as posters up at the Research Station are Merlen's as well. His watercolors have been exhibited by the National Audubon Society in Washington, D.C.

But the art's just a hobby for Merlen. It's science he lives for. Over the past fifteen years he's published more than two dozen papers on a broad array of biologic esoterica, from the scavenging behavior of the waved albatross to the calibration of stable oxygen isotope signatures in coral. He's also written two field guides to the waters of the Galápagos, one on fish and the other on marine mammals.

Even the writing, however, pales next to Merlen's passion for the fieldwork itself. He and Gayle share a house in the village, but one gets the sense that Merlen is most at home on the water, preferably alone.

The water, in fact, is where he is bound the next afternoon, as he unties a small dinghy at the Park Service dock, at a small, sleepy cove just west of the Research Station. The cove is surrounded by mangroves, which, from here into town, have been invaded during the past year by a white, scaly insect that's killing the trees at a devastating rate.

The parasite, known as "cottony cushion scale," showed up in southern California's orange groves in the early part of this century and nearly destroyed them. Now it is here in the Galápagos, attaching itself to the mangroves, sucking the trees' sap and coating their branches with a sweet, sticky secretion. The goo both smothers the trees and attracts a black, sooty mold, which blocks out the sun. The effect in the end, as one scientist puts it, is that the trees are both "vampirized and mummified."

Very visibly, the mangroves are dying, their leaves turning black as their branches turn white. The situation has become so severe that the Station, for the first time in its history, is considering introducing its own nonindigenous life-form to the islands to combat this invader. The creatures they're thinking of sound benign— ladybugs, or "ladybird beetles," as the scientists call them. The bugs have been effective elsewhere, eating the same parasites that are now killing the Galápagos mangroves.

This might indeed be the only way that these trees can be saved, agrees Merlen, but it's still unsettling. Once you start fiddling with the chain of nature, he says, even the best intentions can turn on themselves. Look what happened with the mongooses in Hawaii and Fiji and the Caribbean Islands. Well-meaning scientists brought those animals in to eat the rats that had invaded the cane fields, but the mongooses wound up devouring other creatures as well, including sea turtle hatchlings, whose populations have since dramatically declined. Like the hosts of a party where a guest has turned ugly, these places have found that the mongooses are much harder to get rid of than they were to let in.

Of course, none of this would have been necessary in Puerto Ayora if these parasites had been kept out in the first place. But who knows how they got here. It's hard enough controlling the goats and pigs and dogs and rats that have been let loose in the Galápagos over the decades. Although people knowingly bring in the larger creatures that now swarm over some of these islands, tinier but just as deadly organisms hitchhike in on uninspected produce, inside unchecked packages, on the soles of unclean shoes or the surface of unclean clothing, and most dangerously, in the ballast water of commercial and cruise ships.

Ballast water—the seawater used to balance the buoyancy of large ships—has become an increasingly alarming front line of battle in the global war against invasive species. When a good-sized ship empties its load, be it cargo or passengers, it fills the lower part of its hull with hundreds of tons of seawater to maintain the boat's hydrodynamics. That water is typically filthy, the kind of oily, scum-ridden liquid that laps at the docks of urban ports from Stockholm to Hong Kong. In the hull of a ship, this water becomes an aqueous soup of bacteria, microbes, and larvae, carried hundreds or even thousands of miles from its source, then dumped out in a foreign harbor as the boat takes on cargo or people.

The implications are obvious. As Puerto Ayora continues to grow, the harbor of Academy Bay becomes busier each day with a steady stream of such ships. Several are anchored out there right now, as Merlen's skiff swings away from the Park Service cove and slices across the mouth of the bay, pointing west toward the "other side."

The sky is dark. An afternoon downpour—an *aguacera*—is moving in from the highlands. Merlen pulls a worn canvas cap from his pack and yanks it down on his head.

Off to the right sits a small fishing trawler, empty, anchored, its steel hull flaking with rust and neglect. It's been sitting there for almost two months now, ever since it was seized by the Park Service in November off Wolf Island, where it was illegally fishing, with longlines, no less. Like the *Magdalena*, which still sits in that downtown lagoon, this boat, the *Mary Cody*, is owned and operated by the barons of Manta. Like the *Magdalena*, it's now awaiting legal action, which has been complicated by the fact that the island right now has no judge.

What makes the *Mary Cody* different and even more destructive than the *Magdalena* is the nature of the fishing it pursues. The *Magdalena* went strictly for sea cucumbers, which is harmful enough because of those creatures' critical role in the nutrient dynamics of the waters in which they live. Marine biologists often compare sea cucumbers with earthworms because, like earthworms in farm soil, sea cucumbers aerate and enrich the sea bottom, where they lie by the millions, sucking up muck through their systems then spewing the nutrients out into the water. The abundant sea life in that water, from small fish to whales, depends on those nutrients as the base of their food chain. Removing the sea cucumbers is, as some scientists put it, like sterilizing your farm. No one yet knows the extent of the damage done to the food chain in the Galápagos where *pepinos* have been pillaged.

While that damage goes largely unseen, the havoc wreaked by longline fishing boats like the *Mary Cody* is much more visible. And horrific. The sight of a dolphin or tiger shark impaled on an industrial fishing hook is not pretty. Longliners hang thousands of such hooks from steel-cable fishing lines in deep ocean waters, lines that stretch out as far as seventy miles. The lines are laden with nets and hooks of all sizes, snagging anything that goes for their bait or swims in their way. The wastage, or "bycatch," of such lines is said to be about thirty-five percent; in other words, as many as one third of the creatures caught on these lines are thrown back dead in the ocean. The *Mary Cody* was fishing for tuna the day she was seized, but her bycatch included sea lions, sea turtles, and sharks.

Such boats are barred from the Galápagos Marine Reserve by the Special Law, but that hasn't kept them away. Their owners know how laughably limited the Park Service resources are. The way the fisheries in Manta look at it, losing a *Mary Cody* here and there is a small price to pay for the many more boats that are able to enter these waters, fill their holds, and leave without being detected.

This is the kind of thing Eliecer Cruz and his park wardens are up against. It's helped to have Godfrey Merlen lending a hand. For years, Merlen's alerted them to local poachers he's come across out among the islands as he's doing his fieldwork. When the Park Service got use of a light plane not too long ago to patrol the archipelago from the air, they asked Merlen to fly along as a spotter, which he happily did. There have been times when he's taken matters into his own work-worn hands, boarding an illegal boat that he's happened upon, cutting the nets, and, if possible, releasing the catches. He's faced a machete or two, he says, but such "incidents," as he calls them, have not yet gone beyond threats.

If they did, that wouldn't stop Merlen. There comes a point, he will tell you, where talking to people and hoping they'll change is not enough. He's attended more meetings than he can remember—with the Park Service staff, with political groups, with the fishermen themselves—and all that those meetings amount to in most cases are mere words, for which Merlen has a low tolerance.

"Talking and talking in circles when you *know* people are camped at that very moment on a beach over in Fernandina—that can become infuriating," he says. "I find it deeply disturbing when people make a mockery of the innocence of these islands. Sometimes you've just got to *do* something."

He's in deep water now, midway across the mouth of the bay, the throttle wide open as a white spume of seawater sprays from the stern of his launch.

Abruptly, he cuts the engine to idle. The sounds of the breakers on the ocean reefs to the south are carried in with the afternoon breeze. The clouds have grown thick. The bay water is dark but still clear. To the right, from the harbor, a small fin appears, slicing the surface as it slides toward the skiff.

It closes to ten yards, then sinks. Then another appears, off to its right. This fin, too, is bound straight for the boat and also disappears just off the bow.

Merlen leans over the side, peering into the water as a massive shadow glides directly beneath. The shadow is almost as wide as his dinghy is long, with tiny twin horns jutting from its head, a long whiplike tail in the back, and to the sides, a broad sweeping pair of black, batlike wings. Merlen knew what this creature was when that first "fin" appeared: a large manta ray, about eight feet across.

"Ah, he's a good one," Merlen says, moving to the boat's other side as the *diablo del mar* ("sea devil") moves away. In the distance its pectoral wing tips again split the surface as it turns back toward Merlen.

"Curious, are we?" he says, as if the thing understands him.

The ray slides under the dinghy once more, then heads off toward the sea. Merlen guns the engine and in minutes he's rounding a jetty of cactus and stones—Angermeyer Point, gateway to the "other side." Here he turns toward a large, quiet cove, Bud's Bay, where a lone boat is anchored. The boat, a gray, fiberglass-hulled work vessel, is Merlen's.

"Mm, looks like the birds have been busy," he says, pulling himself up onto a nonskid deck spattered with guano. "I don't begrudge them that," he says, knotting the skiff's rope to a railing.

The water is green here. So are the mangroves. The rain clouds have veered east, and the sun has appeared. The roar of the surf out past the point can hardly be heard in the cove's tree-sheltered stillness. Merlen ignores the splash of a booby dive-bombing nearby, but he raises his head at the screech of a heron somewhere in the mangroves. Another screech and he's into the wheelhouse, from which he emerges in seconds, gripping a pair of binoculars.

"Ah, there it is," he says, training the glasses on the thick, shoreline foliage. "They've got a nest going there, haven't they?"

A yellow-and-blue tarp is stretched over the stern of the deck. Merlen sets down his field glasses, takes off his cap, and moves into the shade. A pelican glides past, skimming the cove's glassy surface.

This is the *Ratty*, a forty-two-foot line-fishing boat built in Norway in the late 1970s. Merlen bought it nine years ago, after the Ecuadorian fishery that owned it went bankrupt. He rigged a mast to the wheelhouse—"I wanted to use the wind a bit"—and has taken it since into just about every nook of these islands. He's done seismograph studies, charted seawater temperatures, and taped the deepwater sounds of fur seals feeding at night. But the boat's primary purpose is finding and following whales.

"That's what this is," Merlen says, stroking his beard as he studies the clouds to the east. "A whale hunter."

The hunting he's focused on lately is a survey of the more than 1,500 sperm whales known to exist in these waters. The study was begun in 1985 by a professor of marine biology in Halifax, Canada. That was six years before Merlen bought this boat. Now he and the professor are partners in a project that may, like much of the fieldwork Merlen conducts, last the rest of his life, or at least as long as the funding doesn't run out.

The subject of money is a sore spot for Merlen. It's no revelation that money is at the root of the problems that have come to plague the Galápagos: the poaching, the development, the influx of immigrants. But the fact that money has also become the determining factor in how those problems might be solved is more than just bothersome to him. It makes him feel ill.

"My first impression of the Galápagos," he says, pulling his knees to his chest as he leans back against a hard metal hatch, "was of an incredibly low-key place. I didn't have any money, and nobody else had any money. And that was fine. It was all the more striking for that, because it was so beautifully . . ."

He hangs on the silence, gazing out at the cove. Then he looks down at the deck. "Remote," he finishes.

It was in 1970 that Merlen first came here, as a crewman on a sailboat called the *Golden Cachelot,* one of the earliest vessels to tour the islands. He was twenty-five then, with an agriculture degree from his native England, a degree for which he'd developed a strong distaste.

"I was very disillusioned with a lot that was going on in that industry, just pouring a lot of chemicals on the soil. So I decided to have a look at the ocean and see what was happening there."

He began as a volunteer at the Station, and over the ensuing decades, through tireless fieldwork, established himself as a bona fide marine scientist. Today he is known as one of the leading authorities on the biota of the Galápagos, albeit one without an academic degree.

"I've sort of taken my own route in things," he says, cracking the smallest of smiles. "I've found it can be just as effective, maybe more so, to come around from the rear and make your way up that way."

The career he's established is truly a labor of love. And like deeply felt love of any kind, there is pain that comes with it. The cascading events of the past decade or so distress Merlen in the same way that they disturb others who have watched the Galápagos they once knew turn inside out.

"Introduced organisms, increasing population, demands for resources, demands for tourism: Everybody's making demands on these islands in one way or another, and the pace of those demands has been exponential, catastrophically so."

A thump from above interrupts his thought. He jumps up to find a gull perched on the tarp. "No, it's all right," he coos, as if soothing a lover, "it's all right. You don't have to go." And it doesn't. The bird sits and listens as Merlen continues.

"Ideology or philosophy alone is no longer enough," he says. "What happens here in the Galápagos is determined now by who has more money. We can't simply say, 'This is an extraordinary thing we have here, and why can't we just be altruistic enough to leave it alone?' No, we have to fight over it, and the weapon becomes money. We've wound up with huge sums of money being spent on both sides to determine the fate of these islands. And it all, in the end, costs the planet.

"That's something people tend to forget, that money does not come from nowhere. It comes from one resource or another. The more that we spend, the more those resources, somewhere, are used up."

He stops. He's self-conscious now, aware that his words might sound a little . . . self-righteous. He looks at his sneakers and at his ship. He scratches his beard.

"One has to be careful not to be two-faced about all this. I mean, I make *my* demands on the resources of the Earth, like anyone else. Maybe not as much, but I have a camera. I have a boat."

He pauses again, hunting for just the right words. "It's all about balance," he finally says. "I think we need to try, always, not to be too demanding. And when we do make demands, I think we must match them with an equal amount of care and responsibility."

That's it, the equation he's looking for.

"This isn't just true for the Galápagos and *pepinos*, or for Ecuador and what's going on there. It's true for any place, with any natural resource, anywhere in the world. If you want to get your hands on a resource, you ought to be responsible for looking after it and not squandering it. At the moment, at least, the attitude here in the islands is if I don't take it, the next boat will. And they're right."

And Merlen doesn't entirely blame them. He writes more than just scientific papers. Sometimes he writes opinion columns for the popular press, for newspapers back on the mainland, or for the Research Station's newsletter, the *Noticias de Galápagos*, which is mailed worldwide to members of the Charles Darwin Foundation. In one of those columns, Merlen boils the *pepino* trade down to its essence:

If I had been born in the Guasmo of Guayaquil, into the abject poverty that occurs there, into a world of harsh survival, into a world without trinkets and fancy toys such as television, Beta-

max, and gaudy clothes, I would jump with glee to be offered
ten thousand sucres a day to pick animals from the sea floor, to
be able to join the wealthy elite, gaining the power to buy my
own baubles and vodka and Nike shoes.

That column was written six years ago, when the "Pepino War"
first began. Those ten thousand *sucres* a day now sound quaintly
archaic compared with the $200 or more a day earned by the
pepiñeros licensed to hunt during the most recent, two-month
"season" okayed by the government. The "season" was an experi-
ment, an attempt to appease local fishermen by allowing limited
fishing of the *pepinos.* The result was a travesty of disastrous proportions. What was intended to be a controlled compromise turned
into a feeding frenzy. Before they could begin diving, each fisherman had to secure a *cédula de colono* (a permit) from the government. The idea was to limit the fishing to islanders. The result was
that more than 20,000 permits were issued—more than the official
population of the islands. Nearly $4 million worth of *pepinos* were
hauled out of the waters during those two months.

"And those," Merlen notes, "were just the legal sales."

There are *pepiñeros* in Puerto Ayora, and in Puerto Baquerizo as
well, but their numbers are miniscule compared with the population of poachers in Puerto Villamil, on the southernmost tip of the
western island of Isabela. Galápagans call Villamil "Tierra de
Nadie" ("No-Man's-Land") because of its almost complete absence
of authority. While Puerto Ayora and Baquerizo present the facade
of regulations and rules, in Villamil anything goes.

"That's the way it's always been over there," Merlen says. "People do what they want. It used to just be a slow, lazy, peaceful, little
town. Now it's like the Wild West."

Villamil was a penal colony until 1959, the same year the Park was
created. Its dusty streets are still unpaved today. There are a few small
hotels, but their rooms typically sit empty. The Research Station runs
a bare-bones outpost operation there, with a staff of ten who are typically out doing fieldwork. Villamil is so far away from the hub of the

islands (sixty ocean miles west of Puerto Ayora) that none but the most adventuresome of travelers go there. There is no tourist "attraction" to see, except for, perhaps, the *Muro de las Lágrimas*—the "Wall of Tears"—a monument to pointless brutality standing deep in the bush, four miles from the village. It is nothing but a wall of rough volcanic stones, piled fifty feet high, some twenty feet wide at its base and a hundred or so yards in length. It was built by those prisoners, back in the 1940s and '50s, who were force-marched each day into the island's interior and made to pile lava boulders and rocks atop one another. The reason, according to one written account, was "to subdue the criminal instincts of the prisoners as well as their depraved passions."

Officially, no more than a thousand or so people live in Villamil today. Almost all are involved, in one way or another, with *pepinos*. The place is just too far away for the Park Service to effectively police, and so the poachers operate openly, unabashedly. There is a café in town called the *Barra Pepino*. The skiffs tied to the village's wharf each carry a gasoline-powered compressor and long, coiled lengths of bright-blue rubber tubing. The compressors run air through the tubes to the divers' regulators, which the divers hold in their mouths as they crawl on the ocean floor stuffing their sacks with *pepinos*. Safety concerns, training, even the most elementary precautions, are ignored, and with predictable results. Last year more than fifty divers from Villamil wound up in Ecuador's only decompression chamber, on the mainland in Guayaquil. Six died. And no one has counted the number of this village's men who lie nearly unconscious in the shade of the town's sun-beaten buildings or who lurch through its streets, their brains addled by the bends and by the oil and gasoline fumes sucked through those dive hoses.

It's from Villamil that most of the islands' illicit fishermen embark to the outermost beaches of Isabela and Fernandina, where they build their camps and cook their *pepinos*. While the *pepiñeros* of Puerto Ayora have been known to rent the entire Quatro y Media for an evening, thus closing the place to the public, the Villamilans have no such luxury within reach. So they import their women, bringing out speedboats of prostitutes to their fishing camps, where the women are paid in *pepinos*, which they eagerly accept.

"A hundred *pepinos* a go," says Merlen, who not long ago encountered a boat called the *Michelle* off a Fernandina beach known as Punta Mangle. Merlen asked the Ecuadorians onboard if this wasn't the boat people have heard so much about, the one known to carry prostitutes out to the *pepiñeros.*

"No, *señor,*" answered one of the men. "They are *cocineras.*" Cooks.

"Cooks, indeed," Merlen laughed.

He was able to help break up a camp that day, but there are so many more camps. And lately the *pepiñeros* have been turning to lobsters, shark fins, sea urchins, and anything else for which there might be a market. In that battle of money which Merlen bemoans, the cash flowing into the hands of the fishermen—from the *pepiñeros* of Villamil to the trawlers based out of Manta—is a deluge compared with the relative trickle of funds coming in to the Park Service and the Station and the organizations and agencies around the world devoted to saving these islands and the islanders from themselves.

Even this high-minded purpose is a sticking point for Merlen. "It's easy for most of us—the scientists and the people who care about the Galápagos and who are trying to get the people to do certain things to protect it—it's easy for us to prescribe solutions because we can afford to do so. If we were in these people's shoes, it wouldn't seem quite so simple."

This is where Merlen turns back to philosophy, which, in the end, is the one place he finds hope. The sun is now setting, the sky to the west turning purple and pink as he unties the skiff's rope from the railing.

"Someone once said that we live by love, by hope, and by example," he says, "and the greatest of these is hope. I think that might be true not just for man, but for animals as well."

He turns his head toward the shore, where the heron's nest sits. Beyond it, barely visible through the foliage, sits a sad, weather-beaten old home.

"Life isn't necessarily easy for any of us," he says, "man or animal."

With that he starts the skiff's engine and points it toward home.

EIGHT

Cobblestones

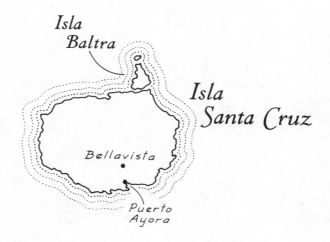

JANUARY 10, 2000

Daniel Fitter, with his father, Julian, Puerto Ayora

The airport at Baltra is on heightened alert. The soldiers on duty, who typically man their positions by napping in the shade of the baggage claim area or laughing over beers at the open-air snack bar, are in full combat readiness. UZIs are slung over their shoulders and grim looks are fixed on their faces as the first flight of the day taxis up to the terminal.

It's the tenth of January, and already the confidence proclaimed by President Mahuad when the new year began is crumbling to pieces. The *sucre* is still free-falling, tumbling ten percent daily, down to 29,000 per dollar just yesterday. Inflation is up, close to seventy percent. Since Mahuad assumed office seventeen months ago, ten banks have shut down, wiping out the life savings of thousands of depositors.

The protests in Quito have grown frightening, with thousands of *Indios* streaming into the city during the past several weeks to join the students burning fires in the roads to block traffic, the bus drivers and teachers and farmers on strike, and the oil workers threatening shutdowns of the nation's most profitable industry. Demonstrations have erupted in Guayaquil, too, and in the city of Cuenca as well, to the south. The protesters are demanding nothing less than Mahuad's resignation and the dissolution of the nation's Congress and Supreme Court.

It is those *Indios*, more than anyone else, who trouble Mahuad. They have long been mistreated: exploited for cheap labor, ignored as second-class citizens, robbed of their ancestral land in the mountains and jungles where most of them live. As late as the 1960s, advertisements in newspapers were still printed that offered rural *haciendas* for sale with Indians included, as if they were cattle or horses. Just last year, when Ecuador's per capita annual average income was tabulated at a woefully slight $1,600, the same figure for Indians came to $250.

Much of the land that once belonged to these *Indios,* deep in the rain forests of east Ecuador's Amazon basin—the river-laced jungle watershed Ecuadorians call the *Oriente*—has now become a denuded grid of oil-fouled roads and industrial pump stations operated by the state-run corporation PetroEcuador. The wells are drilled by major companies from all over the world such as Texaco, which first found oil under the *Oriente* in 1967.

It took Texaco five years to build a 300-mile pipeline up over the Andes and out to the Pacific coast. In 1972 the tap was turned on, the oil began flowing, and the industry—the *petroleros,* as the Indians call them—moved in with a vengeance. ARCO, Conoco, Mobil, Occidental Petroleum—they all began slashing and dynamiting thousands of acres of forests and soil, fouling rivers and fields with tens of thousands of gallons of spilled or dumped oil, bulldozing crude roads through Indian territory, driving the natives and wildlife from their forests and homes as billions of gallons of crude petroleum were pumped into the pipeline and out to the coast. The onslaught continues today.

For two decades the Indians—the Cofans, the Quechua, the Siona, the Secoya . . . more than a dozen tribes, more than 150,000 indigenous Amazonian peoples—suffered and stayed silent in the face of this assault. But by the mid-1990s, the seeds of political awareness planted among the *Indios* by outside activists and Western church volunteers started to sprout. The natives began to rise up in numbers that could not be ignored. Those numbers have swelled exponentially in the past several years as the Indians have organized and begun to press for their rights. With a fierce sense of identity, dressed in ponchos, feathers, and beads, carrying spears even on the downtown streets of Quito, speaking their own ancient languages rather than modern Spanish, the activist *Indios* have aroused their city-bound brethren, the dirt-poor Indians and *mestizos* who have been driven from the jungle and now crowd the streets of Quito's "old town," begging tourists for coins or hoisting huge sacks of vegetables and fruit on their backs, hoping to sell them at market.

It's for good reason that the Indians frighten Mahuad the most. Full-blooded *Indios* make up nearly half of Ecuador's thirteen million people. That figure is closer to ninety percent if the mixed-blood *mestizos* are included. Most of these natives have nothing to gain from the existing government and nothing to lose if they fight it. The language their leaders speak is that of revolution, of a sweeping restructuring of the nation's political power—power that has traditionally rested in the hands of a small number of wealthy aristocrats, most descended from white European stock.

It is a well-known fact that more than half of Ecuador's wealth is controlled by the tiny sliver of the nation's population who are white. The Indians want this to change. They do not hesitate to use the term "revolution," and indeed, voices have emerged among them which, like those of past Latin revolutionaries—Fidel Castro, Ché Guevara—have the passion and charisma to capture the people.

"We are beyond angry," said one Indian leader just last week. "And the shamans say change is coming. They say we are entering the Age of the Condor. They say that the Red Warrior has returned."

Mahuad's response to such warnings has been to forge ahead with the notion of dollarization—dumping the *sucre* and adopting the United States dollar. But that can't be done without a loan from the International Monetary Fund—about $250 million—and the IMF won't give Mahuad a cent until he convinces them that the money won't disappear down the same bottomless hole as the *sucre*. The only way to do this is to stop spending, to cut government services, and to ask all Ecuadorians to tighten their belts; quite a request when so many of those people are already starving.

It doesn't look good for Mahuad. His approval rating is a pathetic nine percent. The past week has seen a cascade of events which, while meant to indicate calm and control, reveal panic more than anything else. Rumors of a coup have grown so strong that Mahuad responded, meeting two days ago for seven hours with his military leaders, who emerged from the room with a pledge of allegiance. The generals even took out a full-page ad in the nation's largest newspaper, *El Comercio*, vowing their support of the president—a signal to the more cynical that the end must be near.

Just yesterday, Mahuad delivered a twenty-minute speech on national television, declaring that the shift to the dollar will proceed. That decision did not go over well with his cabinet, all fifteen members of which promptly resigned. Mahuad's response was to warn the nation's banking executives—those whose banks haven't already shut down—that he will convene a special session of congress and fire the lot of them if they don't go along with his plans. A national state of emergency has been declared—the third time troops have been dispatched to the streets since Mahuad assumed office—and that's why the UZIs are out here at Baltra.

The tourists stepping off of this late-morning flight don't seem worried. Their cameras are busy snapping photos of the moonlike landscape around them as they cross the hot tarmac and step into the terminal. There they line up to each pay a Galápagos National Park "entrance fee" of $100, cash only. No wrinkled or torn bills are accepted. Ecuadorians have a phobia about foreign currency. They will take only bills that are crisp and unmarked.

Once the money is paid, the tourists pick up their bags and are ushered toward a bus by smartly uniformed cruise boat guides. The bus is sleek, air-conditioned, with soft, cushioned seats. It will carry them down to their tour boats, which are parked like floating taxis in an inlet nearby. For the next week or two, those boats will be home for the tourists as they roam the islands. They may make a port call, at Puerto Ayora or Baquerizo or even Floreana. Or they may not. Some tour operators don't take their passengers near the inhabited parts of the islands. There are tourists who have visited the Galápagos and left with no idea anyone actually lives here.

The people who do live here are boarding a bus of their own in the terminal lot. It's dented, rusted, with hard narrow seats, and the windows are shoved open for the blessed relief of an occasional breeze. This is the bus the locals all take, along with anyone else bound overland for Puerto Ayora. Mainland businessmen and government officials, relatives and friends from the continent, the *mochileros*—backpackers traveling solo or in pairs, with their bandannas and guitars—are the riders crowding onto this bus.

It's standing room only by the time the driver climbs aboard. A huddle of Park employees are squeezed in the back, laughing, chatting in Spanish. A couple are swigging cold bottles of beer. After several tries, the diesel engine rattles to life and the bus lurches forward, toward a ribbon of asphalt stretching into the distance, up mist-shrouded slopes and over a mountain, to Puerto Ayora, twenty-five miles south.

After only ten minutes, the bus reaches a canal, the southern border of Baltra. A small ferry bobs in the sparkling water. The passengers unload, grab their bags, heave them atop the roof of the ferry, then climb aboard. In the time it takes a young woman at the rear of the vessel to smoke a single cigarette, the ferry reaches the far side. The travelers squeeze into yet another bus and soon are headed uphill into the highlands of Santa Cruz.

The temperature rapidly drops as the road angles skyward. The stark saltbush shrubs and red-barked *opuntia* cactus that cover the shoreline give way to stands of thin, skeletal trees, their silvery trunks glistening like chrome in the bright midday sun. A rider asks one of the Park rangers if he knows of these trees.

"*Palo santo*," says the ranger, pointing his beer at the forest.

Palo santo. "Holy stick." The trees are a hallmark of the Galápagos. The lower slopes of the larger islands are thick with them. Their branches, rich with a perfumed sap, are prized for their aroma. The twigs are lit as incense in churches here and on the mainland. They're also burned on the patios of homes to keep the mosquitoes away.

Salsa music crackles from the driver's tinny radio as the bus climbs higher and the forest grows thicker. Soon the road is surrounded by high-canopied *scalesia* trees, massive cousins of the sunflower, their ample trunks fuzzy with moss and lichen. Dew-dappled ferns carpet the moist forest floor. The woods grow deeper and darker. *Garúa* clouds gather above. A light drizzle begins to fall. The ocean below fades from sight as the bus moves into the mist.

The bus climbs still higher, and now the forest thins out and the landscape turns tundralike, a lonely expanse of wet, undulant fields, sedge-covered cinder cones and soft, spongy bogs. Dark, moist, menacing, the vista looks and feels like a Scottish moor. Only the occasional palm is a reminder that this is the tropics.

Now the bus reaches the top, slowing as it passes a gaping volcanic sinkhole. The crater's diameter is the length of a football field. A crude fence has been built at its rim to keep people and animals from tumbling in.

Here the road bends downhill, out of the clouds. A horse stands alone in a small grove of balsa trees, worn stirrups dangling from its riderless saddle. The bus passes a hut, the first to be seen since the airport at Baltra. It is fashioned from cinder blocks, rimmed by a fence made of twisted tree branches. A little girl plays in the mud by the gate.

The sky is now clear, the sun shimmering. A road sign appears. *PELIGRO—CRUCE DE TORTUGAS:* "Danger—Tortoise Crossing."

Now the ocean comes into view, a crescent of blue on the horizon below. A pickup approaches, roaring uphill, three Galápagan boys perched on the roof of the cab, their bare legs splayed on the truck's broken windshield. The kids hoot and wave as they shoot past the bus.

More traffic passes: a rusted sedan, a dump truck, a motorcycle. The homes grow more numerous, clusters of cabins and sheds and small gardens. One of those sheds, fashioned from bent sheets of tin, is painted with words whose letters drip toward the ground: *SE VENDE ESTA FINCA,* "Farm for Sale."

The road winds past dirt drives leading off into other farms, the remains of the land the Norwegians first cleared, the Hornemanns and Graffers and old Alf Kasteldan. That land now belongs mostly to cattle ranchers, people like Christy and José-Luis.

There's a weed-ravaged soccer field off to the right, then a clutch of bodegas. And now the bus enters Bella Vista, a small hamlet in the hills above Puerto Ayora. If not for the tortoises lumbering through those trees by the road, and the frigate birds floating over the shoreline below, Bellavista could be any dusty crossroad in rural Mexico. The people who live here try to farm if they can, but most of them work down in Puerto Ayora, if they work at all.

The bus stops here briefly, pulling up to a curb by a small, unlit grocery. A half dozen people climb out, trudging off toward their homes as the bus pulls away.

From here it's a straight shot to the sea. The bus picks up speed, hurtling downhill past unmarked dirt drives that wind into the brush. One of those drives leads to Mary's place, the Quatro y Media.

Finally, after an hour-long journey, the bus pulls into Puerto Ayora.

The driver parks at the wharf and cuts off the engine. The passengers step out into the glare of the sun and the noise of the traffic. Some walk off toward their homes, others to their jobs. A few—the travelers—grab their bags and head toward the closest café to sit down and take stock in the shade with a drink.

That bus ride, from here to the airport and back, is a trip every local knows well. Most take it at least one or two times a year to visit family or friends on the mainland, take care of business in Guayaquil, do much-needed shopping in Quito, see a doctor or dentist, or simply to get off the islands. Jack Nelson will be taking that bus sometime next month to begin the long journey to pick up his father in Thailand. Gayle Davis will be on it next week, when she flies up to Quito for her eye operation. Even the poorest of the villagers here in Puerto Ayora are able to occasionally fly to the continent, with round-trip tickets that cost just $30 for *colonos*—Galápagos residents—a tenth of what tourists pay for the same flight.

It's those tourists that Lobo will be greeting tomorrow when he begins a three-month stint of guiding. Tonight is his last night at home, and it's his mother-in-law's birthday as well, Mariana's mother, Blanca. They're throwing a party at the house Lobo shares with Mariana and Blanca and Blanca's husband, Carlos. Mariana is visiting a friend and won't be here tonight. So Lobo is spending this last evening in town without her.

It's pitch-dark as he picks his way through the sharp stones and volcanic cinders that line the narrow path that leads from the road to the back of the house. Most of the homes deep in the village have yards just like this—cinders and rocks. Most are about the same size: small, simple bungalows with two or three bedrooms, walls made of cinder block, and, if the owners are wealthy, roofs made of ceramic tile.

There is music ahead, around the corner, and the golden glow of a porch light. As Lobo steps out from the darkness, two small girls, his nieces, run to give him a hug. A dozen or so adults are arrayed in a circle of chairs on the back cement patio, with a hammock above them, strung near the ceiling to make room below.

There is Mariana's brother, Mario, and Mario's girlfriend Delilah, who was once Miss Galápagos. Mariana's sister, Sandra, sits beside her boyfriend, Fidel, who just got off work from his job as port captain. Fidel is thirty, the same age as Sandra. They both look like young professionals, he in his pressed slacks and starched polo shirt, she in her tropical dress with her blond, highlighted hair. They've been together about half a year now, ever since Sandra broke up with her former boyfriend, the mayor. She was the woman the mayor pulled out of the disco that night and beat.

It's Blanca's fifty-third birthday. A table is loaded with platters of *empanadas* and barbecued *carne*. There are cold Coca-Colas and bottles of beer, and a dish of fried nuggets that only the brave seem to be eating. *"Bolitas de advenedar,"* says Blanca when asked what they are.

"Guess-what balls," explains Lobo in English as the group bursts into laughter.

The man in the chair beside Lobo's does not laugh. He is older, lean, with jet-black hair and a severe, narrow beard running the length of his chin. The beard, with no moustache, makes him look Amish. The man is Mariana's father, Carlos Dominguez, the principal of one of Puerto Ayora's four high schools. He's not happy with what he's hearing from a woman in a chair across from him. The woman's name is Lijia Parédes. She works for INGALA, a government agency created in 1980 to oversee services here on the islands. Until six years ago, INGALA ran everything in the Galápagos—schools, roads, medical services, utilities. But then the government changed, and power was shifted, sliced up like a pie, with pieces going to sectors that were all given a say in where the money would be spent. Tourism, fisheries, farming, the Park Service, merchants, the military, even the mayor—they were each given a voice and a vote in a new governing group called the Provincial Council.

The result has been, as the head of INGALA, a man named Michael Bliemsreider, frankly puts it, "a bureaucratic monster"—a free-for-all of conflict and competing self-interests, with each group blocking the others over almost every decision, all of them fighting for their piece of that pie.

The pie is not small. More money flows through the Galápagos than through any province in Ecuador. Last year, tourists spent more than $120 million here on the islands, from boats to hotels to restaurants to shops to the Park Service entrance fee. With sixty thousand people visiting the islands last year, the entrance fees alone generated more than $4 million (only foreigners pay $100; Ecuadorian visitors pay less), which has raised questions as to why sections of the road down from Baltra remained unpaved until late last year.

The reason is simply that too many hands are laid on that cash as it supposedly makes its way to the people. Most of that $120 million goes straight to the mainland, to the companies who own most of the tour boats. As for the $4 million in Park entrance fees, it's doled out in percentages to seven different agencies, ranging from the Park Service itself, which gets forty percent, to the naval base, which gets five. The port captain, Fidel, receives five percent to pay his staff of marines. The Provincial Council gets ten, which its members haggle over and divvy up. The municipal government, including the mayor, gets twenty, from which community services such as health care, schooling, and sanitation wind up with crumbs. That, say a large number of townspeople, is a transparent sin. The mayor, for example, is paving the streets while the majority of homes, lacking an adequate sewage system, spill their waste into decrepit septic tanks that leak onto the cinders and stones in the yards.

It's the road paving that's got Carlos Dominguez upset at the moment. Miss Parédes is describing the good work being done by INGALA, the new construction all over town, the trucks lined up at the wharf, all those sacks of cement. Carlos can no longer stay silent.

"What about the schools?" he says, still looking out at the night. "Why does education get so little?"

Education is a woeful issue throughout all of Ecuador, with archaic teaching methods (rote recitation and memorization) used in outdated, overcrowded classrooms. In Puerto Ayora, it's even worse. More than a fourth of the town's population are children, from kindergartners through high school students. The schools are lacking in space and in quality teachers, who are paid far less than what even the legitimate fishermen earn down on the docks.

"Why do we get nothing?" asks Carlos, whose teachers' salaries, as low as they are, are nearly twice what teachers are paid on the mainland. That fact only points out, says Carlos, how pathetic the entire nation's educational system is.

Someone mentions the mayor. Carlos flicks his cigarette's ash in disgust.

"He has cobblestones for brains," he says. Fidel cracks a smile. Sandra takes a sip from her drink.

Carlos did not want to come to these islands when his father first sent him as a young man from Cuenca in the late 1960s. But he grew to love the Galápagos, he says. He has since taught linguistics and philosophy at universities on the mainland. He has read Hesse, Kafka, and Steinbeck—"in Spanish, of course." He has written a poem, "A Hymn to the Galápagos," which he says the critics in Quito reviled.

It has never been easy teaching school here on the islands, Carlos says. But at least there were rewards in the past—rewards that are rarer today. There were students of his who grew up to be parents who sent their own children into Carlos' classrooms. There were those who went on to school on the mainland, to universities and professions and success for which they sometimes sent back notes of thanks. But now, he says, the schools, like the town, are awash with strange faces, floods of children of migrants who come and go in a blur. The sense of connection, much less of completion, is eroding away.

"There is no longer any Galápagos," says Carlos. "I don't think I want to stay."

Blanca stands in the doorway, a dish of food in her hands. The children have been put to bed. The porch is still, a soft breeze from the sea riffling the leaves of the trees overhead.

"Well," says Lobo, breaking the silence. "Can you give me your house then?"

Everyone laughs and the party resumes. A new music tape is put on. More beers are brought out. The tinkle of wind chimes drifts up from the darkness, from the porch of a neighbor. It's late, well past midnight, time for Lobo to get some sleep. He's leaving at sunup to go meet his tour group. Mariana's not home yet, but he can't wait any longer. He stands, bids his family and friends good night, closes the door to the back room beyond them, and turns out the light.

By eight the next morning, Lobo is gone. A team of road workers is out not a block from Carlos and Blanca's back porch. The men carry shovels and picks. One wields a jackhammer, digging the dirt and breaking the rock so the stones can be laid to pave the street. His face is coated with layers of dust, as are the faces of the workers digging beside him.

They stop for a moment as a man pedals past on a bicycle, a slim, bespectacled white man. The workers nod and wave, and the white man nods and waves back. Clearly they know him, and he knows them as well. He doesn't look like a tourist, but he doesn't look like the standard Galápagos *gringo* either. The scientists and deep-rooted locals like Jack Nelson, Christy, and Roz all dress like laid-back islanders, in shorts and T-shirts and sandals and shifts. But this man wears pressed slacks, a button-up shirt, laced shoes, and socks. Least likely of all, he's got a bicycle helmet strapped on his head. No one in Puerto Ayora wears helmets.

The man makes a turn toward the waterfront, where he maneuvers into the morning traffic swelling on Darwin Avenue—the taxis and work trucks, the tour groups trudging up toward the Station, the local pedestrians with their sacks and their satchels. At a bend in the road, not far from the boats docked at Pelican Bay, the man turns up a side street, a narrow, tree-shaded lane that climbs back into the village. He passes a closet-sized hairdresser's salon where the proprietor sits in the shop's only chair, reading a magazine and drinking a soda while a soft breeze blows in through her screenless front window.

The pavement stops here, and the road turns to dust and sharp stones, through which the bicyclist weaves before pulling up to a small wooden gate. Around him are houses, askew, as if thrown down on this slope like a fistful of dice. The houses are small, close together, their rocky yards littered with refuse and weeds.

The man takes off his helmet, opens the gate, and steps onto the concrete veranda of the largest structure by far in this part of the village, the Kingdom Hall of Jehovah's Witnesses. The portico that leads into the church itself is off to the left, but the small screen door against which the man is now leaning is the door to his home. He removes his shoes before stepping inside.

The man's name is Daniel Fitter. His wife, standing at the small kitchen counter just inside the door and squeezing fresh orange juice for their midmorning snack, is Tina. Her brown hair is pulled back in a ponytail. She wears shorts and a blouse, and her tanned feet are bare. A pot of chili con carne is simmering on the four-burner stove. The scent of grilled beef and seasoned tomatoes fills the tiny apartment. There are only two rooms: this narrow kitchen and sitting area, with its rough wooden table and sofa and chair, and off to the left, the bedroom, where Daniel goes to put on some music.

The floor is cement, painted green. The high, whitewashed walls are hung with brightly colored photos of seabirds and reef fish and finches and whales, photographs taken by Daniel. There are black-and-white snapshots as well. One shows a man, a woman, and two boys on the deck of a sailboat on a harsh wintry day. The younger of the boys, a blond-headed toddler, is Daniel.

"That was 1969," Daniel says, walking out from the bedroom. He's changed from his slacks into shorts and a neatly tucked T-shirt. His face is clean-shaven, his hair closely cut. His feet are now bare. The Byrds are on the stereo, filling the apartment with the chorus of "Turn! Turn! Turn!"

"It took us eight months to get here," says Daniel, studying the photo. Eight months to sail from England (where Daniel's father had purchased the boat in the snapshot) back to the Galápagos, where Daniel had been born nearly two years earlier in the summer of '67. People around town say he was the first baby delivered in the hospital in the village, but Daniel demurs. "I think I was third," he says, reaching past Tina to have a taste of the chili.

Sounds of sawing and hammering drift in from the bare, rocky lot next door, where a house is being constructed. Daniel and Tina will move into it when it's finished come summer.

"Our first actual home," Tina says. "With actual windows," she adds, looking up toward the ceiling, where, like a jail cell's, this apartment's small windows are set.

It will be nice, they agree, when that lot's no longer vacant. More than once, Daniel and Tina have been awakened in the middle of the night by strange sounds and voices just outside their door.

"Don't ask me why," he says, "but people come to have sex there. We've gone out in the morning and found bras, knickers, condom wrappers, even mattresses. I've seen taxis parked for an hour out there." He looks through the screen door as a young boy walks past the front gate.

"We should have laid down some mattresses ourselves," he says, "and charged by the hour."

Tina laughs aloud, shaking her head. Like Daniel, she wears eyeglasses. Like his, her accent is British. Like him, she's upbeat, forthright, vivacious, as any Jehovah's Witness would need to be in a place such as this. It's not easy, Daniel says, knocking on doors and spreading the Gospel here in the Galápagos, especially with all the competition that's been cropping up lately.

"The Catholics are very upset," he says, smiling and taking a seat at the table. "It's all marketing when you boil it down, and their 'customers' are leaving. And they're not just coming to us. They're going to the Seventh Day Adventists. They're going to the Mormons. They're going to the Pentecostals."

He picks up one of a dozen or so seashells arranged on the table.

"We've got faith healers now, people speaking in tongues, whatever you'd like." He turns the shell in his hand till it catches the light coming in through the window.

"I think there are at least ten different denominations on this island alone, and that's not counting the odd Hindu, Buddhist, or Jew.

"Then," he adds, with that same subtle smile, "there are the evolutionists."

"And then . . ." A pause. "There are the surfers."

The shelves in the bedroom are lined with back issues of *Watch Tower* magazine, which Daniel and Tina and their fellow congregationists distribute all over the island twice every month. The magazine, Daniel is proud to explain, is translated into 128 languages, with more than 22 million copies of each issue shipped to Witnesses all over the world. Six hundred of those copies, printed in Spanish, arrive every two weeks at Daniel and Tina's door, delivered by truck from the airport at Baltra.

Daniel is one of this church's two "elders"—he and a fisherman named Hugo Ruiz. But he's quick to point out that this is an administrative title, not a hierarchical one. The Witnesses don't believe in hierarchy. And the door-to-door visits Daniel and Tina make throughout the village at least seventy hours each month—"There isn't a door here that we haven't knocked on at least once, if not fifty times," says Tina—are not, Daniel adamantly insists, missionary work. He cringes at the word "missionary."

"To me, that term has a tone of zealotry," he says, "and we're not zealots. We're not fanatics. We're reasonable people who are simply trying to apply the principles of the Bible to our lives. We *enjoy* our lives."

An occasional beer cut with Sprite, for example. That's one of Daniel's small pleasures. Daniel enjoys the CDs back in the bedroom as well—Tracy Chapman, UB40, the Jayhawks—although there is some music he listens to that strains even Tina's comprehension, such as the collection of "Kingdom Melodies" produced by the Witnesses as an eight-CD set, one of which Daniel has just put on in place of the Byrds. An orchestral swell strong enough to rattle the walls of a tabernacle consumes the apartment.

"I recall listening to two of my parents' records over and over again as a child," Daniel says, ducking into the bedroom to cut down the volume. "Peter, Paul, and Mary and the Soviet Army Chorus and Band. Those, and the sea chanties my grandmother would play on her accordion."

Daniel Fitter's roots in these islands run deep, and they begin with his maternal grandmother, Emma Angermeyer. A first lady of the Galápagos, Emma was the wife of Hans Angermeyer, who sailed here in the mid-1930s with his three brothers to escape the horrors taking shape in their native Germany. Emma is still alive today, though just barely. She's eighty-six, living in England with Daniel's aunt, Johanna. Word came not long ago that Emma's got cancer, a tumor in the stomach. Tina's been on the phone all week trying to book a flight back to Heathrow for herself and Daniel sometime next month.

Daniel's father, and his father's father as well, just left the Galápagos last week to fly back to England after spending Christmas and New Year's with Daniel and Tina. Daniel's grandfather, R. S. R. (Richard Stanley Richmond) Fitter, has written more than fifty books on British wildlife, and at age eighty-seven he might not be done yet. Daniel's father, Julian, following his own naturalist path, first came to the Galápagos in 1964 as a crewman on the *Beagle II*, a regal, three-masted brigantine brought from Great Britain to serve as the Darwin Station's first research vessel.

In a memoir titled *My Father's Island*, sold in the village's souvenir shops and up at the Station when they can keep it in stock, Daniel's aunt, Johanna Angermeyer, describes the wonder of watching the *Beagle II* sweep into Academy Bay on a spring morning in '64. She recalls her girlish enchantment at beholding a blond, bearded, "bushy-chested" Englishman singing "I Want to Hold Your Hand" as he swabbed the boat's deck. That young sailor was Julian Fitter. The young woman he would soon make his wife was Johanna's older sister, Mary, daughter of Emma and Hans.

Emma Angermeyer's route to the Galápagos is a book of its own. Born in czarist Russia in 1913, her parents brought her as an infant to America, where she grew up in Lincoln, Nebraska. At the height of the Depression she met a dashing young pilot from Ecuador who was passing through town on a military training tour. Emma married the flier, Marco Antonio Aguirre, in 1936 and moved with him to Quito, where he was an officer in the Ecuadorian Air Force.

Less than two years after that, on a foggy, rain-driven morning, Marco Aguirre flew a light training plane into the side of an Andean mountain, leaving Emma a widow. She was still there in Quito two winters later working as a schoolteacher when she crossed paths with a young German sailor who was visiting the mainland from his home in the Galápagos. Emma had no idea anyone lived on those islands.

The sailor's name was Hans Angermeyer, and not long thereafter, in the summer of 1940, Emma found herself married again. Hans took her home with him to the islands, but the stay didn't last long. In late 1941, with Emma seven months pregnant, the couple came back to the mainland to buy a new sailboat. Their timing was terrible. They hadn't been there a week when the Japanese bombed Pearl Harbor, America entered the war, and Hans, being German, was forbidden to return to the Galápagos, where an American air base was now being built.

Two months later, in February of 1942, Mary was born in a Guayaquil hospital. Not long after that, all Americans living in Ecuador were ordered by the U.S. Embassy to return to the States. That May, Emma and Mary, despite Emma's attempts to resist, were flown back to Nebraska without Hans. For the next three years, until the end of the war, the husband and wife exchanged letters between hemispheres.

In the fall of 1946, Emma finally flew down to Quito with the intent of bringing Hans home with her to America. It was too expensive and difficult a journey to take Mary along, so she left the baby with family in Lincoln. After a grueling five-day trip on a freighter from Guayaquil, Mary arrived in Puerto Ayora that December. During the voyage, she learned that Hans' parents, along with the one Angermeyer brother who had stayed behind when the others sailed away, had been killed in the bombing of Hamburg. It was heartbreaking news for Hans and his brothers. Even more devastating was Emma's discovery when she arrived on the islands that Hans was sick with tuberculosis and would not be allowed to come home with her.

Emma stayed with Hans for nearly a year before going back to the States, where she set out to convince immigration officials to allow her ailing husband to join her and their baby girl in Nebraska. There would soon be another baby for Hans to see—Emma was pregnant again, with the child who would become Johanna.

The following February, in 1948, with Hans still on the islands, Johanna was born in a hospital in Lincoln. Nine months after that, with Emma still fighting to find someone to take up her cause, Hans passed away in a clinic in Quito. He is buried today somewhere in that city, but no one knows where; his remains were lost years ago in a bureaucratic shuffle involving unpaid rent on a cemetery plot.

This is the epic tale Daniel was told as he grew up in the Galápagos. He heard it from Mary and he heard it from Emma, who returned to the islands in the early 1960s with her accordion and her daughters and a piano—the first piano the Galápagos had ever seen.

Even then, the place hadn't changed much from the rugged paradise the Angermeyer brothers had known in the '30s and '40s. It certainly hadn't changed over there, beyond the *barranco*, on "the Other Side," where Hans' brothers still lived. It was a world away over there, not just from the world that had moved into the postnuclear age of Khrushchev, Castro, and Kennedy, but from even the new Research Station being built just across the harbor and from the rustic little hotel run by the American, Forrest Nelson.

The lives that these families on the other side led—the Angermeyers, the De Roys, the Divines, and, once they were married, young Mary and Julian Fitter—were the stuff of a tropical Eden. Rough but romantic. Days intertwined with the tides and the sun and the breezes and birds. Nights overhung by the moon and the stars and those high, looming hills. It was a place where crazy Gus Angermeyer—"The Tractor," they called him, because of his enormous brute strength—quoted Nietzsche and Kant as he carried on deep conversations with the iguanas that crawled through his cavelike cottage overlooking the sea. It was a place where the men would hunt goats with hand-sharpened spears, the women lathered their hair with guacamole shampoo made from crushed avocadoes that fell from the trees, and where Emma pulled out the accordion whenever a party took shape, sending the dancers whirling across her home's smooth, cement floor as the moonlight poured in through the oceanfront window.

This was the world in which Daniel was raised. While Julian took tourists for trips on his sailboat, Mary kept house and took care of Daniel. He was the quintessential island boy, his hair bleached almost white by the sun, his skin a deep bronze, and his bare feet like leather as he stalked the lava shoreline from morning to night, exploring the tidal pools where the octupi hid, the mangrove-draped inlets where the pelicans nested, and the small sandy coves where the sea lions slept.

His teachers were the kids he grew up with, and the grown-ups as well: his uncles and cousins and neighbors like the De Roys. There was Andre de Roy, the father, who had come here from bomb-ravaged Belgium in 1955; Andre's son, Gil, who was like a big brother to Daniel; and Gil's sister, Tui, who years later would capture the glory of the Galápagos with her camera as no one had done before, in photographs that are still published around the world.

By the time Daniel was six, he was rowing his little dinghy each morning across the harbor, a distance of a fourth of a mile, to join the children in town in the public school classroom. But that lasted only a couple of years. One afternoon when Daniel was eight, Christy's son, Jason, who was a year behind Daniel, brought home his assignment, a sentence he'd been told by his teacher to copy fifty times in his notebook. The sentence read, "The sun is the largest planet." That was all it took for Christy and Mary to pull their boys out of school and begin teaching them at home, which they did for the next four years. Each weekday morning, Jason rowed over to the Fitters' place or Daniel rowed to the Gallardos'. If someone was sick or they just couldn't make it that day, they hoisted a red flag outside their house.

Every two or three years Daniel and his parents would fly back to England to visit Julian's family. The year Daniel turned twelve, they moved there to stay. Galápagos tourism, which had begun so quaintly in the late 1960s with most of the rooted locals enthusiastically running small tour-sailing operations, sharing their islands with pride and with pleasure—the Angermeyers selling berths on their sleek, black-hulled *Nixe,* the Nelsons doing the same with their *Orca* and *Vagabond,* and Julian Fitter making junkets on his gaft-rigged Baltic trader, the *Sulidae*—these seat-of-the-pants tour operations had by 1980 ballooned into a mass industry. When the flotillas of engine-powered cruise boats owned by mainland corporations began to move in, Julian decided it was time to move out. He didn't leave the Galápagos behind entirely. Far from it. To this day, he's the moving force, the founder and director of the British-based Galápagos Conservation Trust, an organization devoted to identifying and addressing the needs of the islands. As for Mary, she saw, just like Christy, that she had reached the limit with homeschooling her son. The boys needed a proper education. Christy sent Jason to Quito for his. Mary and Julian decided Daniel would get his in England, which he did, but not in the ways they intended.

"It was complete culture shock," Daniel says, sinking into the room's only soft chair. Besides the British obsession with grades, of which Daniel had no conception, and homework, which his grandmother Emma, who had taught school herself, abhorred—"School is for schoolwork," Emma always told Daniel, "and home is to do what you'd like"—Daniel now found himself in a world defined by values he had never known on the islands, such things as status and winning and wealth.

"I felt like an alien from the very first day," he remembers. "I'll never forget the teacher going around the room asking each of us to tell her our birthday. I didn't know my birthday. Witnesses don't celebrate birthdays. I had to go home and find my date of birth on my passport."

Daniel's religious faith—Mary had been raised as a Jehovah's Witness and raised Daniel that way—faded as Daniel grew into adolescence in the Sex Pistols London of the mid-1980s. By the time he turned seventeen (finished with school but with no sense of a future beyond a yen for photography), his sense of himself as a Witness was nearly gone. He felt rootless, restless, hollow. And so, when a message arrived from Fiddi Angermeyer inviting Daniel to come back to the islands and work with him, Daniel leaped at the offer. Fiddi's father, Fritz, was one of those four fabled brothers, and Fiddi now carried on his uncles' tradition, running the most respected sail-touring operation in the islands.

So Daniel left England and his mother as well, who was dying of cancer. He wanted to stay, but Mary insisted he leave. "She said go, get out of here. Deep down, subconsciously, I think I understood that she didn't want me to see her die."

Two months after Daniel arrived back in the Galápagos in October of 1986, Mary Fitter passed away. Her funeral was held in England, in Dorset, but her ashes were then taken to the islands, where they are buried today in a small, tree-shaded cemetery up by the entrance to the Research Station, just across the road from the Hotel Galápagos.

And so, at eighteen, Daniel had reached a crossroads, a crisis, with the loss of his mother, the loss of his faith, and a sense of identity that was torn and confused. After a year on the islands as a certified guide, he went back to England to sort it all out. He rediscovered his faith, then crossed paths with Tina at a Kingdom Hall meeting. They married in 1993, with a firm stipulation from Tina that Daniel *never* take her to live in the Galápagos.

"I'd read *My Father's Island*," she says, "and it wasn't pretty to me."

So they took a stab at being modern British suburbanites. Daniel got a job in a photo shop. Tina worked as a nanny. They bought a car. Then a friend showed up at a Witnesses meeting, just back from his new home in Africa, and the friend told Daniel he was a fool to be joining this rat race in England when he had such deep roots in a place as rare and real as the Galápagos.

It took some convincing to persuade Tina to give it a go, but she finally relented and took a trip down to the islands with Daniel to see for herself what this place might be like. The bus ride itself, from the airport to town, was almost enough to send her home right away.

"I was shocked, utterly shocked," she says. "When you're a tourist, you don't see *any* of what you see on that bus ride. You don't see any of what this place, this island, this town, is really about."

Tina stops for a second and waves her hand toward the kitchen window, through which the clustered slum homes of their neighbors can be seen. "You don't see any of this!"

The squalor that has spread through the paradise Daniel grew up in is a strong part of what made Tina decide to agree to make the move, which they did in December of 1995. Their work as Witnesses is paramount for Tina. As for Daniel, he's fashioned a balance between his faith and his passion, between spreading the word of the Bible and feeding his soul with the natural wonders that flowed through his blood as a boy. When he's not Witnessing, he works as one of the islands' most respected naturalist guides. His camera is always with him. He's got a book due out soon, a photographic guide to the wildlife of the Galápagos, with pictures by Daniel and text by his father.

The guiding, Daniel will be the first to admit, is as close to his heart as his religion. But unlike his faith, which now never wavers, this profession of tour-guiding here on the islands has changed in ways Daniel dislikes, in the same kinds of ways that drove his father away.

"Guiding can be a dangerous thing, in terms of keeping a healthy sense of one's self," Daniel says. "It can really turn you into an egotist. You've got a controlled audience of people for a week or two who think you're absolutely wonderful and who do anything you ask them to do. The pay is good, it can be very good. And there are lots of pretty girls, which I would say is the main reason probably sixty percent of the guides out there right now are doing this."

Tina's setting the table. The chili is almost ready.

"In the past," Daniel continues, "most of the guides were truly keen naturalists. I mean, you could have paid them a buck a day and they would have done it. There are still some of those left, but now it's much more for the money and for the, shall we say, fringe benefits."

The two faces of Daniel—Jehovah's Witness and naturalist guide—raise an obvious question, one he's faced all his adult life.

How, people ask, can a person so deeply steeped in fundamentalist biblical faith reconcile his religious beliefs with the tenets of biologic science, specifically the science of evolution?

"People ask me all the time, 'How can you be a guide and believe in Creationism as well?' I tell them, yes, I—we—believe that there is a Creator. He is the answer to the question of why, not how. The how, the mechanics of life, is left to the scientists, as it should be. At the end of the day, Adam was the first scientist, the first Park warden."

He again picks up one of the shells. "I believe strongly in biologic evolution—the adaptation of species, survival of the fittest and such. But I do not believe in organic evolution, which is the evolution of life from nonliving matter."

This synthesis of Creationism and evolution has found a small foothold in scientific circles in recent years, as well as a name: "intelligent design theory." The process of natural selection, say its proponents, while valid and useful in studying and understanding plants, animals, and humans, does not answer all our questions about life on Earth, including the most elemental one: Where did it begin? That question, say intelligent designists, is answered only by acknowledging the existence of an intelligent designer, a Creator, a God.

Daniel leaps from his chair and grabs a book from a shelf on the wall. Hard-covered, with well-fingered pages, its title is *Darwin's Black Box: The Biochemical Challenge to Evolution*, written by an American, a Lehigh University professor named Michael Behe.

"This man is my second God," Daniel says, holding the book up with both hands, as if making an offering. "My first God is the God of the Bible, Jehovah. My second God is Michael Behe because he sums up so perfectly the principle of biochemical evolution."

Lunch is now ready. Daniel puts the book back and moves to the table. One of the workers on the house comes to the door and asks in Spanish if he might have a glass of water. Tina answers in Spanish as well, as she hands him the drink. The man downs it in three gulps, thanks her, and returns to work.

"He used to be a drunkard," Tina says, washing the glass. "He'd beat up his wife. They were in a really bad state when we began teaching with them."

Now the man is a member of their congregation, as are almost all the crew working on that house. In the five years since they began Witnessing here together, Daniel and Tina have watched their congregation swell to nearly two hundred. But there's still much work to do. They can simply look out their door at enough challenges to keep them busy for a lifetime. Such as the bus driver and his family who live just across the road.

"They shout and scream at one another all day," says Tina, "with the TV going full blast."

"We've got a pretty good sense," says Daniel, "of the dynamics of that particular family. They've got a pretty primitive form of communication."

And then there's the "dope den," as Daniel calls it, just up the lane.

"Sometimes it's awful, sometimes it's not that bad," he says. "It depends on who's renting it at the moment. The people who just moved out, they kept it a pothole. Constant music, and dope wafting out the windows. We knocked on that door several times."

They'll be out knocking on other doors later this afternoon. Then there will be more calls to make to firm up their flight plans to England to see Emma.

But right now it's time for lunch, which means prayer.

And silence.

And the sounds of the sawing next door.

NINE

Tranquilo

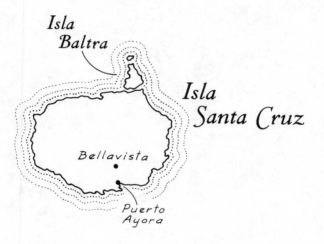

Isla Baltra

Isla Santa Cruz

Bellavista

Puerto Ayora

JANUARY 14, 2000

taxi driver Milton Medina in Puerto Ayora city jail

party of eight checked in late yesterday—five men and three women. Jack was expecting the men: Ricardo Nuñez, with one of his surf groups from the mainland. Nuñez runs the only surf tours around the archipelago—or at least he's trying to get started. He's got a Web site, "Galápagosurf.com," although updating it is sometimes a problem, what with his day job and all. And then there's the small matter that most of the spots to which Nuñez takes his clients are National Park waters, closed to the public, illegal to surf. Only a few designated sites in the islands are open to surfers. But what the hell, the Park Service can't patrol all this water, and the way Nuñez sees it, or his argument, at least, is that he and his customers are doing no harm.

When *Surfer* magazine brought those pros down to do its big story, it was Nuñez who served as their guide. He's been riding waves all his life, starting out on the Ecuadorian coast where he was born and grew up thirty-some years ago. The surf isn't bad there, Nuñez says, but the first time he saw the Galápagos, at the turn of the 1980s, he thought he'd found heaven. He'd never seen tubes like these, and in a setting like this. He worked on a traditional tour boat around the islands for a couple of years, then went back home to Guayaquil to join his family's beer distributorship because he simply had to make money. The beer still pays Nuñez's bills today, but two or three times a year he charters a boat and brings out a group of a half dozen or so surfers, who pay and pay well for him to show them some waves like the ones they have seen on those magazine pages.

That's what the four young men in their twenties with him this Friday morning have come for. Except this group has clearly got more money than most surfers Jack sees, with their hand-tooled leather travel bags, Perry Ellis slacks, Ralph Lauren shirts, and Docksiders shoes—not to mention that chartered pearl-white, seventy-five-foot catamaran anchored out in the harbor on which the group will be living for the next week or so as they circle the islands looking for waves.

The group's apparent leader, the short stocky one with the salon-styled hair, the tight T-shirt, the abs, the biceps—and the shapely redhead in jeans and a bikini top parked on his lap—Jack's never seen him before, but he knows who he is: the son of one of the most influential members of the Ecuadorian Congress. The kid's father is at the moment in Quito, looking out his office window at mobs of Indians facing off in the streets with some of the several thousand soldiers and police deployed just this morning by President Mahuad to keep the protesters from fulfilling their vow to seize Congress when Mahuad delivers his State of the Union address one week from today.

The kid seems less than concerned about the coup his father is facing back home. Right now he and his buddies are hungry for breakfast, which Betty and Albertina and the rest of Jack's kitchen staff have just about gotten ready. The lights were still on in this kid's bungalow when Jack went to bed late last night, and when he passed the room early this morning on his way to the office, female laughter was drifting out its window.

The congressman's son and his friends had made reservations with Jack's office manager, Carlos, but the three girls were a wild card, showing up in their platform pumps, hip-hugging skirts, and tight, lace-up tops. Nuñez said something about them being Hawaiian Tropic models, come for some vague kind of photo shoot, and Jack listened and smiled. He'd seen these women before. "Part of the scene," he calls them, high-priced escorts from Guayaquil, as rentable as that catamaran in the harbor. But Jack said nothing to Nuñez about this. And when he got a phone call early last evening from yet another member of the group, the nephew of a former Ecuadorian president, it all fell into place. The nephew called to say he would not be arriving till today. "Oh, by the way," he told Jack, "some models will be arriving with the group. Please put them in their own room. I'll be paying the bill."

Jack has his doubts about whether he'll ever actually see that

money. The nephew's been here before, and he's "forgotten" to settle his tab when he's left. Sometimes he makes good later on; sometimes he doesn't.

But what the hell. That's how it is in a place like this, a country
like this. The people who have passed through Jack's hotel over the
years—the nice, normal folks, and the con men, thieves, freaks, per-
verts, refugees, rock stars, groupies, scoundrels, scumbags—who is
Jack to judge any of them? Whoever they are, when they get here it
doesn't much matter to Jack where they've come from or where they
are going. He treats them all the same way, just like the elderly bird-
watchers sitting at the table by the back window or the tour group
from Tokyo gathered down at the bar. Jack hopes they have a great
time, that they come and go in peace, and that, in the end, they each
pay their bill. Jack's not the kind to make quick character judgments.
Live and let live; that's pretty much what he believes. But please, if
you've got any class at all, pay your bill.

Now sit down with the congressman's son, and the kid will tell
you what class is. Not five minutes into the conversation, he's
already giving the rundown on that catamaran. "It has everything,"
he says, in English tinged with a sweet Spanish trill. "The cook, the
captain, the people who clean the rooms and make them up."

He makes a circle with his thumb and forefinger, squints his
eyes, and puckers his lips.

"It is as good as it gets," he says. "Believe me."

The others are eating their breakfast, but the congressman's son
is finished with his. His wife just called from the mainland to see
how he's doing. He had to shush the girls at that point by cupping
his hand over the receiver and putting his finger to his lips. God
knows he didn't need his wife asking what those female titters
were in the background. His wife told him their ten-month-old son
misses him, and he told her he misses the boy, too. He's got a photo
of the baby in his wallet, which he pulls out and shows off with
fatherly pride. Someday the family fortune will belong to this boy,
he says, or at least a large part of it.

"Bananas," he says, putting his wallet away. "We have some
plantations."

His father, he says, was the family firm's CEO before becoming a congressman.

"Now that he is a politician," he says, "he is out of the business. It is kind of an ethics rule."

Kind of confusing, apparently, because in the next breath he explains his own position as the company's general manager by saying, "There is nobody higher than me, only Daddy."

His English is excellent, thanks to four years of college in the States at the University of South Carolina, where he got a B.A. in business. He spent a bit of time in San Francisco, he says, but now at age twenty-eight he's back home, running the sixth-largest banana-exporting operation in Ecuador.

"Dole, Chiquita, Del Monte," he says, "they are our customers. We primarily sell in Germany and Eastern Europe and Russia. All developing, emerging markets."

He's been all over the world, closing deals for his fruit, says the kid. "Poland, China, Portugal, Belgium, Germany, Japan, Singapore, you name it," he says. But last year was the first time he visited the Galápagos.

"Sometimes," he says, "it's incredible how you can go all over the places, but not in your backyard."

The redhead strolls past with a cell phone. The kid winks, grins. The office phone rings. It's one of the other men's wives, calling the hotel to see if he's okay. Again the girls—the redhead and the tall one with the tumbling, black hair and the young one, who can't be older than eighteen—cover their mouths to suppress their giggles. The ex-president's nephew will be checking in some time later today. The group will spend one more night at the hotel then take off tomorrow for six days of surfing, if things go as planned.

It's not yet nine A.M. on this Friday morning, and already the temperature has climbed into the nineties. With so much of the islands covered with lava—or, recently, paved with asphalt and concrete—the sun's heat, through both radiation and reflection off the rocks and water, is magnified well into the hundreds. Because of cold ocean currents and the soothing sea breezes, the Galápagos heat often feels less intense than it is, a deception that can prove deadly for unknowing visitors. Locals liken the heat on these islands to that of a fan-assisted oven: The airflow can feel cooling, even as it's sucking the moisture from your body, gently cooking your skin to a crisp.

Max Parédes has seen more than a few cases of severe sunburn in the twenty-five years he's worked at the hospital here in Puerto Ayora, although the vast majority of the thirty or so people a day who come through the clinic's front doors are either stricken with parasites or expecting a child. Pregnancy and parasitic infection are, far and away, the two most common conditions treated by Parédes and the three other doctors on his hospital's staff.

They've got fifteen beds here, although on this particular morning, not one is occupied. At the moment, a half dozen or so men and women and a couple of children are sitting in the waiting area, gazing at a television bolted to the ceiling and watching a program called *Laura en America* via cable from Peru. At this time every weekday, almost every TV set in town—and across these islands, and indeed, throughout all South America—is tuned to this program. It is a Latin version of the *Jerry Springer Show*, starring a professionally dressed blonde who looks not unlike Dr. Joyce Brothers, acting as ringleader to a parade of betrayed wives and cuckolded husbands. When Laura is on TV here in Puerto Ayora, the streets and sidewalks are noticeably empty.

Parédes is in his office, squeezed into a chair that can hardly contain his broad, beefy body. He's forty-eight and "healthy," he says, thumping a fist on his chest. He wears slacks and a sportshirt, not the blue or white scrubs of a doctor on duty—although he is, at the moment, on the clock. Above him, mounted like art on the walls, are an array of stringed instruments—guitars and mandolins. "I give lessons," he says, "when I have time."

It's a slow day. But then almost every day is like this, says Parédes. There's not much illness to deal with here in the Galápagos, he says. He mentions AIDS, saying there have been only five victims here. He brags that the cholera epidemic that swept through South America five years ago took no lives on these islands, although they did treat fifty or so cases in this clinic. Parédes says he wishes his hospital had its own ambulance—the only one on the island is owned by the Red Cross, which lets Parédes and his staff use it whenever it's needed. But then again, he says, it's a relief not owning the vehicle. "If we did have one," he says, "people would abuse it to get free rides to Baltra."

They don't see death often inside these walls, says Parédes. When they do—two, maybe three times a year—the bodies are accident victims from the traffic that has increased so much in the past decade, and from the illegal diving done by the *pepiñeros*. With the nation's only decompression chamber six hundred miles away in in the Guayaquil, there's not much that can be done for those unfortunate divers. And there's little hope that such a luxury will be available here in the Galápagos anytime soon. The very idea makes Parédes laugh. His salary, he says, is six million *sucres* a month, about $240. His colleagues make less, including a young female staff member who's fresh out of medical school in Guayaquil. This is her first job, with a monthly paycheck just a bit more than half of Parédes'.

Parédes' doctors and nurses would all love to have more pay and equipment, but the hospital is doing well enough with what it's got, says Parédes. He emphasizes that he has no complaints about the funding he gets, both from the nation's social security system and from the municipal government. All of his friends on the Provincial Council, says Parédes, are doing a wonderful job.

The mayor himself will tell you the same if you stop by his office down by the waterfront, just across from the police station. The room is upstairs, with its own air conditioner and flags flanking the desk. A bright Galápagos mural is painted on the wall behind the chair in which the mayor sits on this shimmering day, marking some documents with a pink highlighter pen.

His name is Franklin Sevilla. He's forty-one, with a wife and two children and almost four years as mayor under his belt. Before he took office, he was an electronics salesman with a small shop in town. His family still owns a hotel here, the Hotel Palmeras. He made much more selling radios, he says, than the $500 a month he's now paid as mayor. "My family wants me to stop," he says of his public service, "but I have goals, and I haven't finished them."

Those goals, he explains, are much the same as most mayors' in most small towns anywhere in the world: improving the water system, working on trash removal, addressing the sewage problem, upgrading the electricity, and yes, paving the streets.

"I don't like personal propaganda. I don't want people to see my face." He points his pen at the papers. "I want them to see my work."

Or perhaps both. That road to Tortuga, for example. When the paving was finally finished, a ceremony was held featuring the unveiling of a large, wooden sign at the road's entrance, announcing to visitors that this project was the work of Franklin Sevilla's administration. The mayor's name was painted right on the sign in large letters. There were other signs as well, posted every quarter-mile or so along the length of the road, all the way to the beach. The Park Service didn't care much for the placards, Eliecer Cruz in particular. Within days the things were taken down by wardens with chain saws.

Sevilla shrugs off such unpleasantness. "In politics," he says, "there are always two groups: those who like you and those who don't like you."

He says this—he says almost everything—with an unceasing smile. He's peppy, upbeat, a cheerleader for the Galápagos. He knows that his vision of these islands and their future may differ from others', particularly from the people at the Park and Research Station. But hey, he'll tell you, he's lived here all his life, and that counts for something.

He was born in Bellavista, one year before the National Park was created. He saw his first car at age thirteen. "We rode on donkeys and horses. We got our milk from the cows, our food from the ground." And, he adds, "We ate a lot of tortoises. It was free meat, just roaming around."

It was illegal, he acknowledges, to kill tortoises. But everyone did it back then, he says. The Park Service didn't start caring, he says, until the 1980s or so. Back in those days, Sevilla's family, neighbors, friends, and even he himself didn't quite understand why such laws existed in the first place.

"We didn't understand why people would want to protect the animals when God gave us the animals to eat. Even to this day, I feel this way. We respect the importance and rights of the animals, but we *also* have lives, like all human beings. We *also* have needs."

To be frank, says the mayor, it's those foreign meddlers up at the Research Station who are behind most of the problems the islands are having. If those *gringo locos*, as he calls them, would just get out of the way, this town and these islands could prosper in the way they should.

"When we got the desalinization system," he says, "the scientists were against that. They were against the electricity going twenty-four hours a day. Telephones, the bank, the sewage system—they are against all these things because it will attract more people to come here."

There is a gap, says the mayor, between the people up at the Park and Station and the townspeople he represents. "I want to close this gap between the Galápagos and the Park," he says. "We must remember that we live by tourism here."

And by fishing, he adds. He won't say he supports the *pepiñeros*, but he won't condemn them, either. Like any good politician, he knows where the votes are, and there are too many votes in the camps of the fishermen to risk losing them by taking a stand on this issue. Indeed, when a stand must be taken, such as when one of those small, local, illegal *pangas* is seized, the mayor will side with the locals. Since the town's judge was thrown off the island and has not been replaced, the mayor has acted in his stead, prosecuting or releasing local lawbreakers as he sees fit.

"When I'm convinced someone is guilty, I send them to Guayaquil," he says. Most of the cases he faces are minor misdemeanors—"delinquents, drugs, thievery." And, of course, poaching. "If the fisherman is *Galápagueño*, and it is the first time for them, they are pardoned. I have that authority."

If it's the second or third time, well, the mayor won't say. This whole subject of laws and lawbreakers makes him a little uneasy. He's happy to talk about the good works being done, but if you want to discuss crime, he says, it would be best to go talk to the chief of police.

Which is not hard to do. The gate to the Puerto Ayora police station is always wide open. It takes a minute or two for the men in the guard shack to go see if the chief is done with his midday *siesta* and is prepared to see visitors. The chief, it turns out, is as laid-back as his headquarters, with the bay waters lapping outside his office window, kids playing tag under the palms at the edge of the small parking lot, and a woman—the wife of one of his lieutenants—sitting on a curb in the shade just outside his office door, nursing an infant.

Beyond the woman, behind a pair of clotheslines and a junked motorcycle, sits the *cárcel*—the town jail, a small concrete bunker with one steel-barred door and two steel-barred windows. The bars on the right look in on the men's cell; the ones on the left look in on the women's. Right now there is one person inside, leaning on the door, a muscular man in his thirties or so, wearing a tight white T-shirt, with swept-back Elvis-style hair and a glum look on his face.

"*Apesta!*" he says, pressing his nostrils with his finger and thumb.

It does stink—of urine and feces. There is no toilet inside and no lighting either. A wet, rotted mattress leans up against a graffiti-scrawled wall. LA VIDA ES DURA PERO NOSOTROS TENEMOS QUE SER MAS DUROS, reads one message: "Life Is Tough, but We Must Be Tougher."

The man says he was arrested less than an hour ago. His name is Milton Medina. He drives a taxi. He's here because he ran over a bicycle and does not have the money to buy the owner a new one.

The chief won't say what he plans to do with Medina, but he acknowledges the jail is a disgrace. It was built to hold four. "If there's more," says the chief, "they just have to fit in there. If there are twenty criminals, you can't tell them to come back tomorrow."

The chief is a pleasant man, surprisingly young—thirty-nine—to be wearing a captain's bars on the shoulders of his tan khaki uniform. He's in charge of a staff of twenty-nine men. "Not one," he says, "from the Galápagos."

Neither is he. His name is Rodrigo Proáno. He came to Puerto Ayora from Quito exactly one year ago. In fact, he had been here just three days when the march on Judge Avellan's office took place last January. Proáno was inside the judge's chambers that morning when the protesters broke the front gate with the battering ram. "I was the one who suggested he flee the island," he says. "He wanted to stay, but I said that was not possible."

When the judge was led out and was put in the truck waiting to take him to the airport, Proáno was one of the policemen beside him. "Yes," says the chief, his eyes widening in mock terror as he dodges his head this way and that. "Welcome to the Galápagos, with the flying eggs."

The ceiling fan above Proáno's desk turns slowly, stirring the sweltering air. A half-empty bottle of Amaretto sits on a shelf by his filing cabinet. Outside, his staff's only vehicle—a '96 Chevy pickup, the same truck that carried the judge away—is parked in the lot. There is one motorcycle as well, and two boats, but that's it. For the most part, the cops in this village travel just like the townspeople and tourists: on foot.

It's a sleepy job, says Proáno, and he likes it that way. This posting, for him, is a reward of sorts, a respite after doing years of hard time in the streets of Quito and Guayaquil and Cuenca—inner cities where Proáno worked for almost two decades before coming here.

"I have never been in a place so *tranquilo* as the Galápagos," he says. "In all those other places, I always carry a gun on my belt. But here," he says, pulling a handkerchief from his back pocket, "I carry this."

The mainland cities, he says, have become like war zones. In his last year on the beat in Guayaquil he was up at five every morning and often would not get back home until midnight. "Here," he says, "I *ask* people to give me work."

The things he saw in those cities, he says, will stay with him forever. "The way people can treat each other. Murders. Rape. Fathers sexually abusing their daughters. Many things are stuck in my mind, things that I can't forget, things that hurt my heart."

His most nightmarish memory, however, took place not in Quito or Guayaquil but in an Amazonian jungle village called Lago Agrio in the northeast corner of Ecuador near the Colombian border. Across that border, in Colombia's southernmost Putumayo province, more than 150,000 acres of coca plantations, controlled by the 16,000-member Revolutionary Armed Forces of Colombia (FARC), produce nearly half the world's supply of cocaine. The guerrillas have been battling their government for over thirty years now, with more than 35,000 Colombian people killed in the fighting. Nowhere has the violence been more vicious than in the Putumayo zone, where the FARC's most feared unit, the Southern Bloc, holds sway.

Proáno was sent to Lago Agrio in 1993 to lead the community's twenty-man police force on border drug patrols engineered and largely supplied by the United States' Drug Enforcement Agency.

Actually, to call Lago Agrio a village is not accurate. Thirty years ago it was indeed nothing more than a jungle hamlet, called "Nuevo Loja" by the indigenous Cofan tribesmen who lived there. But the Texaco Oil Company arrived in the late 1960s, turning the place into a beachhead for its *Oriente* operations. Before long, ninety percent of the crude oil flowing out of Ecuador's Amazon basin ran through this village, and thousands of petroleum industry workers—foreign and Ecuadorian—began moving in.

Today, 25,000 people live in what has come to be called Lago Agrio—"Bitter Lake"—possibly the filthiest, most violent, disease-ridden hellhole in all South America. Battered dust-coated oil company trucks rumble night and day down trash-strewn streets, past shacks and shanties crammed with Colombian refugees who have fled the killings across the nearby border. Destitute Ecuadorians—indigenous Cofans driven out of the surrounding jungle and impoverished "settlers" from the west, from the cities—hustle everything from wristwatches to pet monkeys to bowls of *boa ceviche* on the dusty roadsides. The hot, humid air stinks of petroleum. At night, as the flames from the refinery plants at the edge of the town throw their light on the surrounding jungle, the thump of disco music throbs from crude strobe-lit brothels where drunken oil workers fistfight and curse and make illegal transactions in dozens of languages. Bloody gunfights erupt in the streets. Execution-style murders by ski-masked Colombians have become common, as have kidnappings and killings of oil workers—some of them Americans—by FARC guerrillas demanding multimillion-dollar ransoms.

The root of this nightmarish violence is America's "drug war," which escalated at the turn of the 1990s with Colombia—and FARC—becoming that war's primary foreign target. Ecuador, dependent on America's oil dollars for its very existence, reluctantly became part of this war, agreeing to host and join U.S. antidrug operations launched from various bases in Ecuadorian territory. Lago Agrio became one of those bases, and this is how, a little over six years ago, Rodrigo Proáno became a soldier in that war.

In the autumn of 1993, using speedboats supplied by the DEA and supported by Ecuadorian soldiers dispatched from Quito, Proáno and his men began patrolling the winding San Miguel River and its tributaries, which form part of Ecuador's 370-mile border with Colombia. Not a month after the patrols began, on a December morning, a letter arrived from the FARC guerrillas.

"It said if we did not stop, then they would—" Proáno makes a slashing motion with his finger across his neck. "We didn't take it seriously."

A week after the warning arrived, Proáno traveled to Quito to visit his family. While he was away, on a Thursday afternoon, just a week before Christmas, a squadron of seven speedboats carrying thirty-six men was ambushed by cross fire from more than 200 guerrillas at a bend in the river.

Proáno pulls a small booklet from a shelf near his desk. With drops of blood drawn on its cover, the booklet is titled *PUTUMAYO: Sacrificio Y Valor*. Typed in Spanish, it is an hour-by-hour account of the events of that day. A rendition in English reads as follows:

> *06:30h: In an atmosphere of comradeship, officials and police troop personnel were having breakfast at the B-5 Putumayo installations. Many of them were emanating professional perspectives while others were missing their families.*
>
> *07:00h: . . . departing to the area of Pena Colorado on the river Putumayo: 1 chief, 8 officials and 20 policemen in 6 motorboats and, in addition, 1 COE motorboat with crew of 7 army men, all Ecuadorian.*

12:00h: The motorized caravan made up of the 7 motorboats had crossed Pena Colorado and were going toward Pinuna Negra.

14:00h: Once the professional activities in the site were concluded, the patrol initiated its return which was not accomplished with the expected agility due to damages in motorboat Pirana. . . . At the communications base, a feeling of preoccupation started to invade.

14:45h: Nature presented an impressive spectacle. Entering a turn shaped by the river, at the height of Pena Colorado, the patrol is attacked from both riversides with fire originated from automatic guns and with hand grenades propelled from the vegetation. . . . The motorboats had no covering so they tried to get away from the area. The river flow was low and the boats started to get stranded. Confrontation continued for approximately one hour and a half.

16:30h: Once the first attack stopped, a white speedboat was seen displacing guided by guerrilla men, to inspect the Ecuadorian boats. They proceeded to take armament and the engine from one of them and to destroy the others.

16:45h: An Ecuadorian helicopter arrived to the area for help. . . . Minutes later, two motorboats arrived, one from the army and the other from the police, to provide support to the attacked men.

17:00h: The motorboats were not able to provide the requested help because their navigation was impeded by machinegun fire.

19:00h: . . . survivors from the attack were under arrest at a FARC guerrilla camp.

21:00h: At the dock, activities were undertaken to receive the wounded and the bodies which came down the river and also to stop drifting vessels.

Twelve men were killed that afternoon, says Proáno, including eight of his police officers. Nine more were wounded. Two have never been found. "This was the hardest experience of my life," he says. "To have my friends die—twenty years old, thirty-five years old. They left children, wives, fathers, and mothers."

If he never sees another dead man, says Proáno, slipping the book back on the shelf, it will be too soon. He doubts he will see many here in the Galápagos, certainly none from such violence. There has never been a murder on this island, he says. Well, he corrects himself, maybe one, up in Bellavista a few years ago.

"It was a problem with two homosexuals on a farm," says the chief. "There was one that was jealous of another and he knifed him." But that, says the chief, doesn't really count. It was a lover's quarrel. Besides, he says, they were homosexuals.

Violent crime has not reached the Galápagos, at least not yet, says Proáno. There are break-ins and petty theft, but nothing like back on the mainland. "There," he says of the cities, "if you put your camera down for an instant, you will never see it again." Here, he says, the camera will be there even if you leave and come back.

Drugs have become somewhat of an issue, says the chief, but again it's nothing like what is seen in the cities or even on other island resorts, such as in the Caribbean. "When foreigners come," says the chief, "lots of drugs come also. It's not that the tourists bring the drugs, but when they're here, they ask for the drugs."

Truth be told, says the chief, he's not much concerned with such things as long as they are kept discreet and no one makes trouble. The Galápagos is, after all, a vacation place, a place to relax. "I still have my pistol," he says, "but it's not necessary here."

As the afternoon ends, the chief orders the taxi driver, Medina, released with instructions that he buy a new bike for the owner as soon as he can.

It's getting dark now. It's Friday night. Darwin Avenue is alive with the pulse of the music spilling out of the waterfront clubs. Nowhere is the music louder than outside the Galápason. The place is packed—bodies jammed chest-to-chest on the dance floor, *latinos* and *gringos* alike, locals and tourists, men and women sharing sweat and saliva as they grind and rub bodies to the beat of the music.

The crowd is three deep at the bar, where a twentysomething kid named Jorgé is mixing *cuba libres* as fast as he can. When he's not tending bar, Jorgé works as a guide on the *Galápagos Explorer*.

When he *is* tending bar, he's never too busy, he says, to take "special care" of the "ladies." On this particular evening, he grabs a stool by a woman named Mona, who's nursing a whiskey and Coke and smoking a Belmont.

Mona is twentysomething herself, Swiss, a nurse, with a dark pageboy haircut, no makeup, and a loose-fitting T-shirt draped over her slim, boyish body. This is her second trip to the islands, she says. The first was three years ago, when she bought a one-week discount package, including a brief, four-day tour on a small six-passenger boat. "Two German girls," she says, "two Swiss guys, me, and my brother." The crew included the captain, a guide, and a cook with whom Mona had sex late one night out on the deck as the boat sat anchored off Seymour Island.

"The sex itself was okay," she says, "but what made it great, what made it fantastic, was it was here, in this place, out in these islands, under the stars. It was so real, so romantic."

Now Mona is back, nuzzling Jorgé as they smile and whisper to each other at the end of the bar. Not far away, among a crowd of men watching surf videos on a TV mounted above the dance floor, stands Bico. He's nursing a beer, killing time before going home. Petra's out guiding, he says. She'll be home next week.

And there's Jason, out on the dance floor with Monica, the two of them moving as if they're possessed, the couples around them giving way as Jason and Monica show the crowd how to salsa.

The song ends, and Jason moves to the bar to buy a cold drink for himself and his girl. Bico is there and they chat as a group of four men and three women come through the front door. The group grabs stools near a table covered with flickering candles. It's the surfers from Jack's place, Ricardo Nuñez and the guys—and the three girls as well.

The girl with the dark, tumbling hair is wearing a tank top, revealing a tarantula tattooed on her right shoulder. No sooner is the group seated than she's mounted one of the men, straddling his thighs as she settles onto his lap and locks her lips onto his.

"Hm," says Bico, "his wife would be interested to see this."

Jason heads back to Monica. Bico finishes his beer and leaves to go home. Mona and Jorgé are nowhere to be seen. Nuñez's group begins to split up, each of the women paired with one of the men.

It's a little past midnight. The surfers' catamaran waits in the harbor, shining like a snowdrift in the light of the moon. Ten or so hours from now it will lift anchor. But for the time being it bobs in the stillness, a single light glowing in one of its berths as the sounds of the discos drift out over the water with no sign of ceasing.

The night is still young.

TEN

Paradise

Puerto
Velasco Ibarra

Isla
Floreana

JANUARY 15, 2000

Dr. Ritter and the "baroness"

The woman is choosy about her soft drinks. She and her tour group, all Americans, just arrived in Jack's lobby a few minutes ago after a midmorning hike to the Station. They're hot, tired, and thirsty. Jack's more than willing to oblige, asking them each what they'd like in the way of a beverage.

"Ginger ale," says the woman, as she sighs deeply and drops her fanny pack on a chair by the window. She gives Jack no more than a glance as she unzips the bag and searches for something. As far as she knows—as far as she cares—this man in his flip-flops and T-shirt and shorts is part of the help at this hotel, just another employee. Which bothers Jack not in the least.

"We don't have ginger ale," he says pleasantly enough, moving toward the bar to fetch the others their drinks.

"Mm," says the woman, still not looking up. "Have you got Seven-Up?"

"No Seven-Up," says Jack, lifting a handful of cold bottles from the cooler. "We've got Sprite."

The woman stops, lifts her head, and with exquisite deliberation turns and gazes at Jack.

"Sprite," she says flatly, as if he's just tossed her a foul-smelling bone. She purses her lips, turns her eyes back to her bag, gives her hair a quick flip, and repeats the word. "Sprite."

Jack doesn't need this grief, not this morning. Nuñez and the surfers checked out an hour or so ago, and indeed, the ex-president's nephew skipped on part of the bill. "There's an old Ecuadorian saying," Jack said with a shrug after the surfers had left: "It's the same shit; they just change the flies."

Maybe, after all these years, Jack's finally had enough of the flies. Maybe it's his dad's illness—the old man's mortality shoving itself in Jack's face so close he can smell it. Whatever it is, the way Jack feels right now, he'd sell this hotel in a minute if a buyer just happened along.

"If someone walked in with a suitcase full of cash and a couple of tickets out of here," he says, setting up a sewing machine on a lobby table after the tour group has finished their drinks and moved on, "I'd be gone. Not immediately, not forever, but I'd be gone."

He fetches some swatches of neon-bright fabric from a room in the back. The scuba boat he owns with his dive shop partner, Mathias, needs some new flags, so Jack's doing what's always been done with such needs around here: He's making them himself. The hum of the sewing machine blends with the sound of the surf floating in through the lobby's screen door.

"Two million," says Jack. That's what he figures the place ought to go for. If someone laid that kind of cash on the table, he'd take it. Then at last he'd be able to settle up with his wife, Patricia, finalize their divorce and move ahead and get married to Romy. He'd love to tie up the loose ends with Romy and Audrey. It would clean things up as well for his daughter, Noell, whom Patricia took with her to California when she and Jack split back in 1992. Noell was two at the time. She's ten now. Jack can't wait to see her next month when he stops in L.A. on the way to pick up his father in Thailand.

California remains a touchstone for Jack, even after all this time. It's where he grew up, of course. It's where his mother still lives. It's where Patricia and he met, before he first came to the Galápagos. And it's where he looked up Patricia two decades later, after she wrote him a letter that arrived out of nowhere. They got married shortly thereafter, in 1987, and she came down to the islands with Jack to help run the hotel. Two years after that, Noell was born. Nearly three years later, Patricia had had enough—of the Galápagos, of the hotel, of the marriage—and went home.

Then came Romy. It's easy to look at the three of them—Jack, Romy, and Audrey—and mistake Jack for Audrey's grandfather. Happens all the time. Jack doesn't care. In fact, he kind of delights in the surprise on a hotel guest's face when they discover that Audrey is Jack's daughter and that the striking Peruvian beauty beside Jack is his wife.

Actually, Romy's only part Peruvian, on her mother's side. The other parts—Italian and Austrian—come from her father, whose family fled northern Italy during World War II and wound up in Lima, where Romy was born in the summer of 1962. Five years after that—the same year Jack first came to the Galápagos—Romy's dad, Armando Antonio Alfredo Hartmann, took his family to South Bend, Indiana, where he spent the next five years at Notre Dame earning his Ph.D. in chemistry. Then he moved his family back to Peru. That explains Romy's fluent English and dead-on American accent.

Romy arrived in Puerto Ayora in early 1986, after a short stint in Germany as a perfumer and a couple of years as a museum guide in Guayaquil. The Galápagos trip was a lark, with a friend who'd gotten a wild hair to visit the islands. For Romy, it was love at first sight— "no traffic, dirt streets, everyone barefoot"—and she wound up staying. She did "the hippie thing," as she calls it, for a couple of years, painting T-shirts and making sand-cast candles to sell to the tourists. Then she went to work at Jack's hotel. She and Jack were "just friends," she says, until Patricia moved out. "Then," she says, "we became more than just friends. I realized I loved him." They moved in together that year. Audrey was born three years later, in 1995.

Now Audrey's four, and Romy's getting a bit edgy about the future, about how life—Audrey's life—will develop if they stay on this island. Audrey's close to school-age now—in fact, that's where she is at the moment, at a little preschool up in the village, where Romy will fetch her in a half hour or so.

Right now Romy's enjoying the downtime, relaxing on a lobby sofa with a hot cup of coffee before returning to being a mom. Her thick dark hair's up in a bun. Her strong, shapely figure is draped in a loose T-shirt and shorts. She's got paint on her hands from a still life she's working on back at the house, a big painting she hopes to have framed and ready to hang by next week. The portrait of Darwin on the wall, the one with the window frame, is Romy's. If all she had to do was paint and pass her days here on this island for the rest of her life, she'd be perfectly happy. That's part of the reason she's stayed for the past fourteen years. This island life, she admits, can be hypnotic, seductive, easy to settle into without even knowing you've done it.

But now there's Audrey to worry about. It would be nice, for starters, says Romy, if she and Jack could get married, which is something Jack's wanted from the beginning. "I don't really care much, myself," Romy says. "I'm not crazy about marriage. But I would do it for Audrey's sake because of social reasons."

Beyond the issue of marriage, the question of raising Audrey in such an insular place is beginning to press on both Romy and Jack. "If we keep her here," Romy says, taking a sip from her cup, "it's like we're keeping her in a bubble. She needs a better education than what she's going to get here."

She takes another sip. "Shit, man," she says, setting the cup down and turning to look out the window at the glimmering bay, "she needs to know there's a world out there, even if it's falling apart."

It does indeed feel as if the world—at least Ecuador's little corner of it—is imploding. The volcanoes around Quito are continuing to blow; newspapers publish eruption alerts every morning. The Colombians are making louder anti-U.S. noises. And the capital city is now under siege from the *Indios*, with hourly news updates barking out of radios perched in windows and on store counters throughout Puerto Ayora.

But up at the National Park headquarters, just off the road to the Station, it's as if nothing is happening, as if the mainland is as *tranquilo* as the finches perched on the pads of the cactus that surround this compound of sea-green, cinder block buildings.

The front door to one of the buildings is open, the sound of a radio drifting from inside. But the radio's not tuned to the news. It's playing rap music—Tupac Shakur chanting and whoofing from a tiny transistor as a woman sits at a computer typing a letter. She's Eliecer Cruz's secretary, and the director is in, if you'd like to have a seat. He'll be free in a couple of minutes.

Which he is. The door opens, a squad of Park lieutenants files out, and Cruz returns to a desk strewn with memos, reports, and fresh faxes. It could seem very hectic, but Cruz is unruffled. The same quiet calmness he displayed when he spoke to the mob from the steps of Judge Avellan's building last year, the easy confidence he exudes whenever he's in public, is here, when he's alone in his office. His English is sketchy, so an assistant is called in to translate as Cruz explains how in the world he can be so relaxed when his job, this Park, the very nature of these entire islands might be completely transformed at any moment.

Cruz settles back in his chair and half-smiles.

"Anything is possible in situations like this," he admits. He counts on his fingers the number of Ecuadorian presidents who have come and gone in the four years he has directed this Park. "*. . . dos, tres, quatro.*"

He smiles.

Four.

"I am always walking a tightrope," he says. There are politicians both here on the islands and certainly on the mainland, he says, who would love nothing more than to see him removed. There are local businessmen and fishermen who would pay for the freedom to pursue their vocations unhindered by aggressive Park wardens enforcing Park laws. Each time the government changes hands, the hopes of Cruz's detractors are kindled. And each time—so far—he has survived.

"*Gatos . . . ,*" he says.

"Cats," repeats the translator. "They have nine lives."

Cruz nods and stands. He's not concerned with the minute-to-minute accounts of upheaval on the mainland. He's in continual contact with Roz Cameron's boss, the head of the Research Station, an Englishman named Robert Bensted-Smith. And he's in touch as well with the U.S. Embassy in Quito. But all Cruz will say about these conversations—all that needs to be said, he says as he smiles—is that "they have promised me they will 'fight like the tiger' for us."

That leaves him free to focus on his job, on the problems at hand, which at the moment include a nasty little situation that's been developing since early last year. It seems that an imaginative entrepreneur from the mainland has put together a unique Galápagos tour package and has begun advertising it on the Internet. Cruz pulls a printout of the Web page from a folder and slides it across his desk. The page is adorned with photos of seals, tortoises, and iguanas. But its title is what catches the eye:

ANDEAN OUTDOOR OUTFITTERS
Conservation Through Hunting

The description of what these tours offer is even more arresting:

**See Charles Darwin's legendary islands and hunt the
extensive populations of feral game.**

The price for six nights and five days, including airfare from
Miami, is $4,800 per person. Two telephone numbers are provided,
one a U.S. 800 number in Boca Raton, the other a number in
Guayaquil. It seems that last March, the company's first customer
arrived here, an American who flew in with his wife. The couple was
met by two "guides" who took them by truck, boat, and on foot for a
five-day foray into the islands that exceeded the clients' wildest
expectations—at least according to an account of the trip written by
the husband, an attorney from Iowa named Richard Meyer, who
summed up his experience for a newsletter called *The Hunting
Report*, published out of Miami.

The excursion, wrote Meyer, was an anniversary gift for himself
and his wife, Lynn. It *"allowed us to get off the beaten path and
really see the Galápagos,"* he explained at the start of his piece. Then
he went into detail:

> The experience is not really a sport hunt as such, nor is it a
> "drive- the-Suburban-out-to-the-pasture" prairie dog shoot.
> Travel to the first shooting area I visited on Santa Cruz
> Island involved at least a one-hour trip by truck and another
> hour by open boat powered by a 50 hp outboard. We saw sea
> lions, sea turtles and manta rays on the boat trip. While I
> walked inland and shot 13 feral donkeys in 3 1/2 hours, my wife
> snorkeled with her guide, who caught fresh lobsters and pre-
> pared a midday luncheon.

That was the first day. The journey went on:

> I spent another day in the Galápagos trying to shoot a wild
> boar that we hunted with the locals' hunting dogs. The boar

was so large that the dogs were unable to turn or stop it, so I did not get a shot. A pleasantly surprising aspect of this hunt was the jolt you got seeing the 400-pound tortoises meandering along in the bushes.

Then came two eventful days on Santiago Island:

The landing on the beach here was rugged and wet. Once through the surf, we set up a traditional "Galápaganian fishing camp" consisting of a suspended tarp to shade the sun and a campfire. In the late afternoon heat, I shot 17 feral goats. The bushes and grass on the island had been stripped by them, leaving little vegetation for the land tortoises and other native fauna.

My wife and her guide snorkeled, hiked, and photographed marine iguanas, pink flamingos, sea turtles and other wildlife. That night, she and I slept in a nylon pup tent on the beach. We were awakened after midnight by a sea turtle throwing sand on our tent as she dug a nest for her eggs. The next morning, I shot 51 goats in about 3¹/₂ hours.

On our last day, we traveled two hours by open boat to the west side of Santiago. We attempted to find wild boar while my wife and her guide snorkeled for lobster. After an hour of unsuccessful searching for boars, we went back toward the beach, where I shot 24 feral donkeys in 1¹/₂ hours. We then went back to the landing site for a wedding anniversary luncheon of wine, fruit salad, and fresh lobster ceviche. After lunch, we boated back to the hotel. That evening, we were treated to a delightful anniversary dinner at a rural restaurant.

In conclusion, wrote Meyer:

A trip there organized by Escobar, even without shooting, would be far preferable to the canned offerings of the tour operators.

Indeed, says Cruz. He recites just a few of the laws broken here: hunting without permits, transporting tourists in open craft between islands without license, camping on Park land without permits, camping in a turtle nesting area, and fishing for lobster out of season without permits.

"It is blatant," says Cruz. "Very blatant."

He doesn't blame the American and his wife, who Cruz assumes were unaware that what they were doing was illegal. But the man who set this all up, the owner of Andean Outdoor Outfitters, an American-born Ecuadorian named Braden Escobar, knows just what he is doing, says Cruz. And if things go as Cruz plans, the next time Escobar arrives for such an outing, he will be placed under arrest.

It's one thing, says Cruz, for the Park Service to struggle with the complex problem of getting rid of the *chivos*—the goats—as well as the wild pigs and other introduced species disrupting these islands. He recognizes that the locals were hunting these goats and pigs long before the Park even existed. He is a local himself, born on Floreana thirty-four years ago. He respects the needs of his fellow *Galápagueños*, he says, both the fishermen and the people who live in the hills. For the former, a licensing system and limited fishing seasons have been created. The latter are allowed to hunt wild game in similarly controlled circumstances.

But outsiders like Escobar, says Cruz, are no better than the mainland industrial fishing fleets who pillage the Galápagos waters with no regard for the future of the animals that live in those waters nor for the Galápagueños who depend on those animals for their very existence.

It's a high-wire act, Cruz admits, controlling the outside invaders while appeasing the people who live here—especially the fishermen. This has become possibly the most critical part of his job: keeping the people who live on these islands happy while educating them about why they must help manage and protect the rich resources that surround them. It's not easy, he admits, to teach people to take the long view in a culture like Ecuador's, a country that has become so conditioned—and understandably so—to living for today rather than preparing for tomorrow.

With the fishermen, it's an admittedly complex problem to deal with, says Cruz, especially with all the recent arrivals from the mainland who have no feel or affection for these islands. But the issue of hunting is much simpler. While thousands of Galápagans' lives depend upon fishing, he says, very few, if any, are as dependent on hunting. Bagging goats and wild boars is a supplemental activity at best for the farmers and cattlemen who live in the highlands. As for the claim made by people like Escobar that they are performing a public service by helping the Park get rid of these unwanted animals; well, says Cruz, that claim is as absurd as it is insincere.

To begin with, he explains, there are tens of thousands of wild goats on these islands—250,000 to be somewhat precise, nearly half that number on Isabela alone. With the kind of hit-and-miss excursions run by freelancers like Escobar, their "customers" wind up shooting maybe a few dozen goats at best, and in a completely random fashion. What use, Cruz asks, is that?

This is a science, he says, getting rid of animals like this. It must be systematic. It requires planning and preparation, which Cruz's people, working with advisors from the Research Station, have been applying for quite a few years now. Cruz is proud to point out, as are the people at the Station, that the feral goat and pig populations on several islands—Española, Plazas, Santa Fé, Rábida—have been completely eradicated during the past two decades, thanks in large part to Park wardens like a man named David Sáles, who just returned from a fifteen-day pig hunt on Santiago.

Men like Sáles are called *matar-chanchos*—"pig stickers"—and they are proud of the title. Sáles has been part of a pig-hunting team for four years now, since he joined the Park Service at age twenty-six. He was born and grew up here in the highlands of Santa Cruz, where his family still raises cattle today. He's a good-humored man with an easy smile that spreads widely beneath his Zapata-like moustache. And he is in tremendous physical condition, which is easy to understand once his job—"one of the most dangerous jobs in the Park," he points out—is explained.

The *chanchos*—the wild pigs, which ravage sea turtle, tortoise, and iguana nesting grounds—are hunted separately from and, critically, *prior* to the goats, says Sáles. This, he explains, is because the goats ravenously feed on the bushes and grasses that grow thick in the highlands. "If we killed the goats first," he says, shrugging his shoulders with the obvious logic of what he is saying, "the vegetation would grow up so densely we would never find the pigs."

Pigs first, then goats. That's the drill, explains Sáles, whose work routine has its own precise rhythm: fifteen days out on an island, four days back home, then back out again for another fifteen-day hunt. The pig hunters are put ashore on a targeted site in twelve-man teams, he explains. Each man is equipped with a hand-held Global Positioning System locator, a VHF radio, a gun (Sáles' own weapon of choice is a bolt-action . 22 rifle) and a dog. "You never get close to a pig without a dog," explains Sáles. "A pig will tear you to pieces."

He pulls from a backpack the jawbone of a young boar he killed on a hunt not long ago. The jagged, tooth-studded bone is more than twelve inches long. A pair of sharp, three-inch tusks juts from its chin. "That was a young one," says Sáles, "about two hundred and fifty pounds." Full-grown boars can weigh as much as a hundred pounds more, he says, with tusks that extend nearly a foot. Sáles says he has seen dogs disemboweled by such tusks. One of his own dogs was eviscerated by a pig not long ago. Now he's got a new one, a mongrel halfboxer he calls Bambi, trained to kill, as are all *matar-chancho* dogs.

The wild pigs do not need to be trained to kill; they are born with that instinct. It is a mesmerizing sight, says Sáles—chilling but hypnotic—to see that instinct unleashed. Sáles describes watching a colleague's dog maul a pig it had caught. Believing the pig was dead, the dog relaxed and backed off. In a blink of an eye, the pig suddenly rose up and took the dog down by its throat. "Tore it wide open," says Sáles. The pig then charged the dog's owner, who shot it point-blank. Again, they thought that was it. "The pig kept coming," says Sáles. "He had to club it with the stock of his rifle. He finally killed it, but the rifle was bent beyond repair."

Despite such risks—or, Sáles admits, because of them—he simply loves hunting pigs. Before the Park Service paid him to do it, he did it for fun, going into the woods from the time he was a boy, on weekends and with friends after their farm work was finished. "The chasing," he says, "you've got to run like hell, sometimes for hours, keep-

...with the dogs. And then comes the actual shooting. For a ...ays with a satisfied smile, "this is the ultimate sport." ...eams, each man fanned out from fifty to two ...to twelve miles a day through terrain ...They cross fields of wicked *'a'a* ...s of American-made, ...e. They run ...a low-

...cer's, back at the ...y afternoon, Felipé's ...o large, horned skulls ...," he says, glancing up at ...es—from Pinta."

...killed on that island in the ...work that makes Felipé smile. ...es is his specialty. It's what he ...States, in Hawaii, and in Colorado, ...t Scholarship to learn, as he puts it, ...ints."

...his education pursuing an undergraduate ...e early 1980s from the University of Con- ...e loved watching the dark-rumped petrels ...t washed up on the beaches of his home island, ...ung man, he saw those same birds nearly wiped ...s, pigs, dogs, and donkeys that had infested that ...ners. Midway through his college career, he had an ...which led to the Fulbright.

...ded that, shit, as just a scientist studying this stuff, I wasn't ...o get anything actually done. I realized, hey, in order to save ...rds, I'm going to have to learn to destroy these animals."

Felipé is the seventh of his parents' twelve children, eight years ...lder than his brother Eliecer. "Lucky seven," he says with a grin, flicking an ash and taking a seat on a bare picnic table. The landscape

Still ahead (once Sáles and his team have completed their job) are the 80,000 or so goats that now roam Santiago. At the moment, however, the focus of the Park Service's goat-hunting efforts is the island of Isabela, where an assault on the scale of the invasion of Normandy is soon to be launched. Eliecer Cruz, like his counterparts at the S[...] tion, is careful about talking too much about this one. It's politi[...] touchy, the image of helicopter gunships carrying crews of [...] shooters with automatic weapons spraying death on herd[...] goats. Cruz would prefer that his brother, Felipé, talk[...] which Felipé is more than happy to do.

Felipé Cruz's office is in a building beyond Elie[...] rear of the Park Service compound. On this earl[...] outside having a smoke. Behind him are tw[...] mounted to the bars of a window. "Ah, yes[...] the trophies, "the last two goats—big on[...]

These were the last two of 38,000[...] mid-1970s. That's the kind of clean[...] Dealing with nonindigenous spe[...] studied in college in the United[...] where he went on a Fulbright[...] "how to efficiently kill varm[...]

Felipé actually began [...] ornithology degree in t[...] necticut. As a boy, [...] *skim the waves tha*[...] *Floreana.* As a yo[...] out *by rats,* ca[...] island *and o*[...] epiphany, [...] "I dec[...] going t[...] my b[...]

hundre[...]
number. Last y[...]
have found only one or[...]
finished, Sáles emphasizes, un[...] "an[...]
left pregnant with babies," he says, [...]

around him is overgrown desert, thick brush and cactus stretching off toward the north where the highlands are framed against a bright, turquoise sky. He wears a Park Service ball cap, a white T-shirt and shorts, and thick, hand-sewn sandals on his tough, calloused feet. He's lean, sinewy, perpetually restless. He hates meetings, of which he's attended two already today. He'd much rather be here, with his men and their weapons, or out in the field.

He stubs out his cigarette and moves into his office, where a wall-sized relief map of Isla Isabela looms over his desk. The map is a prism of colors: forest-green volcanic craters and cones ringed by orange and yellow mountainside slopes, edged by coastlines of pink, and, surrounding it all, a deep-cobalt-blue sea. Beyond the map stands a bookcase of binders with handwritten titles: *"Chivos Santiago"*; *"Chanchos Santiago"*; and, most conspicuously, *"Isabela Sur: Animales Introducidos."*

The sanitary term for Felipé's specialty is "eradication." His title at the moment is Technical Director of the Isabela Project, whose goal, he explains, again using sanitized biospeak, is the "ecological restoration" of the northern half of that island. Boil it down, his job is to kill all the goats.

If there is one place in the Galápagos that illustrates the nightmare of introduced species, it is Isabela. By far the largest of the archipelago's thirteen main islands—eighty miles long from north to south, fifty miles wide at its thickest—Isabela is home to the Galápagos' largest population of giant tortoises. The animals feed and nest on the slopes of the island's spectacular volcanoes—Wolf, Darwin, Alcedo. Eighteen years ago, in the summer of 1982, when the first comprehensive study was made of the wild goats on Isabela, only ten of the animals, apparently left by fishermen, could be found on the island. Today there are more than 100,000.

"Goats are born for one thing," Felipé says flatly. "To reproduce." That reproduction, he explains, is explosively exponential. A wild female goat reaches sexual maturity when she's seven months old. The typical nanny gives birth to two kids at a time. She does this, on average, three or four times a year for the length of her life. "Do the numbers yourself," says Felipé. "They multiply fast."

The havoc these animals wreak as they devour the landscape is difficult to describe with mere words, says Felipé. This is why he carries a set of slides when he speaks to visiting tour groups or scientists. The photographs, taken by Tui de Roy, show specific locations on the rim and slopes of Volcán Alcedo, the island's largest volcano and a prime tortoise feeding ground. The first set of photos, taken in the mid-1980s, shows lush verdant foliage, Amazonian in its richness. The second, taken just ten years later in the same locations, shows a landscape of death, utter defoliation, barren, eroded dirt slopes with hardly a bush or a tree to be seen. "Like in Vietnam," says Cruz, "after they used Agent Orange."

It was the shock of such devastation that prompted the Darwin Foundation, through both the Station and the National Park, to launch an unprecedented counterattack on these animals. With funding from a group called the Global Environmental Facilities—a branch of the World Bank—funneled through an arm of the United Nations called the U.N. Development Project, the pieces are now almost in place for the most expansive and expensive governmental assault on wild animals in the history of man.

It will last for two years, with another year of follow-up study. It will use two helicopters brought in from either New Zealand or Australia—the bid is still out—with flight crews and sharpshooters supported by ground teams of Galápagos Park Rangers. It will cost $6 million. And in charge of it all is Felipé, who now steps outside into the midafternoon heat, lights another cigarette, and crosses a small dirt courtyard that leads to a bunkerlike building and a locked metal door. He pulls out a key with the pride of a parent showing off a new baby.

Inside is an arsenal worthy of Patton.

Eight AR-15 .223-caliber semiautomatic rifles, each in its own cushioned carrying case—"a military-caliber, assault-type weapon," says Felipé, lifting one of the gleaming, unfired long-guns from its container. "Very efficient."

Eight Benelli twelve-gauge shotguns with "box-shot" ammunition—"just one big piece of lead," he says, pulling one of the shells from its carton and flipping it into the air, "rather than many small pellets."

Four dozen Ruger .223-caliber, bolt-action rifles—"for the ground crews," he says.

He opens a closet containing hundreds of boxes of bullets. He pulls down from a shelf one of twelve velvet-soft sacks, each containing a sleek rifle scope. On wooden, warehouselike shelving that runs from one end of the room to the other are arranged dozens of pairs of gleaming black combat boots, radio chargers, portable generators, solar panels, sleeping bags, cases of insect spray, GPS monitors—all that his rangers could possibly need as they work their way over those hills and ravines, shooting every goat they see.

"This is the largest area in the world where an eradication program has ever been attempted," says Felipé. "And I know we are going to get hell for it. That is what happened in Hawaii, where they had a tremendous problem with feral pigs. They used snare traps there, and the animal rights people were very upset."

He steps back outside, locks the door, and lights another cigarette. "I know these animal rights people are going to try to do some hassle with us," he says. "They want more humane ways of killing these animals? Come on! I mean, pigs are not human. Goats are not human. And the point is, they don't belong here. Look at the damage they're doing."

He shakes his head. "Let's be real, man."

He takes a seat back on the table behind his office, gazing up at the hills, where a bank of cottony cumulus clouds have now gathered. It's funny, he says, that someone like himself should become a target of animal lovers. No one has lived with and loves wild animals more than he.

"Being a naturalist," he says, waving an arm at the landscape before him, "it's in my blood."

And in his brother's. And in the blood of the other ten children raised by Emma and Eliecer Cruz Sr. on the island of Floreana.

Floreana. To Galápagos tour groups with nothing to go on but their guidebooks, this southern island with the lyrical name is known for two things: the beach-mounted mailbox used by David Porter's warship, the *Essex,* during the War of 1812 (a replica of that box still stands on the same spot today, offering visitors a novel way to mail a postcard home), and the scandalous multiple murders that transpired there in the mid-1930s. The tale of those murders—of nude farming, sex slaves, and poisoned meat—is told eagerly to enraptured tourists by guides who embellish its edges with their own imaginations. As with many such stories massaged over time by both memory and myth, it's hard to tell where fact blurs into fiction.

This much is known: A Berlin doctor named Friedrich Ritter, along with his lover, a woman named Dore Koerwin Strauch, left Germany in 1929, bound for the Galápagos, about which Ritter had read in a best-selling book of the time called *Galápagos: World's End*. Published in 1923 by a writer named William Beebe, that book brought more attention to these islands than anything that had come before it, including Darwin's writings. Beebe painted a portrait of a tropical paradise, albeit with a few unpleasant realities; still, more than a few readers envisioned a heaven on earth. It was Beebe's book that lured the first Norwegians to the Galápagos in the 1920s, and it had the same effect on Dr. Ritter.

A vegetarian, nudist, disciple of Nietzsche, student of Lao Tzu, and an avid astrologer, Friedrich Ritter had decided by the late 1920s that Berlin was not for him. Nor was Germany or Europe or any place on the planet where people were living. He was sick of society and envisioned life as an Adam in his own self-made Eden. So he sought out an Eve, whom he found in a former patient, Dore Koerwin Strauch.

Strauch happened to be married at the time, as was Ritter. But their utopian vision overwhelmed such a minor inconvenience. They informed their respective mates that they were leaving for the Galápagos Islands and offered the somewhat stunned spouses an invitation to come along if they'd like. Ritter's wife and Strauch's husband, not surprisingly, refused, and so the doctor and his lover turned to their preparations, which, according to some accounts, included the forty-eight-year-old Ritter pulling out all his teeth and forging himself a set of stainless steel dentures. He intended this to be a permanent stay.

It turned out to be, at least for the doctor. It wasn't easy carving

a farm and a home on the slopes of a dorment volcanano in Floreana's tangled highlands. When the couple arrived, they soon
learned why this island, which had once housed a penal colony,
was now uninhabited. Wild cows, bulls, and pigs—the progeny of
the animals once raised by the prisoners—feasted on whatever Ritter and Strauch tried to grow. When the couple built fences, the
animals tore them apart. True to his vegetarian beliefs, Ritter had
brought no weapons. But he had brought cases of dynamite to blast
the volcanic rocks from the fields he was planning to farm. He soon
found that the explosives were handy for blasting wild animals, too.

But nothing could hold off the mosquitoes, cockroaches, and ants
that infested the couple's home. The house itself, a geodesic dome of
sorts built of logs cut from the surrounding forest, looked fine, solid,
positively Germanic—until the first rainy season arrived. The logs
warped, green shoots began to sprout from the walls, and tree
branches grew up from the floors.

Still, with time the couple settled into their Eden and began to
enjoy the fruits of success: bananas, papayas, oranges, coconuts,
guavas, lemons, pineapples, and plums, all of which grew abundantly
in the soil Ritter was able to clear. Vegetables were plentiful, too, as
was fresh water from a trickling spring. They called their rustic estate
Friedo—a combination of the couple's first names. Flush with pros-
perity, they began writing letters back home, which were delivered by
sailors and yachtsmen who passed through the islands.

The Berlin press, which was well aware of the doctor's scandalous departure, eagerly published the accounts, which soon drew
curious visitors to the island to see the place for themselves.
Among the first was an Englishman named J. F. Schimpff, who for a
time lived in a cave not far from Ritter and Strauch. Schimpff wrote
of his experience in a 1932 article published in a magazine called
American Weekly:

*Naturally I felt somewhat embarrassed at intruding on these
people, and thought it best to announce myself. I did this by
singing the German national anthem, in honor of the fact that
Dr. Ritter is from Berlin, and his Eve, Dora Koerwin, I had
heard, was the wife of a Dresden school teacher. Before I had*

finished the second line, two absolutely naked figures, beauti-
fully tanned, ran out of the roundhouse, stared at me a moment
with open mouths, and then darted back again.

. . . The doctor soon reappeared, dressed in canvas pants and
a white shirt. Eve soon followed in a light blue cotton dress,
under which there was nothing but Eve.

. . . Afterward I learned that this Adam had also paused to
insert his false teeth. . . . I have read of savages losing their wits
at the sight of a white man taking out his glass eye—well, these
teeth had almost that effect on me. They were not made of
porcelain, to resemble human teeth, but of glittering stainless
steel.

Visitors were the last thing Ritter wanted. He treated guests
rudely, but they continued to come to check out what a *Time* magazine reporter at the time described as "a free-love, back-to-nature
colony." Most of the visitors quickly left, turned away by the
island's brutal realities or by the brutal temper of the good doctor
himself.

In the late summer of 1932, a German named Heinz Wittmer
and his young wife, Margaret, arrived on the island and stayed.
They built a home far enough from the Ritter estate that the doctor
was not too disturbed. Less than three months later, however, in
the autumn of that same year, a newcomer arrived who would turn
out to be more than merely disturbing to both the doctor and
Strauch, as well as the Wittmers.

She called herself a baroness, though her credentials were suspect and never confirmed. A *Newsweek* magazine account of this
woman's arrival on Floreana—culled from reports relayed by
passers-through to the islands, as most Galápagos news was at this
time—reads like pulp fiction, with the hint of a titter on the part of
the writer:

The most recent newcomer is not even mildly annoyed by Rit-
ter snubbings. She is Baroness Bousequet de Wagner of Vienna.
With her she brought three men known only as Philipson,
Alonzo, and Arends.

As she stepped ashore, the Baroness removed all her cloth-

ing except a pair of pink silk panties, flourished a .22 caliber revolver, and proclaimed herself Empress of Floreana. Since she had the revolver and no one else wanted to be Empress, her reign is undisputed.

Ecuadorian officials, sent to investigate strange goings-on, were shocked when they first saw the Empress. They caught their breath a second time when they found the Ritters wearing nothing but hip boots to keep thorn bushes from scratching their legs. When the investigators submitted their report, Ecuadorian Government officials sadly shook their heads, carefully put the report away, and forgot about the whole matter.

The matter, however, was far from concluded. Over the course of the next year and a half, the friction among the neighbors increased. The baroness built her own highland dwelling, not far from Friedo, and gave her place a much more dramatic—and, she hoped, commercial—name: Hacienda Paraiso. Never mind that the hacienda was in fact hardly more than a hut. The baroness had plans to build a resort hotel here, to turn Floreana into "a sort of Miami," as she put it in a quote published in *Newsweek*.

She never got quite that far. In November of 1934, two years after the baroness' arrival, a news report burst from the Galápagos Islands that both shocked and captivated the world's reading public. The remains of two bodies had been discovered on a beach of an island called Marchena, 120 miles north of Floreana. Photographs of the small, shriveled corpses, cooked by the sun and curled up like mummies on the black lava sand, were dispatched to newspapers and magazines throughout Europe and the United States. A flurry of news stories soon followed in publications ranging from the *Los Angeles Times* to the *Times* of London to the great, gray *New York Times*, each rife with speculations about the identities of the bodies and whispers of murders of passion on this tropical island.

Over the ensuing weeks, a string of facts began to emerge from the fog of innuendo and rumor. A long-running feud had indeed developed among the baroness and her neighbors. The woman had clashed with both Ritter and Strauch, and with the Wittmers as well. To make matters worse, the doctor and his mate were not the best of friends with their neighbors, the Wittmers.

Events had begun escalating when one of the baroness' housemates, the man they had called Arends, was wounded in late 1933 in an unexplained shooting accident and was evacuated from the island. The following spring, in late March or April, the baroness vanished along with her housemate Philippson (whose name now had three *p*s in updated news reports). That July, the baroness' third housemate, the aforementioned Alonzo—now identified as Rudolf Lorenz— turned up missing as well. Finally, that December, not long after the discovery of the bodies on the Marchena beach, Dr. Ritter fell dead from a sudden case of botulism after eating, of all things, a pot of bad chicken.

The string of strange deaths prompted wild speculations and questions that remain unanswered to this day—questions not only encouraged by guides and debated by tour groups, but also explored over the years by a slew of would-be detectives and novelists.

Among the most obvious puzzles: What happened to the baroness and Philippson? Were they lost? (This is quite possible in a place such as this.) Or were they killed in an accident? (This is just as conceivable.) Did they commit suicide? The baroness, according to both Dore Strauch and Margaret Wittmer, who were questioned by government investigators in the wake of the deaths, had grown increasingly distraught as her vision of a booming resort on this island faded with each passing month. Suicide was not out of the question.

Or were the pair murdered? If so, by whom? Lorenz emerged as the prime suspect here. He and the baroness' other two housemates had, in Strauch's words, been "slaves to the woman, even to the extent of sleeping together with her in one bed when commanded to do so." After the exit of Arends, Lorenz had apparently been rejected in favor of Philippson, and in a fit of jealous rage might have murdered them both.

This would explain Lorenz's hasty departure that July. In an agitated state, he managed to hail a passing Galápagan fisherman and persuaded the sailor to give him a lift. No one will ever know Lorenz's ultimate destination. A heavy sea blew the small boat off course, its motor failed, and then the wind stopped, leaving Lorenz and the unfortunate fisherman at the mercy of the tides and sun. These were the two bodies found that November on the sand of Marchena.

As for the death of Dr. Ritter, the first question everyone asks is, How in the world did this avowed vegetarian wind up eating a plate of cooked chicken? It turned out, according to Strauch, that the doctor was a closet meat eater and had been for years. He had potted that fatal chicken himself and ate it with relish the day before he died.

Strauch herself was a suspect in this one. Margaret Wittmer, who had seen Strauch and the doctor squabbling many times over the years, arrived at Ritter's bedside during the man's final hours and witnessed, at least according to her account, Ritter cursing Strauch with his last dying breath.

Strauch's account differs. It throws the light of suspicion on Frau Wittmer, who had had her own run-ins with the doctor several times, at least according to Strauch.

Dore Strauch left Floreana that December of 1934 and sailed home to Germany, where she wrote a book on the affair, titled *Satan Comes to Eden*. Margaret Wittmer wrote a book of her own, *Floreana*, which is still sold today in the souvenir shops in Puerto Ayora. Frau Wittmer will sign a copy for the occasional tourist lucky enough to catch the old woman at the small seaside hotel that her family still runs on the same Floreana beach that Margaret and Heinz first arrived at in 1932.

The hotel was built in the late 1940s with the best of the pine from the air base at Baltra. Some tourists today mistake the elderly woman who serves meals on the hotel's screened-in patio for Margaret, but that's actually her daughter, Floreanita, born here in 1937. Margaret's upstairs in bed most of the time. She's in her nineties and not doing well.

Floreana remains to this day little more than a remote outpost, the smallest by far of the four Galápagos Islands where people are permitted to live. Fewer than eighty souls make their home in the island's seaside village of Puerto Velasco Ibarra. Most of them are

Ecuadorians who have drifted here over the past several decades, settling into a cluster of small houses arrayed near the shore, around the Wittmers' hotel, by the village's simple cement wharf. Some of them fish. Some of them farm. And one of them emerges from a house near the wharf when the whine of a boat engine tells him visitors are arriving.

His name's Walter, he'll tell you, extending his hand as he helps tie up your boat. Walter Cruz. He looks like a native, an old-time islander with a thatch of white hair on his darkly tanned chest and a salt-and-pepper beard and wild random curls framing his round, ruddy face. But he sounds like an American, which he might as well be, after spending the past two dozen years in Miami. He just returned to Floreana last month, two days after Christmas, to resettle this house by the beach and a farm in the highlands, the place where he and his siblings grew up.

Walter knows they think he's gone nuts, his younger brothers Felipé and Eliecer and the others. They can't understand why Walter's come back to this island at this stage in his life. He's fifty-four, with a wife and two kids and a professional career in America. What in the world, they all want to know, is he doing back here?

"I know, it seems crazy," he says, leading the way up to his house. But his children are grown, he explains. And his wife, a schoolteacher, will soon join him when she wraps up her obligations back in Miami. As for that professional career of his, well, fixing boat engines for wealthy yacht owners around Biscayne Bay might have fattened his wallet, but it did not feed his soul.

"I just couldn't take it anymore," he says, walking barefoot and shirtless across the dirt of his yard. "The city life, driving a car every day, running the rat race. I'm not made for that. Now this," he says, lifting a coconut from a pile drying out at the end of his porch. "I am made for this," he says, hacking the fruit open with a heavy machete.

A vehicle appears off in the distance, churning up dust as it descends from the highlands. It's a four-wheel-drive Jeep with a man at the wheel: Walter's younger brother Claudio. The three little boys chasing each other around the back of the house are Claudio's kids. Walter has to explain this because, unlike himself, Claudio—

the eighth of the Cruz children, born just after Felipé—has never moved off this island and speaks only Spanish.

The Jeep pulls up to the house, the engine shuts off, and the boys rush out to leap into the arms of their father. Whereas Walter is short, Claudio stands tall. Whereas Walter is thick, his brother is thin. Whereas Walter's beard is speckled with gray, Claudio's is black through and through. But they share the same wide, easy smile.

"Twice a day he goes up to the farm," explains Walter, as Claudio and the boys head into the house. "The rest of the time he's down here," meaning the village with its seventy-five residents.

"Seventy-six," Walter says, "counting me."

There's not much to this community, just three dirt lanes, a single small schoolhouse, the Wittmers' hotel, and the homes, which are laid out along a mile of waterfront. There are a couple of power lines, fed by a generator in a small building down by the beach, that Claudio tends when he's not up at the farm. "He's the technician," says Walter, not just for the village's electrical system but for Floreana's telephone system as well, which last month expanded from one phone line to eight. "Hey," Walter laughs, "we don't have to line up to make outgoing calls anymore. Now we can even call each *other*."

Walter's laughter is brief. Those new telephone lines are a harbinger of more changes to come. There is talk that an airstrip might soon be put in for Park Service use, which has most Floreanans quite excited. "They think it's fantastic," Walter says. "But I don't like it. I'm probably the only one opposed to it." He draws a deep breath and smiles.

"But then," he says, "I was one of the few idiots against putting that road across Santa Cruz." Another deep breath.

"But *then*," he says, "look what has happened to the Galápagos after they built that."

Walter and Claudio are all that's left here of the clan that some argue is truly the first family of Floreana, perhaps even the first family of the entire Galápagos. Enough of the Wittmers, they say. They're history. And the Angermeyers as well. Now the Cruzes, they say, there's a family that has really made something of themselves. Look at Eliecer and Felipé and their Park Service success. And their brother

Augusto—Georgina Cruz's husband, the father of Sebas—look at that cattle farm Augusto and Georgina have got over on Santa Cruz, and their own tour boat business and the beautiful house they live in above the *barranco*, perched right there on the harbor, looking down at the town.

Even Walter's is a success story of sorts, how he was one of the island's first tour guides, helping lay out and mark the first landing sites and Park Service trails back in the '60s and '70s. And how he worked with the scientists up at the Station and how he finally met his wife and moved with her to Miami.

So maybe Walter knows what he's doing, coming back here to the island this way. He certainly seems to be happy, hiking down to the water at lunchtime and grabbing a couple of lobsters with his bare hands, bringing them back to the house and sautéing the buttery meat on his small kitchen stove. It doesn't take much to get him to drive you up to the *chacra*—the farm, which happens to be the old Ritter estate. The drive is a rough one, on a gravel and dirt road rutted by rain. It takes a while to get up there, which gives Walter time to tell his family's story—or at least a small part of it.

It begins, naturally, with the patriarch, Eliecer Cruz Sr. He was born, says Walter, in the Ecuadorian province of Ibarra in 1916. After finishing school, he went to work as a typographer in Quito. "But he didn't like sitting in an office," says Walter, "so he went looking for adventure."

He found it for a while in the early 1930s working a farm in the northernmost coastal province of Esmeraldas. One day, however, a wealthy landowner showed up and told Eliecer, as wealthy men often did at that time, that this land was rightfully his, not Eliecer's.

"What could he do?" Walter asks. "There was nothing he could do. But my father had heard of the Galápagos, and so he came here."

That was in 1935. Eliecer spent two years fishing on San Cristobal, then sailed over to Floreana to try his hand once again at working the land. It was now 1937, three years after the baroness mess had blown over. There were only three families on the island at that time: an

American couple named Conway, the Wittmers, of course, and an Ecuadorian named Zavala with his wife and children. "Them," Walter says, "and from time to time a few soldiers."

He downshifts and slows and turns off the road onto a rugged dirt drive sprinkled with fresh horse droppings. The surrounding gullies and brush resemble Texas hill country. Ahead is a makeshift barbed wire fence, a thick stand of trees, and a small wooden gate. Walter parks the truck, climbs out, opens the gate, and steps into . . . paradise.

High-arching *scalesia* and *acacia* branches drape cool shadows over a well-tended path rimmed by pink and white pansies. A freshwater rill trickles through a carpet of emerald ferns and moist, spongy mosses. Splashing the greenness are bursts of roses, dahlias, and lilies. Blood-red hibiscus, pink bougainvillea, and broad, green banana leaves point the way up the slope to a small, one-story house ringed by fruit trees—papayas, mangoes, guavas, and plums. The house was built by Walter's uncle, Eduardo, in the late 1950s, on the same soil Ritter and Strauch had cleared decades before. These flowers were theirs. They planted the fruit trees. But the only trace left of their actual hands is a small mound of vine-covered stones and a rough wooden cross up past the plum orchard, in the dark of the forest beyond the barbed-wire fence. A barely legible number is etched into one of the stones: 1934.

"Dr. Ritter," says Walter. "That's where he's buried."

By the time Eliecer Cruz Sr. fetched his wife, Emma, and brought her to this farm in the late 1930s and they had their first baby, Walter, in 1945, Ritter and Strauch and all the others were ghosts. That's how Walter remembers the stories of these strange German people who once lived here. To him they were ghost stories.

But Frau Wittmer was no ghost. The photo of Hitler that hung in her living room in the late 1930s was taken down by the time Walter was born. But Mrs. Wittmer was just moving into the prime of her life, and she became Walter's flesh-and-blood godmother. "She convinced my mother to call me Valter," he says, grabbing a ripe plum from a low-hanging branch. "Valter, Valter, Valter. I finally said 'I don't like Valter. My name's Walter.'"

Once he was born, he says, it was if the floodgates were opened for Eliecer and Emma. The babies kept coming. And coming. And coming. "It got to a point where I said, when is this going to end?"

It ended with twelve, enough little Cruzes to keep the place going. The family raised livestock. They grew corn and cabbage and carrots and coffee. After a while they became fishermen, too, trading some cows for a boat and an engine. "A Briggs and Stratton," says Walter. "Three-horsepower, bronze shaft, homemade prop, direct-forward drive, no neutral, no reverse. Just crank up the engine and go."

There was no formal tourism yet, but the occasional yacht would pass through, and little Walter would run down with a sack of fresh oranges and trade them for bullets for his .22 rifle. He could speak English, which stunned more than a few of the yachtsmen, this barefooted Ecuadorian island boy chatting them up.

"My Uncle Eduardo taught me," he says. "He learned by reading books. He had cases of books, a very literate man. I said if my uncle can learn English like this, from just reading a dictionary, so can I."

Until he was ten Walter was homeschooled by his uncle, his mother, and sometimes Margaret Wittmer. Then he began taking classes in the small port-captain's building down by the beach. The port captain was the only government official at the time on the island, the only one other than Eliecer Sr., who, because of his reputation throughout the Galápagos and because of the respect of his neighbors, had early on been named Floreana's *intendente*—a loose blend of mayor and judge. One of his first official acts was to throw the police off the island.

"They were more trouble than anything else," Walter says. "All they did was grow grapes and get drunk and fight. My father finally kicked them out. He said we don't need any police here. And the government agreed."

There are photos of Walter's father all over this house, old, faded snapshots of a bony, barefoot, shaggy-haired man with a beard just like Robinson Crusoe's, eyes as warm as the sun and a smile even warmer. In most of the photos he stands beside a short, portly woman, caressing her as if they are teenage lovers. Eliecer never left Emma, not even for a quick chore, says Walter, without kissing her full on the mouth. "You've never seen two people who loved each other so much."

In the spring of 1956, near the end of Walter's first year in the port captain's "classroom," two Ecuadorian Navy warships showed up off the island's shoreline. The massive vessels dropped anchor, and one sent a motor launch into the village. Aboard the launch was the nation's president, His Excellency Dr. Valasco Ibarra, whose name would soon be given to this village.

"They had us line up to greet him," Walter recalls. "Eight kids. We sang the national anthem to him. Then he took my sister Rita out of the line and said, 'I promise you a schoolhouse.'"

They eventually got it, though it took several years. "The materials were first shipped to San Cristobal," says Walter. "And they stayed there for quite a long time, until my father finally traded some of our cattle to get the stuff here."

There were other Ecuadorian presidents after Ibarra who dropped in at Floreana over the years. Celebrities stopped in as well—movie stars, sports heroes, all eager to meet these islanders, Emma and Eliecer Cruz, who became celebrities of sorts themselves. They were fun to sit with and laugh and drink a glass of Emma's famous *vino de naranja*—orange wine. In 1970, she carried a jug of the wine with her, along with some jars of plum marmalade, when she went to the mainland to visit the leader of the nation's new ruling military junta at the time, a general named Rodriguez Lara. "Everyone," says Walter, "loved my mother's wine."

The year he turned nineteen, Walter's life was changed by a visit to Floreana from some scientists from the Research Station on Santa Cruz. Among them was Dr. Robert Bowman, the American who had been one of the Station's earliest trailblazers. Beside Bowman was a geologist from Berkeley named Alan Cox. Cox asked Walter if he'd like to work with him as a field assistant. "The next thing you know," Walter says, "I was out on the islands drilling holes in solid lava sites for core samples. You can still see my little holes here and there."

Walter moved to Santa Cruz later that year, 1965, and lived in the highlands with old Mrs. Hornemann on her family farm. "*Mutti*," he says. "She was my second mother." When he wasn't out drilling with

Cox, Walter earned extra cash guiding small groups up to the tortoise reserve in the Santa Cruz highlands, an all-day trip by horseback from Academy Bay.

By the late 1960s Walter had hooked up with Karl Angermeyer and began taking some of the first tour groups out onto the islands. "We decided where were the best places to take the people, then we went there," Walter says. "A lot of the trails the tour groups use today, we made them back then."

He worked on tour boats—the *Lina*, the *Iguana*, the *Encantada*— into the mid-1970s, which is when he ran into a particularly difficult pair of clients, a couple from France. "They were the first vegetarian passengers we had ever had. I can tell you, they were a pain in the ass." The husband spent each day off taking photographs while the wife wound up hanging around Walter. "They left, and the next thing I knew, I received a letter from her, from New York. I almost didn't answer it. This crazy passenger. And she was married."

He answered the letter. One thing led to another. And by the following summer, the woman was back in the Galápagos, this time as a crew member aboard Walter's boat. A year after that the two were married and she became pregnant. A year after that, in November of 1976, they moved to Miami.

"Which pretty much brings us to where we are now," Walter says, taking a bite of the plum. He's done with the tour. It's starting to cloud up. By the time he's back down by the beach, the rain's falling in sheets.

He hustles inside the house, where Claudio's boys are watching TV. There's lobster left in the fridge, which Walter pulls out and broils. The boys have no interest. "They don't like lobster, they're sick of it," says Walter. "They'd rather have eggs."

Which Claudio is frying right now.

Then everyone sits. The men eat their lobster, and the boys eat their eggs.

The afternoon rain that's moved down from the mountains sets the village palms swaying. It wets down the dust and sweeps over the rooftops of this house, of the others, and of the hotel down by the beach, where Margaret Wittmer lies sleeping.

ELEVEN

The Other Side

Isla
Genovesa

JANUARY 22, 2000

Gus Angermeyer

ye-bye, Jamal. Bye bye!"

Albertina is beaming, glowing like a diva as she dances among the Hotel Galápagos' dining room tables, setting the places for breakfast. Outside the sky is gray, overcast. The hotel's four guests this morning are still sleeping. In the kitchen, Betty, the cook, slices a bowl of papayas while a transistor radio perched in a window delivers the news.

"*Hasta la vista*, baby," chirps Albertina, ducking in for a handful of silverware. "*Adios!*"

Mahuad has been ousted. It happened late yesterday, and it is still playing itself out at this moment—Ecuador's first coup in twenty-one years. More than fifteen hundred protesters armed with pickaxes and shovels broke through the barbed-wire barrier surrounding the National Congress in Quito yesterday afternoon. They stormed into the building, leaned out windows, and pushed onto balconies to the roaring cheers of ten thousand people below, all calling for Mahuad to resign.

He resisted at first. Barricaded in the presidential palace just twenty blocks down the street, he appeared live on nationwide television, pointing at the camera and shouting, "I am *not* going to abandon you."

But by nightfall he was in hiding, whisked away in an ambulance while thousands of *Indios* joined by Ecuadorian soldiers outside the palace danced and sang and shot bullets into the air.

Once the smoke cleared—what little smoke there had been—a mere eight protesters had been wounded in both Quito and Guayaquil. Two more lay dead, but they were not shot by soldiers or police: They had tried looting in the midst of the chaos and were each killed by the owner of the store they had raided.

That was early last evening. By midnight, a three-person junta—a military colonel named Gutierrez, a former Ecuadorian Supreme

Court justice named Solorzano (who tried to proclaim himself president during a similar upheaval three years ago), and an *Indio* leader named Antonio Vargas—had declared themselves in command of the country. One Ecuadorian congressman dismissed the triumvirate as "the Three Stooges." U.S. State Department officials promptly decried the takeover, calling it a "proto-coup" and warning of "disastrous consequences for all Ecuadorians."

The junta apparently listened. General Carlos Mendoza, the same man who had warned of just such a coup not two weeks ago but who had also vowed his allegiance to Mahuad both in person and in a full-page newspaper ad, ordered Gutierrez to get lost and then took his place in the ruling triumvirate. Mendoza then promptly dissolved the junta. At three A.M. the threesome stepped aside, and by sunrise Mahuad's vice president, Gustavo Noboa, had emerged as Ecuador's sixth head of state in the past four years.

At this moment, this morning, according to radio reports, Noboa is in Guayaquil, meeting behind closed doors with the president of Congress, deciding what to do next.

"*Ese hijo de puta!*" spits Albertina. "That son of a whore." She does not like Noboa.

"Okay," answers a voice at the door, speaking, like Albertina, in Spanish. "Who do *you* want?"

It's José-Luis, with Christy, come for a quick cup of coffee before starting their day.

"I want the generals," says Albertina as José follows her into the kitchen. "I know we're going to suffer, but I'd rather see the military in there than all these 'politicians.'"

José comes out with a roll in his hand. "She is absolutely right," he says, shrugging his shoulders and taking a seat. "This is bad, and it's going to get deeper."

Christy sits down beside him. She takes off her hat, leans back, and crosses her legs. "Bad, bad, *bad*," she says, taking a sip of her coffee. "This is the worst I've ever seen."

"Well," says José, gazing out at the gray clouds hanging over the harbor, "we do have a lot of presidential material here in Ecuador."

The door opens again. In comes Jack, a knapsack slung over his shoulder. "Good morning," he says to Christy and José-Luis. He sticks his head in the kitchen then moves down to his office. "The shit is now hitting the fan." He speaks with no trace of emotion, as if he's describing the weather outside.

He flips on his own radio and drops his sack on the desk beside a small sheaf of papers, including the receipts for the surf group—Nuñez and the others—who checked through yesterday on their way back to the mainland after their week of wave-riding. None of them seemed too upset about events in the capital. And they left with their hotel bill still unpaid.

Jack, however, has larger concerns at the moment. Romy recently found out her visa's expired, and the government official she's been dealing with in Quito for the past several weeks to renew it is now pushing for a bribe—he calls it a "fee"—of $5,000. So Jack needs to put in a few calls to some friends on the mainland who can go talk to this asshole and straighten things out. No way is Jack going to pay that kind of money for a matter as simple as this.

But it's the trip to Thailand that's got Jack worried most. He'll be leaving soon, and with the government now in a shambles, all bets are off in terms of such things as international flights through Quito or Guayaquil. To make matters worse, outbreaks of dengue fever and leptospirosis have been reported in Guayaquil. Dengue—also known as "breakbone fever" and "dandy fever"—affects tens of millions of people each year, mostly in tropical countries. Carried by mosquitoes, the virus causes fever, nausea, vomiting, shock, and, in one out of twenty cases, death from internal bleeding. Leptospirosis is no more inviting. Caused by drinking or even just swimming in water contaminated by the urine of infected animals, this bacterium causes severe headaches, chills, vomiting, jaundice, diarrhea, kidney damage, meningitis, and, in some cases, death. It looks like Jack will be spending quite a few hours on the telephone this morning.

The day's guests have now arrived in the dining room and are having their breakfast: a Spanish couple with their young daughter, and an American from North Carolina, a computer programmer named George. Christy and José-Luis have moved on, but another visitor has arrived. He's a large man, a *gringo*, wearing white trousers, cowboy boots, and a white, long-sleeved shirt. A pair of aviator sunglasses covers his eyes, and a thick, walrus moustache droops down both sides of his mouth.

"Steve Divine," he says, extending a hand. He's here for a cup of coffee before fetching his little boy, Stevie, and driving up to his farm in the highlands. The mud-splattered maroon Diahatsu pickup parked outside belongs to him, and within minutes he's behind the wheel, whipping it down Darwin Avenue toward the harborfront home he shares with his wife, three kids, and his mother, Doris. Until a couple of years ago, Doris Divine could still get around, but she's gone down-hill lately. Now, much like Margaret Wittmer over on Floreana, Doris spends most of her days upstairs in bed.

"Mentally, she's lost it," says Steve, waiting for a group of straw-hatted tourists to stroll past before pulling into his driveway. "At eighty-four, though, that's not surprising."

Steve's wife, Jenny, is at work at the travel agency she operates just up the street. Their daughter, Janine, the thirteen-year-old, is in bed sleeping late this Saturday morning. Fifteen-year-old Jennifer is up, parked in front of the television, watching an MTV video dubbed in Spanish. She has no interest whatsoever in joining her dad and her brother for a day on the farm. Neither does her sister.

"Getting either of them to go up there is like pulling teeth," Steve says. "But Stevie likes it. The horses, tortoises, wasps, ants—he really gets into it."

As if on cue, nine-year-old Stevie bounds out of his bedroom, barefoot, blond, deeply tanned, and very, very excited. "One time I take a ant," he says, speaking in clipped, broken English, his eyes wide with amazement. "This big!" he says, holding his finger and thumb a half-inch apart. "And you know what? I throw him in a—what—a spider web. And the spider, he suck the ant's blood. And I watch it. It was fun."

Steve grabs a laptop computer on the way out the door. "For Stevie," he says. "So he can play that video game Quake."

"Oh, yes," says Stevie, following his father out the front door, "I love those monsters."

Stevie climbs in the truck's backseat and urges his dad to stop at the grocery on the way out of town. This is the best part, says Stevie, of living down here instead of up at the farm. "Is many places," he says, "to buy things for eat!"

Steve relents, and they make a quick stop at a tiny *bodega*, where Stevie picks out a container of yogurt with graham-cracker crumbs.

"Junk food," snorts Steve.

"It's delicious," says Stevie with a grin.

Before climbing back behind the wheel of his truck, Steve suits up, slipping a cloth ball cap onto his head, draping a wraparound scarf down over his neck, and pulling on a pair of long, white gloves. In the hat and the hood and the gloves, along with the shades and the trousers and the white, long-sleeved shirt, he looks like a beekeeper. Or a nuclear power-plant worker.

"It's the sun," he explains, buckling his seat belt. "Even on a morning like this," he says, looking out at the gray sky, "you've got at least twice the UV rays you get on the sunniest day in southern Florida. Remember," he says, gunning the engine and pulling away, "these are the tropics. Those rays are coming straight down."

Steve's concern with the sun is a recent obsession. He didn't bother with sunscreen until he was in his late twenties. That's when he began noticing spots on his skin. "Little, scabby, wartlike things. Precancerous *keratosis*. I had them burned off. No big thing. Ten or fifteen a year."

Early last year that number leaped to near fifty. Then, just this past October, only three months ago, the doctors removed more than a hundred spots from Steve Divine's skin. More than half of those were from his left arm alone, his driving arm, the one he hangs out the truck's window when he's at the wheel, like today.

"That woke me up. That's when I got serious. Something like that tends to get your attention. Before was like heartburn. This was a heart *attack*."

Between here and Bellavista the landscape is brown, sunbaked, barren. Then the road starts to climb, the air becomes cooler, and deep-green forests of *cedrela* and *cascarilla* trees rise up on both sides. The sun breaks through the clouds, and horses appear, along with herds of burgundy-and-white cattle grazing in elephant grass that rustles like wheat in the soft morning breeze.

"If it was up to just me, I'd never come down from here," Steve says, pulling up to a barbed-wire gate at the side of the road. This is the entrance to *Rancho Mariposa*, the farm his father, Bud, named nearly a half century ago.

Bud Divine. There are few names more fabled among these islands than Steve Divine's dad. Remember Forrest Nelson, the man who earned such respect as a can-do *gringo* in those hard, early days at the turn of the '60s? Well, Bud Divine was on this island years before him, in the early 1950s, running a small store and a bar—in a shack made of pitch pine—in the village and raising his family on the "Other Side," across the harbor in a small house beyond the *barranco*. The serene little cove by that house, near the path to Tortuga, is still called Bud's Bay today because that's where old man Divine anchored his boat for so many years.

But woe to the person who called Bud Divine "old" to his face. Right up to the day he died, Bud Divine was a man who'd kick your ass roundly if you rubbed him the wrong way. He was a fair man, make no mistake about it. And he could be a hell of a lot of fun. He knew how to drink, no question, and he smoked like a chimney. His bottom line, always, was that he valued in others the qualities he demanded of himself: no bullshit, no slack, work hard, play hard, and expect no more or less from this life than you can carve out of it with your own honest hands.

The men who worked for Bud Divine were at first dumbfounded when payday arrived and they found they'd been charged for each of the cigarettes they'd bummed from him during that week. Divine jotted the numbers they owed him in neat, minute script on empty Marlboro packs he used for notepaper, then subtracted the sums from their paychecks. Once they got over the shock, they realized this was just the way Bud Divine was, a bit of a tight-ass, but fair if you thought about it. This was, after all, the Galápagos, not Guayaquil, or, God forbid, a place like New York. There was no room for excess here. Each drop of water, each bite of food, and, yes, each cigarette was a thing to be treasured, to be worked for and savored. Generosity, sharing, helping out someone who's truly in need—these things all had their place. But to reach out for something you hadn't paid for or earned, or to throw away something you had, was unheard of.

Waste in a place such as this was a sin. People still talk about the time Bud Divine saw someone toss an old, broken broom handle from a work site out into the harbor. Divine leaped into his skiff, the one with the twenty-five-horsepower engine (the most powerful motor on the island at that time) and roared out toward the small, floating stick, bellowing at the miscreant: "Jesus Christ, man, you can use that for something!" He fished the pole out of the water to keep for himself, which cost him more in boat fuel than he would have paid for a new broom, but that wasn't the point.

This obsession with waste made Bud Divine's death seem all the more wasteful. It happened in 1983, four years before the old man would have turned seventy. He was riddled with cancer, all but housebound, needing help from Doris and Steve just to make it through the day. It was torture. That's the reason he'd come to these goddamned islands in the first place. It was just about the last place left on Earth where there was nothing that stood between a man and his existence but his hands and his head and his heart and his will.

Bud Divine had spent his whole life staying one step ahead of the bullshit: the government and the politicians, the lawyers and their laws, societies built on dependency and need. He'd worked as a prospector back in the States and as a cowhand, too. (He still wore that ten-gallon hat and brown rawhide boots when he first came to the islands, but he soon traded the hat for a baseball cap.) He took an epic trip once in the '40s on horseback from Arizona up to Montana, got snowed in at the end there, and came away with some frostbite, but who cared about that? It was a hell of an experience.

He owned a ranch for a time in Arizona, the Butterfly Ranch. That's where the name *Rancho Mariposa* came from for this spread in the Galápagos hills, a Spanish translation of Bud Divine's old place in the States. His first taste of the islands came during the war when he worked manning a barge that hauled fresh water from San Cristobal to the troops over on Baltra.

After the Japanese surrendered, Divine wound up in Seattle, where he met Doris (a newspaper reporter) and swept her off her feet. They bought a sailboat—the *Symbol*, as a matter of fact—in 1947, and two years after that they sailed the thing to the Galápagos. By the time Steve was born in 1954, the family was settled here on Santa Cruz, with a house down by the ocean and the farm up in the hills.

That's how Bud Divine came to these islands, pushed by the need to live life his way. And that, in a sense, is how his life ended. Riddled with cancer, having to ask others to do for him what he could no longer do for himself, was no way to live. And so one evening in the autumn of 1983, down in that house by Bud's Bay, he sent Doris out for an errand. Then he fished out his .32 revolver, put the barrel to his mouth, and pulled the trigger.

Of course, some called it cowardly, a terrible thing to do to the loved ones he left behind. Sure, Steve admits, it still hurts, thinking of his dad dying that way. But Steve understands. As for Doris, well, who knows? Her memory's gone. She passes her days in the upstairs room in Steve's house in town, just a husk of the young woman she'd been all those decades ago back in Seattle, when Bud Divine walked into her life and swept her away.

Steve climbs out and opens the gate to the ranch. The smell of horse manure hangs in the air. When Steve was a boy growing up in the '50s and '60s, horses were the centerpiece of this farm, both for working the cattle and for sheer transportation. The only way to the town in those days was on horseback or on foot. They had close to a hundred horses back then, recalls Steve, but now there are maybe thirty, and only a half dozen of those have any real use.

"The rest are just family," says Steve, pulling the truck through the gate, then closing it back behind him. "I could get maybe thirty dollars each for them now, which is nothing. Actually, I'd be lucky to get that. Since the road was put in, the value of horses on this island has gone to almost zero. Sometimes you can't give 'em away."

He's got a few cattle on his 750 acres up here, but any income the farm generates these days is mostly from tortoise-watching—from the tourists who pay three bucks a head to hike through these forests and fields and photograph themselves among the dozens of Galápagos tortoises who make their highland home here.

Divine averages five tour groups a day. The groups range from a half dozen to as many as a hundred. Last Wednesday a group of sixty from the cruise ship *Polaris* came up. The next afternoon there were fifty from the tour boat *Santa Cruz*. Sometimes the tourists pay Divine out of pocket, but typically he collects from the tour boat operators, who don't always come through with their payments. The *Galápagos Explorer*, for example, says Steve, hasn't paid him in over a year. Right now, he says, they owe him more than $1,000.

"It's not fair," he says. "A ship that size, with that kind of money behind them, not paying their bills? I could understand if it were a small operation having a hard time. I can let things like that slide. But this, this pisses me off."

This is a slow day. There's only one group scheduled, a class of sixteen biology students from a school in the United States, a place called Calvin College in Michigan. They're down in a meadow, circled around their professor and a good-sized pair of tortoises as Divine pulls up and parks in the shade of a massive teak tree beside a low, cinder-block building.

The view is breathtaking. White cattle egrets in full breeding plumage soar over rolling green meadows that slope down toward the sea. Far below, the ocean spreads out like a hazy, blue blanket. To the left, on the southern horizon, beyond the gray haze that hangs over Puerto Ayora, sits a dark, rounded hump framed by billowing white clouds: Floreana. To the right, the west, looms the outline of Isabela—large, dark, and cragged, it appears close enough to reach out and touch.

A distant whinny drifts from the moss-draped forest above. A yellow warbler chirps in a nearby stand of smooth, gray-trunked balsas. From the far side of the house, where an open veranda looks down on the sea, come the sounds of rumbling, groaning, and electronic beeps.

Stevie's got the laptop plugged in, and he's shooting the monsters on his video game.

"At least he still likes coming up here," sighs Divine, lifting a couple of cases of bottled water from the back of the truck. "The girls prefer it down there in town, where everything's happening. They get bored up here."

A woman named Juanita, whose husband Efrain runs the ranch for Divine, stands at a stove by the veranda cooking lunch. An infant sits strapped in a stroller beside her. Efrain is off repairing a fence on the west end of the spread. Later today he'll move a few cattle. Then he'll get back to clearing the brush and spraying for *mora*, which has become a chore without end since the vines first appeared here a dozen or so years ago.

"I didn't realize how bad it could get," says Divine. "I had no idea. For the first couple of years, I was reluctant to use herbicides, and then the *mora* just exploded. Now there's no alternative. It's either use the Roundup or go under."

A young Ecuadorian man wearing a Park warden's uniform sits at the veranda's open-air counter, drinking a bottle of beer and nodding his head at Divine's words. The man's name is Washington Parédes Torres. He's guiding today—that's his group down in the meadow, the Michigan kids. They can take care of themselves for the moment, says Washington, so he's taking a break and having a beer. He doesn't mind jumping in on this talk about *mora* because his own family is fighting the same stuff on their farm just up the road, the farm he grew up on.

"The, how you say, scientists," Washington says, taking a swallow of beer. "They always do the same thing. They come and they study and they study. And then they leave, and then another scientist comes and *he* study and study. But nobody *does* anything.

"We have one scientist last year who helped," he continues. "He was named Billy. He give us thirty, forty gallons of Roundup and we use it. And it worked. But you need the same gallons three or four more times for each hectare because the mora come back again. It is in the ground, the seeds, and it doesn't go away, even with the poison."

There is a movement just past the teak tree, a slow-crawling shadow. A head pokes into view: hairless, leathery, reptilian. Then a long, outstretched neck lined with deep wrinkles. Then a smooth, weathered shell, the size of a coffee table, supported by four elephantine legs. The thing moves in slow motion, oblivious to all that surrounds it—the people, the cooking, the sounds of the computer.

"That one's probably about eighty years old," says Divine, hardly looking up from the bottles he's unpacking as the immense tortoise comes into full view. "We've got some here as old as a hundred and fifty.

"You can pretty much tell the age by the smoothness of the shell," he continues. "The smoother it is, the older they are.

"It's kind of funny that way," he chuckles. "We get wrinkled, they get smoother."

Hang around here long enough, says Divine, and you hardly notice the tortoises anymore. They come and go just like this one, in silence, stopping every couple of slow, deliberate steps to chew a mouthful of grass, or to sink in the mud of one of the forest's wet spots, or to gulp the freshwater they find in the highland's puddles and ponds. The one time they openly announce their presence is during mating season, when the male's bellowing roar can be heard like a lion's, echoing through the treetops as he couples with his mate.

But it's not mating season right now, and the hillside is silent, serene. Steve grabs a bottle of water and settles into a chair overlooking the ocean below. Juanita has mentioned the government overthrow on the mainland, but, to tell the truth, Steve's just not that concerned. This stuff has been happening in Ecuador ever since he was born—ever since Ecuador was born. What matters to Steve is what hits closer to home, what actually happens *here*, on these islands: this *mora*, for example, or the goats and wild pigs that have been spreading like crazy, or those freighters from Japan sitting on the horizon, filling their holds with *pepinos* and such.

"They're raping this place," Divine says of the illegal fishing, "turning it upside down just so half of Asia can get their dicks hard."

He takes a hit off his water. "I'd love to see Greenpeace come down here," he says. "Or the Sea Shepherd," he adds, referring to the vigilante ecowarriors whose ships roam the world's oceans, enforcing international fishing regulations in places where those laws are blatantly violated.

This is about as far as Divine's concerns go. The world beyond these islands' shores remains for him much as it has been all his life—a universe away. Steve's got snapshots of himself as a baby, in a bassinet fashioned from an old tortoise shell. He's got memories of old Christian Stampa, one of those first pioneering Norwegians, talking with Bud and Doris on the porch of their house down by the bay about the trips Stampa used to make over to Floreana and the run-ins he had with the baroness herself.

"He'd go over there to hunt wild cattle," says Divine. "She actually pulled a gun on him, or at least that's what I heard. She was a little bit wacko."

He takes a deep breath. Washington's gone now, back to rejoin his tour group. Stevie's still engrossed in his video game. There's a wasp's nest Steve would like to go find and hack down a bit later. The wasps have been stinging some of the horses and cattle lately, and Steve's got a pretty good idea where the nest might be. But there's plenty of time to do that. Besides, he says, it's good for Stevie to be around people speaking English like this, to hear this language and maybe speak some of it himself. Stevie's sisters can speak hardly a word, and that bothers Divine.

"They need to learn English," he says. "It's the language of business. It's the language of travel. And here in the Galápagos, it's the language of tourism. That's one of the reasons I like to bring Stevie up here, so it's just me and him talking."

English, says Steve, was the language of choice among the expatriate community he grew up with down on the "Other Side." With both his own parents born and raised in the States, it's no surprise that Steve, though he calls himself Ecuadorian, walks and talks like an American. He didn't even visit the United States until just five years ago, when he and Jenny and little Stevie flew to upstate New York to see some relatives and friends.

"I couldn't believe how fast-paced everything is," he says. "Everyone's in a rush. Too damned aggressive, if you ask me. That's one problem up there, is that so many people are just downright ornery."

But then, he adds, there's a bright side to all that rushing around. "I like the way everything works up there. I mean, you pick up a phone, and there you are. It works. And everything's so organized. The superhighways, for example. I mean, it would scare me stiff to actually drive on the things. My wife did the driving while we were up there. But navigating is so easy. Everything's marked, which it's not in Ecuador. Highway signs down here are conspicuous by their absence."

Steve was blown away by the bus trip he, Jenny, and Stevie took during that U.S. visit, from Buffalo all the way to Miami—a trip Steve enjoyed immensely, although Jenny (an urban Ecuadorian whom Steve married after meeting her in 1983 while she was leading an island tour from the mainland), did not.

"Yeah, she almost killed me for that one. We went by Greyhound, thirty hours straight through. I loved it. I've done a lot of busing in Ecuador, back and forth from Guayaquil to Quito and such. Let me tell you, a Greyhound bus is paradise compared to Ecuadorian buses."

He takes a swig of his water. "First of all, you've got legroom. Your knees aren't crammed up in your chin. And no one's carrying chickens and pigs. And you've got a rest room. It might not be clean, but at least you don't have to wait and hold it till the next stop. And," he adds, standing and stretching, "nobody's smoking."

Steve's been thinking hard lately about taking the whole family, including the girls—"especially the girls," he says—up to live for a while someplace in the United States so the kids will be forced to learn English. He's been giving it a lot of thought lately. He's considered Miami. It seems as if everyone he knows around here goes to Miami. He and Jenny have got friends there so it wouldn't be hard to find a place to stay. "The trouble is," he says, standing and tossing his empty water bottle in the trash, "everyone speaks Spanish in Miami."

If he had his choice, Steve would prefer someplace a little less urban, a bit more like this farm, with hills and trees and wide-open spaces without all the crime they've got in a big city. And yes, a place where his kids could learn to speak English. Someplace like . . . Arkansas.

"I've heard Arkansas's rural, quite cheap, and beautiful country," says Steve. "Not a place to go for a job or anything like that but a good place to vacation. Of course I've never been, but it could happen. Maybe this summer. We'll see."

Stevie's done with his game. Lunch is ready. The tour group has left, gone back down to the town, where the morning grayness has moved off toward the west, toward the "Other Side," and the sun is now beating down.

It's early afternoon, *siesta* time, and the harborfront is deserted. A couple of water taxis putt back and forth among the tour boats anchored out in the bay, but other than that there are no people in sight, not at this time of day, not in this heat. The tourists are resting inside their cabins out on the boats. Or they're back at their hotel rooms having a nap. Or they're eating a late lunch in one of the restaurants. Or perhaps they're doing some shopping in one of the waterfront shops, such as the Angelique Art Gallery down by the wharf, where a hand-painted banner fashioned from a bedsheet and strung loosely between two rooftop poles proclaims:

PEACE ON EARTH
Angelique Art Gallery
Wishes You A Happy New Century
www.sarahdarling.com

Inside, behind a small desk, sits a willowy, darkly tanned woman. She looks about forty and is wearing a white peasant blouse and a long skirt to match, with brunette braids brushing her bare, freckled shoulders and a smart, little straw hat pulled tight on her head. The shop is tiny, no wider than the empty tour bus parked at the curb just outside, just deep enough to allow four, maybe five, customers to step in at one time and take a look at the artwork arranged on the walls.

The woman is, of course, Sarah Darling. Her paintings are hallu-
cinogenic swirls of fluorescent colors in the shapes of various Galápagos animals. When she goes home at night, she locks up the shop
and walks down to the wharf. There she unties a small motorboat
and takes it across the lagoon, out past the point, into the ocean
beyond the *barranco,* and around to Bud's Bay. This is where she
and her husband, Gus Angermeyer's son, Franklin, have lived since
they met and married back in 1989.

Franklin's at home at the moment, working on one of several
sailboats that—in true Angermeyer fashion—sit in various stages
of construction or repair. Meanwhile, Sarah, like everyone else in
this town on this day, is glued to the radio, listening for updates on
the fall of the government. She comments occasionally, in her thor-
oughly British accent, using terms such as "dreadful" and "vile."

She's upset about all of it: the grief on the mainland, the ugli-
ness that's invaded these islands, those "horrid" industrial fishing
boats slaughtering the innocent animals. She's been working with
the school system on that last one, she and a local "shaman"
named Pepé. Sarah would like to use her artwork and Pepé's storytelling to teach the local children about the preciousness of the natural wonders around them. We can't even see all the damage we're
doing, she says. The shamans will tell you, she says, that there are
things none of us can see with our eyes alone. There are a half
dozen or so "medicine men," as they call themselves, in this village. Most have drifted here in recent years from the mainland,
where the tradition of shamanism is deeply embedded in Ecuadorian culture. There are some people in town who take these men at
their word, who believe that these ponytailed strangers are truly
plugged in to the mysteries of the ages. There are others who call
them "shams," not shamans, and say they are nothing but dope-
smoking charlatans riding the coattails of a venerable tradition.

Franklin couldn't care less either way about this shaman bullshit. Now, give him a good bottle of tequila, a willing circle of
friends, and a clear, starlit evening, and he'll pull out the musical
instruments from the old, wooden chest he keeps down in the living room where he's set up an old rowboat as a bar—an honest-to-

god, full-sized skiff that he hauled right into the house when it had no more use on the water. He'll dig into that chest and pull out the beat-up ukulele, the bongos, the guitar, the maracas, and the small, four-stringed *quatro,* and he'll deal them out to his friends like a wild deck of cards. Then he'll lead the group onto his back porch, and they'll all find a seat, and the music will start, and the bottle will pass from one hand to the next. And Franklin will show them the way, a mad grin creasing his face, sweat beading up on his broad, weathered forehead, his tangled, brown hair knotted with sea salt and wind, the muscles on his ropy forearms straining as he bangs on his bongos, exhorting the others to sing and to dance and to bark at the moon.

"From the *soul,* man!" he shouts, his hands beating the drums braced between his bare legs. "Shake it, but don't *break* it, baby!" he bellows, as the group follows his lead, and the porch shudders and shakes, and the music rolls out into the purple night air up toward the moonlight-washed volcanic peaks. The shadows of Franklin's uncles—Fritz, Hans, Karl, and Franklin's own father, Gus, back when they were all Franklin's age and did this same thing—their spirits hover above these cactus and rocks and float out over the still, dark bay waters that lap at the front side of this house.

Franklin does not give a damn about shamans, but Sarah's done her time in Nepal and India and throughout the Far East. She's got a tattered paperback in her shop—*Southeast Asia on a Shoestring*—which she carried with her back in the old days, in the late '70s, long before she met Franklin, after she left her family's wooded estate in Wiltshire, England. She'd grown up there riding horses and all that and went searching for—well, searching for something. She finally found it here, in the Galápagos, where Franklin whisked her right off the deck of a tour boat (his tour boat) and now—what, eleven years later?—here she is, although she's not completely settled with the idea of being an Angermeyer woman, even after all this time.

Just look at Gus' wife, Lucrecia, who separated from Gus in the late 1960s and now lives in Quito. Gus still lives here, spending his days across the lagoon in that small, roughshod house on the *barranco*, the place he calls his "cave." It's a playpen of sorts, and God knows Gus has always known how to play, which is both a curse and a blessing. Sarah will tell you, the same way Lucrecia would, that Gus Angermeyer is an easy man to love but a hard one to live with.

"He's slept with more women than you've eaten hot dinners," Sarah says of her father-in-law. "He was dreadful that way, always out on his boat, chatting up and charming the women. A free spirit. Kind of a German hippie who never grew up."

There's a lot of that spirit in Franklin as well, although Sarah's determined not to wind up like Lucrecia. It's all very complicated, she says, the magnetic allure of these Angermeyer men, of their Galápagos way of living. That lust for life in a setting like this can be very seductive. To have those parties take shape at the drop of a hat, to travel to work each day not in an automobile but in a small boat (or to not travel at all), to work with your own hands as Franklin does, to build and sail your own boats through channels and inlets you've known and explored since the day you were born, and to step out your door and see frigate birds float on the breeze and blue-footed boobies dive into crystal-clear water that laps at your porch—Sarah adores all these things. But it worries her as well, the fact that while this is all so eternally timeless, it's also impermanent, if that makes any sense. Sarah wonders sometimes if it does make any sense, the gnawing anxiety that comes with the sweetness of living this life, the lingering fear that it could all come to an end at any moment. Because that lust for life cuts in so many directions. It can turn out the light as suddenly and as intensely as it switches it on.

Maybe that's why Sarah's artwork has come to mean so much to her. Every time one of those cruise ships pulls in, Sarah prays there's a patron on board, an angel who'll take one look at her paintings and bring them to New York or Paris, hang them in a gallery or in the gallery of a friend, sell them to the world. No matter what happens with Franklin, no matter what happens on this island, whether Sarah stays here for the rest of her life or flies out of Baltra tomorrow, her artwork is with her forever.

There's so much that Sarah's unsure of, but one thing she knows is she doesn't want her life or Franklin's to wind up like Gus'. Don't get her wrong, she says. She loves Gus, she adores that old man. She's heard what so many people in town say about him: He's nuts, wacko, gone out of his mind, hanging around the waterfront, bothering the tourists with his insane ramblings about God and the cosmos and the iguanas, who supposedly share all his feelings.

Sarah knows Gus isn't crazy. Although he can seem that way to the more adventurous visitors who catch one of those water taxis, cross the lagoon, and come upon the grizzled old man perched on the cement steps that climb up the *barranco* from the small concrete wharf where the motorboats dock.

He sits by himself, in a T-shirt the color of limes and faded swim trunks the color of coral. His skin, dark as mahogany, is wrinkled and scarred from an incomprehensible lifetime of barehanded, barefooted labor. It's clear why they called him "the Tractor" back in the old days. His massive hands could clamp around the trunk of a fallen tree like the jaws of a vise; his shoulders could lift that tree up and out like a steam shovel. Even his toes were powerful tools, able to grip a boat's oars as Gus rowed with his legs, with the force and the sureness of two normal men's arms.

They called him the "King of the Galápagos," the magazine and newspaper reporters who came here over the decades to see these legendary brothers for themselves. They'd ask them to pose for corny photographs, to lean on a tortoise, smoke a pipe and look thoughtful, or to wear phony feathered caps on their heads, like tropical Robin Hoods. And the brothers went along with this game because, what the hell, it was fun. It was *all* fun—goddamned hard work, but a blast just the same, living like they did, in those days when there was hardly anyone else on the islands.

Now things have changed. Time has moved on. Hans and Karl are dead. Fritz is still hanging in there, just up the way from this wharf, in his own modest waterfront house. He can't hear a thing anymore—he's been stone-cold deaf for a few years now—but he's still alert, able to enjoy a drink or two in the evening with friends.

As for Gus, well, it's hard to tell how Gus is doing. When a passerby stops to greet him, he looks up, the snowy stubble of his unshaven chin glinting in the sunlight, the thatch of thin silvery hair on his head shining as well. "You don't know me!" he says with disgust. Then he grins, shakes his head, and turns away. "You are crazy," he murmurs in English with a thick, German accent.

A woman is down on the wharf, with a small blond boy, a toddler, who stands by the edge gazing into the water.

"You're stupid," Gus says, spitting his words at the woman. "You're really *stupid*. I would *never* let a little child close to the water like that."

The woman is unshaken. She laughs. "I'm a good grandmother," she says in a calm, soothing voice.

And Gus then laughs, too. It's a game they are both playing. They know each other well. They are neighbors. Her name is Anita, and that's Robert, her grandson. Anita and her husband have lived on this island for years. They run a large restaurant across the harbor, above the town, on their farm in the highlands. The tourists drop in and eat at her place after taking in Los Tunéles, the lava tunnels near Media Luna. You can call her anytime, she says, on her marine radio, Frequency 23-A.

"Ahhh, Galápagos," says Gus, leaning back on the steps, crossing his legs and looking up at the sky. "Galáaapagos."

Suddenly, he sits upright, furrows his brow, and spits toward the water. "Galápagos is kaput. Not only Galápagos, but the whole *world* is kaput."

Anita laughs. Gus relaxes his face, and now he's laughing, too.

"I'm no pessimist," he says. "I will never be. I am the biggest optimist on the planet Earth." He stops speaking, gazes out at the frigate birds floating over the bay, drifting on thermal upwellings, each of them motionless and suspended in the air, as if held in place by the strings of a puppeteer.

"Those are *my* birds up there," says Gus. He leans back, extends a knuckled finger, and begins counting.

"*Eins, zwei, drei* . . ." He stops at six. "Where's the seventh?" He squints his eyes, searching the gray, wispy clouds laced across the bright-turquoise sky.

"Ah, there he is." He smiles, nods his head. "My birds. So beautiful. You would not believe. These birds, they know me, they know who I am."

A water taxi shoots past in the distance, the drone of its engine like a nest full of hornets.

"Man stirbt nicht," Gus says slowly, as if reading the words. *"Man bringt sich um."*

He repeats himself, this time in English: "Man does not die. He kills himself."

A small splash hits the glassy water below. Then another. And now the harbor's surface is dancing with the droplets of a light afternoon drizzle.

"Angel's tears," Gus says, squinting up at the clouds.

Anita and Robert hurry up the steps, say good-bye, and hustle down the path toward the home of a friend. Gus rises as well, and moves a couple of steps toward a rough wooden gate by a hand-painted sign at the edge of the lane. The sign warns, *"PRIVADO."*

As Gus steps through the gate, a gray-striped tabby cat appears from the mangroves by the edge of the little home's small, stony yard. The cat follows Gus as he finds cover beneath the overhang of the cabin's back patio. He takes a seat on a large slab of wood. The cat curls beside him.

"What is beauty?" he asks, stroking the animal. "And what is not?

"Die Schönheit," he answers himself, *"ist ein Licht in dem Herz."*

"Beauty," he translates, "is a light in the heart."

The rainfall makes a light hissing sound as it lands on the black lava stones in the yard. "This is an incredible creature," says Gus, caressing the tabby. *"You* see only a cat."

He shakes his head. "This creature knows things you will never know, things you will never understand."

A small lava lizard darts from the brush onto one of the wet, glistening rocks, its bright-orange throat throbbing against the dull brown of its body.

"You see that creature?" asks Gus. "He, too, knows." He sighs deeply. "It is incredible what you can learn when you observe."

He sighs again. Then he shoves the cat off the bench onto the patio's hard concrete floor, where it lands and darts off into the brush. "*Piss* on him! And shit, too, if you can."

He leans back, closes his eyes, and his face softens. "*Gott ist Liebe,*" he says.

"Do you know what that means?" His eyes are now open. "Our mother would tell us this when we were children: 'God is love.'" He shuts his eyes again. "Our mother, she was the most truly, perfectly beautiful person, believing in God."

It has been sixty-five years since Gus said good-bye to his mother in Germany. Sixty-five years since he and his brothers sailed here to the Galápagos. Gus is thinking about that right now, about his brothers and sisters when they were all young, their parents back home in Hamburg.

"Heinzi, Guschi, Hansi, Karl, Fritzi," he says, his eyes turning moist. "There was Lene, the daughter, she was first. Then the last, Ane Lise." He grins, shakes his head. "Between two very foolish females came five brilliant men."

He turns, spits in the dirt, and stands. "This is shit talk, *Scheiss,* you know that?" When he stands like this, he can see beyond the rocks and the brush and out over the harbor.

"That yacht now that is going out there," he says, watching a good-sized ship move off toward the sea. "How many yachts have been here? How many yachts cruise through here? How many cruise and cruise and cruise?"

He sits down again. "Some find what they are looking for. Some keep on sailing and never find." He looks at the lizard, which still sits on the rock. Another lizard appears, and the two begin chasing each other, skittering over the slick stones.

"What do you see?" asks Gus. "Are they playing?" He pauses, then answers himself. "They are not playing. I have observed these animals for many years. They are like man, like human beings. Jealousy. Territory. That is what's happening."

The rain's falling harder now.

"*Seele, ach meine Seele,*" he says, so softly the words can hardly be heard. "*Noch ein Kind zu sein.*"

There is silence for a moment.

"Soul, oh my soul," he says, just as softly. "A child still to be."

Silence again.

"Ich bin noch ein Kind."

His fingers curl gently around the cat's head. "I am still a child."

The cat is purring now, as loud as the rain.

"Something my mother said to me when I was a little boy."

The cat's eyes are closed. The lizards are gone. The rain falls on the rocks. The harbor is still.

"Du bist wer du bist; du bist was du bist."

He stands one last time. "You are who you are," he says, pulling open the door to his hut. "You are *what* you are."

He steps into the house and closes the door.

Twelve

Cigars and Wine

Isla
Española

FEBRUARY 14, 2000

Galapagos Explorer II

I t's Valentine's Day, and Jack Nelson's cozied up with a late-evening scotch and a week-old *Wall Street Journal* left by one of the guests who checked out this morning. Romy and Audrey have drifted off to bed. Jack will be joining them soon, but right now it's time to relax. He's got Billie Holiday cued up on the stereo, the lamps are turned low, no one else is around. If it weren't for the palm and the *muyuyo* tree framing the view out the lobby's rear window, the twinkling deck lights of those cruise ships anchored out in the harbor could pass for the Manhattan skyline. Or, muses Jack, an oil refinery.

He's finally leaving tomorrow to get his father in Thailand. And, truth be told, it will be a relief to get out of here for a while. It's been a long week, one thing after another, beginning with a yacht sinking over at San Cristobal.

It happened last Sunday. Jack was asleep when the VHF radio he keeps tuned by his bedside to an open marine frequency crackled to life with an emergency transmission at about three A.M. The voice was frenetic, shouting in Spanish, calling for help from the waters off Cristobal.

It was hard for Jack to hear clearly over the static. San Cristobal is at the extreme edge of his radio's range. Closer to home, on Puerto Ayora's local frequencies, you can hear everything—and you will, if you listen in long enough. There are people in town who keep these radios on day and night, for sheer entertainment, eavesdropping and sometimes joining in with whatever comes over the air. Some people like to get on and make obscene sounds or tell dirty jokes. Some set up their radios in their bedrooms and broadcast the noise of their lovemaking. But for Jack, this is business, part of his job as the islands' U.S. consulate warden. And what came across his radio last Sunday woke him up in a hurry.

Apparently, a yacht had run aground at the south end of Cristobal, hitting a reef in the dead of the night. The boat, apparently American, had gone down with two men on board. There may have been a fatality; Jack couldn't be sure. The voice on the radio came from an Ecuadorian naval speedboat racing from the site of the sinking back to Puerto Baquerizo. It was calling for oxygen and medical supplies to be ready when it arrived. A victim, seriously injured, was aboard, bleeding heavily from the head.

This was all Jack could gather from the radio. By sunrise, he'd spoken with the *comandante* of the naval base in San Cristobal. The sunken boat was indeed American—the *Pacific Star*, out of San Diego. A father and son were aboard: a retired doctor named Vernon Koepsel, in his eighties, and Koepsel's fifty-year-old son, Edward. The father was apparently at the helm when the boat hit the reef. The sea was calm at the time, so weather had not been a factor. The old man may have dozed off, figured Jack. Or he may have had a heart attack. There's no telling.

In any event, the son was asleep down below when the boat hit the rocks. The father was thrown over the side by the impact, which broke open the hull. The ship went down almost immediately, leaving the father dead and the son fighting for his life, buck naked in the roil of the sea breaking over the reefs. "No money," says Jack. "No documents. Not even any clothes."

The son suffered only mild injuries. A young Ecuadorian naval lieutenant, however, was hurt badly during the rescue. The radio alert Jack had overheard was for him. By late morning, there was concern the lieutenant might die.

The younger Koepsel had by then been stabilized, somewhat in shock, but other than that, doing fine. The primary problem was how to deal with the father's body—a question Jack discussed at length during the day in a series of phone conversations with the U.S. Consulate's office in Guayaquil. The issue, in nuts-and-bolts terms, was how to keep the corpse from rotting on this remote tropical island.

"Look," Jack told the government official on the other end of the line, a woman named Carla. "This man is already fourteen hours dead. It's hot here, and there's no place on that island to keep the body. No morgue. No freezer space."

There would have to be an autopsy, he told her. "So you're going to have this body cut up. And there's no embalming, nothing like a professional mortuary."

A coffin would have to be found for shipping the body to the mainland, and a mere wooden box would not do. "You can't just ship a dead body in a wooden box," Jack explained, "certainly not by air. You have to get an air-transport casket, a large, hermetically sealed, aluminum casket."

In the last of several phone calls to and from Carla and her colleagues—who by late afternoon had spoken by phone with the younger Koepsel himself—Jack summed things up. "They'll probably find somebody over there with a large enough freezer to keep that body for four or five days while everybody gets their act together," he said. "After that, you're gonna have a stinker on your hands."

By that evening, the navy personnel on San Cristobal had managed to find a makeshift holding facility for the elder Koepsel's body—in the base's small movie theater. As for the lieutenant, he was still alive, but just barely. It looked like he'd have to be medevaced to the mainland.

Any flight to the mainland has now become dicey, with the nation still reeling from the coup just two weeks ago. The Indians have refused to recognize the new president, Noboa, after he announced his intention to carry through with the dollarization changeover begun by Mahuad. *Indio* leaders have told Noboa he has three to six months to change his mind about that. They've presented a list of demands: increased spending on education for their children; bilingual training; prosecution of bankers and politicians who had profited from the nation's most recent economic crisis; and an end to this dollarization nonsense, which the *Indios* point out will penalize poor, rural Indians who've never seen a dollar in their lives. If these demands are not met, warn the *Indios*, there will be real revolt, even a civil war. Those are the very words they are now using—"civil war."

"This time it was peaceful, the next time blood will be spilled," one *Quechua* was quoted in newspapers this week.

"The situation is still hot," agreed *Indio* spokesman Antonio Vargas. "The next uprising could be much more radical, much more hard-line."

Michael Bliemsreider would not argue with that. The Galápagos INGALA director just got back last week from the mainland, from Cuenca, where he happened to be the day the mob seized the presidential palace. He spent the ensuing thirty-six hours with a telephone pressed to his ear, talking with government officials as the pieces on the Ecuadorian political chessboard were madly rearranged. On the night of the coup alone, Bliemsreider figures, he spent at least three million *sucres* on cellular phone calls.

"It has been crazy, like a frenzy," he said last Monday morning, the day after the *Pacific Star* sinking. Vernon Koepsel's body was still on San Cristobal. Ed Koepsel was there as well, waiting while Navy and government officials figured out what to do with his father. Meanwhile, the injured lieutenant had been sent to a Guayaquil hospital, where a day later he died.

In the shade of a palm at the edge of Pelican Bay, Bliemsreider assessed the typhoon of events swirling over the mainland and blowing through these islands. He is not a man who is easily ruffled. At thirty-three he's a seasoned political player here in the Galápagos, having run everything from the National Park to INGALA. His father is German; hence the last name. But he's all Ecuadorian, born and raised in Guayaquil, like his mother. Trim, tall, and athletic, he could pass for a professional soccer player in this country where, as in all South America, soccer is a religion.

Bliemsreider is that rarest of creatures, a bureaucrat who actually gets something done, a man respected by most Galápagans as part of the glue that has held these islands together in the face of the onslaught they've faced in recent years. It's people like Bliemsreider who have fed information and advice to the Ecuadorian government for years now, helping shape such legislation as the recent Special Law.

Bliemsreider knows as well as anyone how difficult it is to get such statutes passed. He also knows how, in the hands of this new Ecuadorian presidential administration, the laws may be changed or

even erased in the bat of an eye. The way things have shaken themselves out since the coup, he's afraid that's exactly what might happen. He looked so relaxed, leaning against that palm tree with his
arms crossed on his chest and a smile on his face as soft as the fronds
waving over his head, but his words were severe.

"Let's see," he said, glancing out at the harbor. "This new govern-
ment took office on a Saturday. By Sunday, Noboa had scratched the
Ministry of Environment. This was one of the first things he did.
That's a pretty clear signal.

"Just look at the new ministers he has named," he continued.
"They're all industrial people—fishing, mining, forestry. Noboa's
son-in-law is Gustavo Gonzales. He owns several ships in Manta.
It's pretty obvious that environmental protection is not this government's priority."

In fact, said Bliemsreider, it is only because of outside pressure—
most notably from the United States—that things are not worse. The
flurry of phone calls Bliemsreider made while in Cuenca included several to Ecuadorian ministers in Quito, who told him that the U.S.
Ambassador herself, a woman named Gwen Clare (who stepped into
this ambassadorship just five months ago), had laid it on the line with
Noboa.

"What's that typical U.S. Embassy phrase?" Bliemsreider asked.
"'Lo veriamos con buenos ojos . . .', or 'It would be nice if . . .' It's a
diplomatic way of putting it, but it means: 'You better watch out.'
That's how I was told that she said it to him. That no matter what
happened, the Park here in the Galápagos needed to be left alone."

Apparently, Noboa got the message. "He issued a statement pri-
vately to the local politicians here in the Galápagos," said Bliemsreider, "that the Park is not to be touched."

Everything else, though, is apparently up for grabs. Including,
Bliemsreider said with that smile and a shrug of his shoulders, his
job. Fanny Uribe, it seems, has been out to get him for some time.
The congresswoman hasn't forgotten that Bliemsreider was with
Mathias Espinosa in that raid on her house, the one where they
shot the video footage of the *pepinos* up on her roof.

"That woman just hates me," Bliemsreider said. "She has been a pain in my ass from the beginning. But I always had the government on the mainland behind me. Now I have no political support at all."

Bliemsreider knows his days are numbered, but until he's replaced he intends to show up at the INGALA headquarters each morning, if for no other reason than to make sure the building's furniture and equipment are not looted. It's no joke, he says. Right now his job is that basic. "I'm just watching over the office so no one carries anything away."

The next morning, Tuesday, thin plumes of oily smoke could be seen coiling up from the waterfront near the wharf. The intersection outside Sarah Darling's art studio had been blocked off with a crude barricade of black lava rocks, and a pile of truck tires had been set afire by a small, angry crowd. The same scene was transpiring at the north end of town, where traffic from Bellavista and Baltra—trucks, taxis, buses—was backed up by protesters refusing to allow any vehicles into the village. Bewildered tourists were unloading their luggage from the buses and taxis and were hiking from there into town.

It turned out that TAME had raised its airfare for islanders in the wake of the sudden shutdown of Saeta airlines the weekend before. Saeta had been struggling lately, not just financially, but in terms of literally keeping its planes in the air. A number of near-accidents in recent months had prompted the government to ground a large portion of the airline's fleet for mechanical inspections. One of its planes bound for San Cristobal just a few weeks ago had lost an engine and plunged several thousand feet toward the sea before the pilot was able to pull out of the dive. Another had been forced by mechanical problems to turn back to the mainland just a half-hour before landing at Puerto Baquerizo. With half its planes now on the ground, Saeta finally decided to throw in the towel, which left TAME in business by itself. And so came this price increase. A ticket to Quito, which until this week had cost 700,000 *sucres*—$28—was now 1,700,000, an increase of $40. Airfare to Guayaquil had been raised the same way, and the townspeople were furious.

While groups of men and young boys manned the barricades at both ends of town, a crowd of two dozen women—some of them TAME employees—had gathered in front of the airline's downtown offices on Darwin Avenue. They were seated on long wooden benches they'd pulled into the street. They laughed and joked, sipping bottles of soda and munching bags of potato chips, chatting with friends passing by while a van parked at the curb blared a pop song from a pair of speakers mounted on its roof.

> *"Believe me when I say how much I love you,*
> *believe me when I say how much I care. . . ."*

It was the mayor who had called for the people of Puerto Ayora to boycott TAME. The voice of the town's *comisario*, the mayor's chief lieutenant, barked from a radio held by one of the women. The *comisario* was urging the people to protest. Word was that a small caravan of protesters was speeding toward Baltra to set up barricades there.

"They won't get too far," said Jack that afternoon. He was out on his hotel's back patio, in the shade of a rough wooden arbor, dabbing some paint on a mobile of fish designs he'd cut out from old copper mesh window screens salvaged from the U.S. barracks at Baltra. The radio in his office was tuned to the local station. News of that morning's strike rattled out through the window.

Jack could understand the people's anger at this rate increase, but this barricade nonsense made no sense at all, he said. The town's bread and butter is those tourists, who couldn't be too happy lugging their own baggage by foot into town, sweating like sherpas. They couldn't be too impressed by that flaming pile of tires or the unsettling sight of townspeople protesting in the streets. These tourists didn't pay thousands of dollars apiece to be caught up in the theatrics of some third-rate banana republic.

The mayor should know better, said Jack. He should know the townspeople are harming only themselves with this so-called boycott. But what does the mayor care? He's out to get votes, said Jack. He wants the people to know he's on *their* side, by God. The next election is less than two months away, and the mayor is seizing the moment, preying on fear and emotions for political capital, as all good populists do. Bucaram did it. The presidents before and after him did it. And the mayor is doing it right now.

"That's the way populism works," said Jack. "You don't do what's effective. You don't do what's right. You don't do what will truly produce positive change. You do what's popular. You shoot for the lowest common denominator, and, as in this case, you almost always wind up shooting yourself in the foot."

That caravan headed toward Baltra? They're running on sheer emotion, said Jack. They're not even thinking about the reality of the situation, he said, about what awaits them at the airport. But they'll find out soon enough, the same way they did last year when they tried the same thing after a similar airline-rate increase. Baltra is a military base, for God's sake. There are soldiers armed with automatic weapons. These yahoos in their Hondas won't get any farther than the canal, said Jack. The soldiers on the other side will see to that. There will be a lot of shouting and posturing. Then everyone will get hot. And they'll get tired. And then they'll get bored. And then they'll finally turn around and come home.

Jack was right. By that evening, the protesters were back in their homes watching television. The next day the barricades were pulled away and traffic began flowing as usual. The TAME rate hike remained in effect. And it was on a TAME airliner that Vernon Koepsel's body was finally flown back midweek to the mainland in an air-transport casket shipped from Guayaquil.

So Jack is now able to leave for his trip in relative peace. The next morning, he'll take a cab to the airport, where he'll catch the day's first flight to the mainland. Then it will be on to California. Then, finally, to Thailand.

Even as Jack is on his way up to Baltra the following morning, a small crowd has gathered outside the police station jail. Inside are six boys, all teenagers, arrested on charges of possible murder.

The details are sketchy right now, mostly rumors. There was apparently some trouble late last night, at a small weekend rodeo up at Bellavista. Someone was killed. No one's sure if there's been one death or two. Word is the police have drawn a pair of chalk outlines of bodies on the road near the turnoff to Quatro y Media.

The crowd at the jail are families and friends of the boys in the cell. There are about two dozen people, mostly women. They're chattering at the kids, passing them food and bottles of soda through the door's bars. A rusted white pickup truck—hauled in, it turns out, with the suspects—is parked outside the chief's office. But the chief is not here, says a police lieutenant, who is happy to share what he knows.

A body was found this morning about six A.M., on the road near Bellavista. "It was destroyed," says the lieutenant. "The head, the legs, everything."

The boys in the cell, says the lieutenant, were among the last to leave the rodeo last evening, at about four A.M. They hitched a ride in the back of a pickup. An older man also hitched a ride in the same truck, a fisherman from San Cristobal who had come over this week to see his daughter graduate from school.

The man had been drinking, says the lieutenant. The boys got into some kind of argument with him. Then they decided to rob him. They beat him, then pushed him out of the truck, leaving him on the road. One of the kids said that they threw rocks at the man's body as the truck drove away, but the lieutenant says he can't be sure of this. In fact, he's not certain of anything here. He says the people at the hospital would know more, at least about the dead man.

They do. Max Parédes has been in his office for hours doing the paperwork on this . . . incident. He says the body was brought in by the police early this morning, at about a quarter to eight. Parédes was not here at that time, but he heard that the body was in pretty bad shape.

"Part of the brain was gone," says Parédes. "The head was—" Parédes stops himself and sends for the doctor who was on duty when the body was brought in. Her name is Paola Vargas. Parédes gives her the seat at his desk. She's young, twenty-seven, small-framed, with thick, dark, shoulder-length hair. She's calm and straightforward, peering over the tops of her eyeglasses whenever she's making a point.

She was at the end of a twenty-four-hour shift, she explains, that began yesterday morning at eight A.M. She was exhausted, ready to head home when the hospital doors burst open and the police brought in this body, found on the road up near Bellavista just after dawn by a man driving in to work in Puerto Ayora. The body had been run over sometime during the night, Vargas says, crushed badly by an oncoming vehicle.

"The head looked like a coconut split in half," she says. "There was no brain. It was empty. And the legs, one was not there." This was the first autopsy she has ever done, says Vargas. Her finding, she says briskly (the cause of death, as she has reported it), is "a transport accident." That's it. No more details. Parédes dismisses the doctor and excuses himself.

By the next afternoon, candles have been lit outside the house of the dead fisherman's relatives, up in the village. Black crepe paper hangs from the home's door and windows as the family observes the *velorio*, the wake.

Meanwhile, Police Chief Proáno will answer no questions, not yet. "The investigation," he says, "is continuing."

The next day is the same. And the next. Finally, on Friday, the chief is ready to talk. All but one of the six boys have been released. Still behind bars is an eighteen-year-old, the "leader" of the group.

"Let me summarize the accident," says the chief, settling behind his desk and opening a thick folder. "It's just another one of so many accidents. What has magnified it is the fact that this group of kids is underage."

The kids ranged in age from twelve to eighteen. "The victim," says the chief, "was totally drunk" when he began walking home from the rodeo at about 3:30 A.M. The kids were walking as well and fell into step with the victim. "He started offering drinks to the older ones," says the chief. "The younger ones noticed. 'Ah, he's got some money.'"

It was the eighteen-year-old who "tried to rob the man," says the chief. None of the other boys took part in the attempted robbery, he says. "They felt bad and were afraid and felt sorry for him."

The victim wrestled himself away, says the chief, and "ran into the vegetation" in the darkness of night. The kids kept on walking and were soon picked up by a passing truck. The victim says the chief, then rushed out of the bushes, desperate. "He asked the driver for help from this assault," says the chief.

The victim climbed into the cab. "He started misbehaving," the chief says. "Just a typical drunk. Very excited and loud." The driver grew tired of the man and stopped the truck. "He made him get out and told him to ride in the back."

The man had no idea the boys were back there, says the chief. Before he could flee, the boys attacked him and heaved him out of the truck.

"The older one," says the chief, nodding toward the cell where the eighteen-year-old is still being held, "he kicked him in the face."

The group has sworn that the victim was conscious when they drove away. The eighteen-year-old swears it. "He said, 'Okay, I kicked him in the face,'" says the chief. "'But when we left,' he said, 'he was standing up.'"

The chief unfolds a large map on his desk. It shows the road south of Bellavista. The shapes of two human figures are drawn on the map, just as the two chalk outlines were drawn by the chief's investigators on the actual blacktop road. The outlines show the position of the body before and after it was struck by whatever vehicle ran over it.

"You see," says the chief, pointing at the drawings. "It crashed into him here and dragged him 3.37 meters, to there." This, says the chief, is why it was rumored at first around town that there had been two deaths. Two chalk outlines, two deaths. An easy assumption to make, says the chief, if you don't have all the information.

The vehicle that ran over the victim has not yet been found, says the chief, and he holds out little hope that his men will ever find it. "I would very much like to know where it is," he says, "but it is not an easy thing, not with the body lying down as it was. If he were hit standing up, it would be entirely different. There would be visible damage to the vehicle that we could look for. But with this, at most this might have damaged the suspension, and that could easily be repaired somewhere up in the highlands."

What the chief is left with is a charge of "attempted assault" against the eighteen-year-old. What bothers him about all this, he says, is the absence of information from the hospital. He can't do his job, he says, if they don't do theirs. And in this case, he says, they didn't do theirs.

"The autopsy report was of no use to me," he says. "It is no good because it doesn't specify if this man died before he was run over or after. It doesn't tell me how long he had been dead. It doesn't tell me anything."

The chief folds up his map and sticks it back in the folder. "It's amazing, just incredible," he says, "not to have the right kind of doctors to give a specific, professional autopsy."

He doesn't blame Dr. Vargas, though. "It's not her fault. There are doctors with a lot of experience here. Why didn't *they* do it? If I, as a police officer, don't do my job the way they didn't do theirs, then we're all screwed."

To hear Michael Bliemsreider tell it, these islands *are* screwed, at least at the moment. Just yesterday morning, Bliemsreider resigned from his INGALA position, as he had said just last week he would. But he doesn't seem too upset, not about that. He's certain he'll land on his feet. He always has. What bothers him is what's going to happen to this town and these islands with virtually everything but the Park up for grabs and with people like the mayor and Fanny Uribe and their lot smelling opportunity and power and all that comes with it. Just a few months ago, Bliemsreider had several international agencies with a special interest in the future of the Galápagos lined up to spend millions of dollars on improving the town's school system, its water, sewage, and social services. But with the coup and the unrest that has followed, those millions are all on hold.

And Bliemsreider doesn't hold much hope that that money will be seen here anytime soon. "We were getting there," he says, "but now it's scratched, back to zero. The Park is the only keyhole of hope right now, not just for the islands, but for the people on these islands. The Park is going to be okay, but the town now is a mess. And it's going to be worse with the upcoming election."

There have been rumors around town the last several days that a gambling casino is about to open in the basement of the Hotel Palmeras, the hotel owned by the mayor's family. "Oh really?" says Bliemsreider. "That's the first I've heard of that. But I'll tell you this," he says with a chuckle. "I wouldn't play there if I was you."

He's not sure if the casino is anything more than mere gossip. But the luxury resort that a local entrepreneur named Furio Valbonesi is said to be building up in those hills above Bellavista—Bliemsreider has seen that project with his own eyes. It's far from finished, but it's definitely taking shape, he says. And he has mixed feelings about it.

"On the one hand, this can be a good thing," he says. "If Furio succeeds in filling this hotel, it will bring new boats, big boats, which will stay a while, which is not necessarily bad. That would be a lot of money for the Park. And in terms of the other businesses that exist in this town, I don't think this will do any harm. The people who want to spend $1,200 a night for one of Furio's rooms—none of these people would stay at the other places that exist here right now. The other hotels will not be hurt by the competition, because this is not competition. If anything, it may raise the standards in town.

"However," he says, "I don't know if that is what the Galápagos wants to become. This is supposed to be a natural environment in which you learn about an incredible legacy. It's not necessarily supposed to be a rich person's playground, like in the Caribbean."

Through Furio Valbonesi's eyes, that is precisely what the Galápagos is supposed to be: a playground for the rich. Furio is unabashed about this, sitting up on the veranda of his open-air restaurant, among the peaks of the highlands. A glass of chilled white wine is in his hand, and a dish of gnocchi sits on the table before him.

Pavarotti is piped through the sound system, the strains of "Come Back to Sorrento" floating out into the afternoon mist.

Furio surveys the ocean far below. The *Galapagos Explorer II* is in port, and a man named Felipé Dégel, an officer on the *Explorer*, is up here, wearing his white crew member's uniform but speaking and acting like Furio's right-hand man. Dégel's own glass of wine is almost finished, and he wants to know if the boss is going to drive up to the work site in his own car, or if he needs Felipé to take him.

"I'll drive myself," says Furio, lighting a cigarette as a young Ecuadorian woman removes his lunch plate. A small tour group has just left, after finishing their own lunch—$14 apiece—and are taking a tour of the lava tunnel located just a short hike uphill from here. The "tunnel visit," as priced on the restaurant's menu, costs $4 a person, which the guests here at Mutiny, which is what Furio calls his restaurant, are happy to pay.

"Mutiny," says Furio, in clipped English laced with an Italian lilt, "is a very good hotel-discotheque in Coconut Grove, in Miami. I like the place. I like the name. So I use it here."

Furio looks like he belongs in Miami, perhaps playing golf. He's wearing an electric-blue Lacoste sportshirt and plaid shorts. And deck shoes, no socks. A pair of wire-rimmed eyeglasses dangles from a cord looped around his neck. He's slim, tanned, bald. To hear him tell it, he's always been quite the *bon vivant*. He's had his share of lovers, for example, but he's never been married.

"Hey, I'm crazy," he says, "but I'm not stupid." That's one of his favorite lines. He uses it often. "There are three billion women in this world," he says. "That speaks for itself. There is always another one nicer than the one you are with, and that nicer one always comes along."

Ask him about his background, and Furio hardly knows where to begin. He's fifty-four, he says, born in Tuscany, into a family whose fortune has seen him through more than a few failed business ventures. He studied medicine, he says, in Paris, and worked for a time as a doctor in the early 1970s in New York. He traded steel for a while in Quito he says. He owned a shipyard in Brazil with a partner who he says wound up betraying him. "He had the know-how," says Furio, "and I had the money. Then he disappeared. Now he has the money, and I have the know-how."

It was in the mid-1970s, says Furio, that he first visited the Galápagos and bought this property, about two hundred acres. "No matter what has happened to me, I have always had this land," he says. "In the worst of situations, I have never sold it."

According to Furio, there have been some bad situations over the years. He owned a couple of tour boats here in the 1980s, but "they tended to sink." By 1990, he says, "I'd had it with tourists." Or at least he'd had it with tourists on boats. So he moved up here and opened this restaurant, which, three years ago, burned to the ground.

"People were thinking I must have done it for the insurance," he says. "But I had no insurance." He was able to rebuild this place, he says, only because the Franciscans in town allowed him to live in one of their church's outbuildings while he pulled things together. "I lived the monk's life," he says, smiling and sipping his wine. "I can be realistic when I need to be."

And he apparently can seize an opportunity when it presents itself, which is how he fell into the money both to resurrect this restaurant and to finally begin building his personal Xanadu up in a 400-acre section of forest at the top of this property. He has "a very rich friend" who made a fortune publishing a magazine called *Auto Trader* in England. The friend, says Furio, gave him the rights to publish the same magazine in Latin America and Malaysia.

"Both were big successes," he says, grabbing a couple of issues from behind the bar. The magazines are replete with photos and descriptions of used cars and trucks for sale by their owners. It's not rocket science, says Furio, but it's lucrative. So much so that he not only was able to reopen this restaurant two years ago, but late last spring he finally broke ground for his dream palace, which, though it's still more than a year from opening, has reached a point where he can show it to visitors.

"Let's go take a look," he says, climbing behind the wheel of a late-model Jeep Grand Cherokee. He settles into the soft leather seat, flips the air conditioner on high, and heads up a dirt road toward the hotel. A couple of copies of *Architectural Digest* are tossed in the backseat. One features Frank Sinatra's home in Palm Springs. The other displays David Bowie's lagoon-side estate on an island in Bali.

Furio's hotel right now has no name, he says. "The Nameless Hotel, I call it," he chuckles, downshifting as the rock-rutted road becomes steeper. "I will give one thousand dollars to someone who gives me the right name."

A thousand dollars, he says smiling, would not mean much to the kind of clientele he expects to fill his hotel's rooms. "They're successful, young-to-middle-aged people, full of energy, but they don't want to be wearing a backpack. If they ride a horse, someone is there to take care of that horse for them. If they have a picnic, someone is there to lay it out.

"You get the adventure," he says, "but you get all the comfort and luxury, too. You get your wine, your caviar, your smoked salmon, whatever. Successful, achieving people, but not with the intention of sweat," he says. "That is who this experience is for. Soft adventure, that is what this is."

As the road levels off in a grove of crimson-leafed *cinchona* trees—an introduced species that has become a nightmarish pest for surrounding farmers—the hotel grounds appear up ahead, terraced and sodded, bedecked with flowers and ferns. More than fifty workers, all Ecuadorian, scramble in and out of half-finished buildings like aroused ants, in a meticulously bucolic setting as carefully manicured as a botanic garden.

A waterfall tumbles down an arrangement of boulders, cascading into a grottolike swimming pool. A tennis court has been cleared in the woods to the left. To the right is where the golf course and airstrip will sit. Up the tree-shaded slope to the rear are the guest quarters themselves, each its own private residence, each built in a distinctive, exotic, "indigenous" style designed by Furio's architect.

The bungalows are cozy, stuccoed, painted bright peach, each with a cone-shaped thatched roof. "Authentic, indigenous," Furio says of the roofs. "The Indians from the mainland, we brought them out to do the weaving."

The "cabins" boast fireplaces, private Jacuzzis, copper bathroom fixtures from a metalsmith in Cuenca, hand-forged iron door fittings with massive medieval keys from antique shops in Guayaquil, ceramic-tiled floors, and hardwood beams and rafters. "The best of everything," says Furio.

"Is exquisite, no?" he asks. Rooms and rates range from the "Imperial" suite, at $1,200 per evening, to what Furio calls the "Victor Hugo" rooms—two of them—which go for a mere $150 per person per night. "They are for the 'miserables,' get it?" he says.

He's proud of the rooms, but Furio is even prouder of the resort's central complex of buildings—thatch-roofed as well—where the guests can dine, drink, play, and be pampered. There is a gymnasium—"With the big mirrors, you know?"—and a spa, Turkish bath, dry sauna, and massage room. There is a library with leather sofas and chairs, a wet bar, a computer and fax machine. "And a printer," says Furio smiling, "so you can work."

There is no air-conditioning, "except for the cigars and the wine." But there is an observatory, which will soon have its computerized telescope installed. "So you can take the picture of the star if you'd like," says Furio, his voice echoing off the tiled floor of the dome-ceilinged room, as a worker by the doorway slaps paint on the wall.

There is a chapel—"multidenominational, of course," says Furio. There is an underground art museum where three wooden crates of pre-Colombian pieces have already arrived. "I have several contacts," Furio says of his source for the artwork.

There is a rooftop terrace with a sweeping view of the ocean and of Isabela Island on the western horizon. And there will soon be a helipad, not far from the swimming pool, "so you can come in on your boat with the helicopter and then fly straight up here," Furio says. The clientele he's prepared for would just as soon not be bothered with the "hassle," as he puts it, of making their way up through the town. "That is not how people like this travel," he says. "They are accustomed to comfort. From the boat to here, that's what they want. If they want to see the town, they can go see the town, but that should be their choice."

The hotel has seventeen rooms for thirty-four guests at most.

Furio's staff—"Maids, cooks, bartenders, reception people, massage girls, everything"—will number forty-five. And they will all be kept busy by what Furio has no doubt will be a booked-up hotel from the first day it opens, which he hopes will be by the end of 2001.

Furio steps out onto the central lodge's rooftop terrace. The air is cool. The sounds of the forest—the insects and birds and the swish of the wind through the leaves of the trees—drift down from above, from the peaks to the east. Furio is flush with the mood of the moment. He is a philosopher, he says, even a poet, as much as he is a doctor and a hotelier. He has mused about many things, and right now he is considering the fate of such places as Bali, the Greek Islands, Belize, and, yes, the Galápagos. "In Europe, in the States, in the Caribbean," he says with a sigh, "you see everything being changed and destroyed. So fast."

Felipé Dégel appears, in case Furio needs something. The boss waves him away and continues his thought. "Here in these islands, things change not so much," he says, lighting a cigarette. "Especially up here."

He stops, leans on a rail, and looks out over the hillside that slopes to the sea. "I knew down there would become what it has," he says, tossing his head in the direction of Puerto Ayora. "But up here is still different."

Down there, in the harbor, the empress of the Galápagos tour fleet sits at anchor. White as milk from bow to stern, it's as long as a football field and tall as a six-story building, with a warshiplike array of radar beacons and antennae on its top deck. It dwarfs the yachts and tour boats around it, boats like Bico Rosero's *Symbol*. It makes them look like mere toys. In every respect, with its piano lounge, five-level elevator, and VCRs in each room, the *Galápagos Explorer II* aims to impress.

And it does. Shoppers and strollers down by the waterfront stop and pull out their cameras. Sure, there are a few locals—like Christy Gallardo, for example—who turn their backs, even pull their windowshades at the sight of the thing. They look at that black smoke curling from the *Explorer*'s massive twin funnels, and they know full well it comes from the bunker fuel that feeds the ship's engines. They know that at night, while its passengers are sleeping and it moves in the dark from one island to the next, the *Explorer*'s crew sometimes dumps the waste from its toilets straight into the sea—or so some of the crew say.

But the tourists don't know this, or maybe they don't want to know. This is supposed to be a richer, more environmentally intimate experience than the traditional cruises vacationers book to the Greek Islands or the Bahamas or Alaska. This is ecotouring. Roughing it a bit. Hiking with backpacks and water bottles. Getting your feet wet when you climb from those wave-tossed dinghies onto the slick, shoreline rocks of these islands. Granted, if you're on the *Explorer*, you've got all the shipboard comforts you could desire. But it's an honest-to-god adventure you're getting here as well, communing with the plants, animals, and fish in this natural setting.

It's Felipé Dégel's job to see that the *Explorer*'s guests get it all— the roughness *and* the comfort. He's the ship's "expedition leader," the head honcho in charge of the *Explorer*'s battalion of guides. Right now his troops are ashore, shepherding their groups to the Research Station. After that, they'll stop at some shops, buy a few souvenirs, then maybe grab a bite or a drink at a restaurant.

The *Explorer*'s brochure, a glossy pamphlet filled with color photographs, features quite prominently the ship's many ameni- ties. Images of the islands and animals are almost an aside to the wide-angle shots of the vessel's lavish cabins, its sumptuous meals, its piano lounge's gleaming brass fittings, recessed lighting, and gold brocade curtains.

The *Explorer II* was built in Italy nine years ago for Mediter- ranean cruising, which it did until the company that owned it went bankrupt. Nearly two years ago, after the first *Explorer* ran aground at Wreck Bay, the Conodros corporation, the largest ecotour com- pany in Ecuador, leased this vessel and named it the *Explorer II*.

Conodros had already made somewhat of a name for itself back in 1996 by launching an "ecolodge" resort deep in the Amazonian rain forest in southeast Ecuador. The compound, called Kapawi—designed and built by the same architect who created Furio Valbonesi's place—was built with the agreement and cooperation of the local, indigenous Achuar Indian tribe, to whom ownership of the land and lodge will revert in 2011. Until then, for a fee of $2,000 a month, which Conodros pays the Achuars, the company is permitted to fly in up to forty tourists at a time—each paying Conodros $1,260 for a one-week stay.

The guests arrive in small planes at a private landing strip in the jungle. The lodge compound consists of twenty lushly furnished, thatch-roofed cabins built on stilts and overlooking a jungle lagoon. "Isolation from the rest of the world doesn't mean a lack of comfort," reads the company's brochure, "at least not in Kapawi." Each room has a private bath with electricity and a hot shower. Meals are served in an open-air veranda. The bar is open till midnight. Canoe trips and hikes are led by Achuar guides, accompanied by Ecuadorian translators, and include a visit to a nearby Achuar village, which has aroused some controversy among those who consider such activity an intrusion.

No such controversy exists here in the Galápagos. The *Explorer*'s guests expect the best, and they get it. They pay top dollar for the ship's choicest suites ($525 per person per night at the height of the season, which it is at the moment).

They are ferried ashore twice a day with military precision. The outboard launches that carry the guests in small groups to each island's landing site are code-named *Alpha* and *Delta* and are dispatched in half-hour intervals. Each morning, the *Alpha* groups hit the shore while the *Delta* groups tour the coastline from the water. In the afternoon, they rotate. "That way," explains one of the guides, "everybody gets to do both things, and it's not too crowded."

It's midafternoon now, and there's some commotion out on the deck. The *Explorer II*'s guests are returning from town, three *pangas* full, and the crew is taking their places to greet them—help them up the ladder, hose off their feet if need be, remove their life vests, and let them know dinner will be served at six.

"There are not that many people today," says a woman watching the guests climb aboard. She is young, in her twenties, short and stout with a tight ponytail. She wears an officer's uniform: white blouse, white shorts, white shoes. Her name is Camila Aroseména, the *Explorer*'s director of public relations.

"We have only twenty-three passengers right now," she says. "Friday we pick up ninety-one, a charter group of Americans. I think they are flying up from Easter Island."

About seventy percent of the *Explorer*'s business is American, says Camila. "Then comes probably the Germans," she says. "Then the Japanese and the Netherlands. And Switzerland. Switzerland is coming on strong." The average guest's age on this ship is about sixty, says Camila. "It makes sense," she says. "It is mostly older people who have the wealth."

The ship's crew, says Camila, numbers seventy, and all, like herself, are Ecuadorian. There is, she says, pressure to hire Galápagans. That was part of the deal when the boat was first brought here, she says. That's part of the deal with almost all business enterprises here on the islands—that jobs should be provided to locals whenever possible. But it's been tough, says Camila, who is from Guayaquil.

"The problem," she says, "is if people are not educated enough, it is difficult to do this work where you are dealing with tourists. So many people from the Galápagos hardly speak English and are culturally deprived. They haven't been exposed to the computer, to the Internet, to TV. These things are all new to them. I was born with these things. They were not."

The result is a caste system among the *Explorer*'s crew that literally follows the waterline: The higher one climbs on this vessel, the fewer Galápagan employees one finds. The men steering the ship's fleet of motor launches are almost all islanders. Down in the heat and grease of the engine room, a few local mechanics can be found as well. But up here on deck, except for the guides, everyone hails from Guayaquil, Cuenca, or Quito. The maids, the waiters, the cooks, the bartenders, the front desk staff, and of course, the ship's officers, are all from the mainland.

That's where Giovanni Celi, the *Explorer II*'s captain, is from.

Heads turn as he enters the dining room for dinner, and rightfully so. He's a dashing man, with a sly smile and a neatly trimmed, salt-and-pepper goatee. His uniform, with four bright gold braids on each sleeve, only makes him look more swashbuckling. It was, in fact, the sailor's uniform that first drew Celi to dream of the sea.

"From the time I was a boy, always I liked the uniform," he says, settling into his seat at the table of honor. Each evening, several of the *Explorer*'s passengers share their meal with the captain as guests at his table. This night, the chosen include Don and Abby, a husband and wife from Atlanta. Don's a pilot with Delta; Abby's an internist with the Centers for Disease Control. They're young for this crowd, in their thirties, newlyweds, married just nine months ago. They had planned to make this trip for their honeymoon, but the ship was in dry-dock at the time. "So we went to Tahiti," says Don. Now they're finally here, and they're loving it, says Abby. "He's the water guy, the diver," she says nodding at Don. "I'm the bird-watcher."

Don is peppering the captain with questions, which Celi gracefully answers as the waiters silently move among the tables, the silverware tinkles, and soft, piped-in music floats through the air.

"My father is from Florence," says the captain, explaining his surname. "But I was born and raised, like my mother, in Quito." He entered Ecuador's Naval Academy as a teen in the late '70s, then spent seventeen years in the merchant marines. "It is interesting," he says as the waiter removes his soup, "that most of the people in our country's navy come from the highlands, from the mountains, not from the coast. Highland people in Ecuador tend to obey more easily than those from the coast."

He now lives in Guayaquil with his third wife and children. "It is very difficult," he says, "for a seaman to keep a marriage. You are away so long." It was normal, says Celi, to be gone for more than two years at a time when he was sailing cargo and container ships around the globe. That's why he leaped at Conodros' offer in early 1998 to bring the *Explorer II* from Istanbul to the Galápagos and to stay on as its captain. "Now I am home much more often," he says.

But these past two years have been strange times in Ecuador, says Celi, both here in the islands and back on the mainland. "All the animals were dying when I came here," he says, "because of El Niño. Then came the crisis with the dollars. Then the volcanoes. And then this coup."

He shakes his head at the current state of his nation. "We never go all the way to the bottom because we are so rich in the things we have," he says. "In much of our country, you need an orange, you reach up and there is an orange. You put a hook in the water, there is a fish. So we do not really know what deprivation is."

He takes a bite of his salad. "But with people moving so much to the cities, we are learning. The people want what they see on TV. And they are angry when they don't have it."

What, asks Don, does the captain think can be done?

"Well," he says, "maybe something like how Pinochet did in Chile."

Don can't believe the captain has invoked a despot like Pinochet. But the captain is unruffled, dabbing his mouth with a napkin. "Look at Chile today." Celi smiles. "It is one of the best countries in South America. It is doing much better than Ecuador."

He leans back while the waiter sets down the main course. "Our democracy is not like your democracy. Sometimes"—he shrugs—"is necessary to die innocent people along with the guilty."

After dinner, the guests move to the bar or out onto the deck to look at the stars. Then they head to their staterooms and beds. While they are sleeping, the ship lifts its anchor and moves to the north side of the island, off a spot called Cerro Dragon. The next morning's 6:30 A.M. wake-up call comes in the form of gentle whale cries and dolphin trills drifting down from bedroom-wall-mounted speakers. Breakfast is a buffet, with a chef cooking custom-made omelets, and an array of every imaginable fresh fruit except for bananas piled high on the table beside him.

"I can't believe they are out of bananas," says a wife to her husband. "Out of bananas in Ecuador?"

Breakfast is brisk, then the guests file onto the deck, where they split off into small groups of seven or eight, each with a guide who helps them into their life jackets. Don and Abby's group includes a couple, Marcelle and Sibylle, from Luxembourg; a thirty-two-year-old financial consultant from Connecticut named Sylvia; and a seventy-four-year-old retired cardiologist from Pasadena, Robert Peck, who, with his wife Ruth, is making his second trip to the islands.

Dr. Peck has been all over the world, he says, but not as a typical traveler. He's more what one might call a witness to history. He went to Zimbabwe just after the revolt in Rhodesia. "It was wonderful," he says. "Uplifting." He visited Nicaragua when the Sandinistas finally, as he puts it, "had the contras on the run." He was in Berlin when the Wall came down—"to cheer them on."

"I'm a human liberationist," explains Peck. "I like to go where the fires are." He's been that way all his life, he says, from his days as a self-described leftist premed student at USC in the '40s ("We formed a club called We Are One, which allowed the only four Negro students on campus to have lunch on a regular basis with some good-hearted white kids"); to his stint in the '50s as a resident at the University of Chicago hospital, where he refused to sign a McCarthy-era "loyalty oath." In the '60s, he treated poor coal miners in West Virginia, spent the "Mississippi summer" of 1964 caring for poor blacks in that state, and worked with war-injured Vietnamese children toward the end of the decade. Even now, he's still active with Physicians for Social Responsibility, of which he's been a member since the group was started.

"I'm no utopian," he says. "But I do believe that every act we do, and everything we are as human beings, either makes things in this world better or worse." That's why, Peck explains, he has always vacationed as he does, either in a place where people are changing the world for what he believes is the better or in a place where man is dwarfed by the power of nature and time.

"To go someplace and get away from the technology, from the settings of our modern lives, and just feel the magnificence of the Sierras, or share the reverence of a Navajo guide or an old Hopi woman, to be in touch with the ancestry and eternal flow of man and nature," he says. "There's nothing that compares to that kind of experience."

That, says Dr. Peck, is what's great about the Galápagos. "It's a natural. Darwin. The theory of evolution. The sense of time before time. It's a powerful place."

It's time now to go ashore. Don and Abby's group's guide, an elfish young woman named Colette, ushers them into a dinghy and in a matter of minutes they're on land, following Colette up a narrow trail that winds through cactus and shrubs to a muddy lagoon. Don has his video camera out, taping the scenery with a running commentary of jokes and asides.

"Shh," says Colette, stopping and pointing. There, halfway out in the broad, shallow pond, stands a flamingo.

"It's not very pink," says Marcelle.

"Like the ones in the zoo?" says Colette with a wink. "They feed carotene to the ones in the zoo, to bring out the pink."

The group moves on as Colette leads the way. While the guests all wear hiking boots or tennis shoes, Colette walks barefoot as she climbs over rocks and tree roots. "You get used to it," she says, giving Sibylle a hand up a steep section of stones.

Colette Moine is one of Puerto Ayora's more colorful residents, pedaling around town on her unicycle. She's got a tightrope as well, a trapeze, and a well-worn set of juggling pins, all from the two years she spent as a young teenager at a circus school in her native Paris. She left there eight years ago, at age fourteen, to join her father in Quito. Her parents had split up when Colette was two, and her father had moved to South America. Colette came to the Galápagos to stay six years ago, moving in with one of her father's three ex-wives. The woman, an Italian named Sylvana, ran a popular waterfront restaurant called The Four Lanterns. Colette worked there as a waitress, but soon found herself managing the place when Sylvana suddenly took off for Tahiti.

"'Good-bye, I'm going.' Just like that, I was in charge," says Colette with a heavy French accent. "I was sixteen," she says, smiling and shaking her head. Since then the restaurant has closed, and Colette has become a certified naturalist guide and a dive master. Her friends are pushing her to become the Galápagos' first female tour boat captain, but she's not sure if she's ready for that, at least not yet. "I'd like to get on a sailing boat—the right boat," she says, "and go anywhere in the world and see what's happening."

At the moment, however, Colette is here, guiding the group up a bluff overlooking the sea. The view below broadens as the trail climbs higher. The ocean spreads out, bright-blue and sparkling. A dirt-orange land iguana the size of a terrier stands motionless under a tangle of brush. At an outcrop of rocks, the group takes a break, kicking back in the blaze of the midmorning sun. The coolness of the breeze on their sweat-soaked skin, the tweets and whistles of birds in the foliage around them, the soft whoosh of the surf far below: It's a transportive moment.

Until Don begins talking about the price he paid for a chateaubriand dinner with wine at a hotel in Quito. He wonders aloud if his and Abby's flight home on Friday will be leaving on time. When he asks if anyone here knows that David Letterman just had a heart attack the other day, Dr. Peck has finally had enough.

"Colette," the doctor says gently. "There's an old saying: Seize the day. Can we stop this talk about airplanes and schedules? Let's move back into this island."

And they do. Marcelle takes a hit in the arm from the thorns of a cactus. Dr. Peck struggles a bit with one of the trail's rockier stretches. But all in all, it's a magical morning. When the group gets back to the ship, lunch is ready, a lavish spread served outside by the pool.

That afternoon the group does Seymour Island, where the foliage is thick with a colony of male *fragatas* (frigate birds) displaying their lust-inflated, ruby-red throat sacs to the females soaring overhead. The boobies are here, too, doing their odd, little courtship dance among the low-lying shrubs and stones, oblivious to the camera-clicking humans.

The day winds down leisurely as smooth sets of translucent, green waves roll in from the west, backlit by the setting sun. Outlined against the flame-orange sunset are the rugged contours of Daphne Major, the island where Peter and Rosemary Grant are still at it after thirty years, continuing the ornithological research described in *The Beak of the Finch*. As a dinghy waits to return the group to the ship, Sibylle hangs back. Mesmerized by the vista from a cliff overlooking the waves, she's silhouetted by the last of the day's sunlight.

That evening, Dr. Peck and his wife join the group at the captain's table. The conversation wends its way to the captain's vision of his own future.

"My dream," he says, "is to have a sailboat and just go on it, go around the world, alone or with my son."

What about his wife? someone asks.

He frowns and shakes his head. "The woman on board is bad luck," he says. "The Greeks, if they had a woman on board, they would throw her over."

It's hard to tell if the captain is joking. No one presses the point. The evening moves on.

The next day the sun rises over Española Island, where the ship has now dropped anchor. The morning is spent in a motor launch, puttering along the island's wave-washed cliffs. Colette points out the bird life, the blood-red barnacles, and the bright-orange Sally Lightfoot crabs scuttling over the rocks. After lunch, the group goes ashore for a two-hour hike along the crests of those cliffs.

That evening, it's time for farewells. The ship's "master musician"—the same pianist tinkling Beatles tunes in the bar two nights earlier—plays "The Shadow of Your Smile" on the lounge's piano as the captain, flanked by Camila and the rest of the *Explorer's* officers in full dress uniforms, raises a toast to the guests.

"We salute you," he says.

The lights dim, the chairs and tables are pulled back, the disco ball in the ceiling starts spinning, and taped salsa music begins thumping from the room's speakers. But it's late. No one feels much like dancing. Camila and one of her shipmates give it a whirl, but within a half-hour the party is over and the room empties out. A half-hour later, the chairs and tables have been moved back into place, ready for the next day, when this load of passengers will check out and the charter tour of Americans will check in.

THIRTEEN

Cerrado

*Isla
Pinta*

MARCH 8, 2000

Wreck of the Jessica

The muffled heaves of a child's sobbing float through the warm evening air over the lantern-lit path from the Red Mangrove Inn. Polo Navarro is there, in the apartment above the hotel's lobby and bar, where he and his wife Monica and her three daughters make their home. But Monica's gone, flew out of Baltra this afternoon with a man named Ulysses, a young Venezuelan surfer Polo hired not long ago to help put up a "sports club" across the road from the hotel.

The club—the Mangrove Adventure, Polo calls it—is actually more of an open-air bar, with a durable pool table and a cooler stocked with sodas and beer. Candlelit tables and chairs sit under a thatch-roofed outdoor arbor. They rent surfboards and bicycles during the day to the tourists, and there's a tree-shaded racquetball court of sorts off to the side. So it's fair enough, the townspeople figure, to call it a sports club.

This time of night, there are typically at least a few people there. Polo is usually among them, wearing one of his bright, flowered tropical shirts unbuttoned to his belly to show off his tanned chest, whacking the pool balls around, laughing, listening to music, having a few beers. But tonight the place is empty, dark, and deserted.

It was only this morning that Monica stopped into the TAME ticket office down by the police station and booked two seats on the day's second flight to the mainland. By the time the plane lifted off, the entire town knew Monica was on it with her lover, Ulysses, headed for Guayaquil and . . . well, who knows what their plans will be after that.

Some saw this coming. After all, hasn't Monica had a history with this sort of thing? Three daughters by three different fathers. Her first girl, the nineteen-year-old, she had with that guy Norman, a languid character who lay around in his hammock nine or ten hours a day. People still laugh about the day Monica finally got fed up with Norman's routine, marched right out with a large kitchen knife and cut the thing down, with Norman asleep in it. Then came the musician from Boston, with whom Monica had her second daughter, who's now fourteen. And then there came Polo, with two kids of his own from a previous marriage, who now live in the United States with their mother.

Lest anyone be too quick to judge Monica for leaving, the fact is that Polo has been no more faithful than she. Neither has he been gentler: Monica has had to explain away the occasional black eye or bruise during the years they've been married. She and Polo have one child together, who turned seven not long ago. It's she, the seven-year-old, who is up there in the bedroom above the hotel crying so deeply because there are no words to console her, no way to explain why her mother has left.

Down the road, in town, where the bars and restaurants are busy on this early March evening, a squad of camo-uniformed police officers, a half dozen of them led by a baseball-capped lieutenant, is sweeping in and out of each nightclub, checking the passports and papers of the people inside. They are checking the patrons as well as the employees, spot-checking for undocumented nationals—Ecuadorians without IDs or papers. It's the authorities' way of sending the message that the laws will be enforced here in the Galápagos—at least some of them. They already shut down one business about an hour ago, the Galápason, and no one knows when it will reopen. The CERRADO sign hung on the club's padlocked front gate doesn't say.

Farther downtown, a few blocks from the waterfront, a crowd is gathered outside the Hotel Palmeras. No police are in sight. And they won't be, not tonight, not tomorrow, not as long as the mayor's family is running the place.

The crowd is waiting to get inside. You can hear it out on the street, a vibrant hum filling the stairwell inside the front doors, rising from the building's basement, where the El Bucanero gambling casino is now open for business.

A large, bearded man wearing a red soccer jersey, baggy swim trunks, and flip-flops stands outside the front door, looking like a bouncer. His name is Luis Solis Macias, but most people in town call him Galaxy. Or so he says. He points to the sign hanging over his head, over the hotel's front door, with a bearded pirate and the words "El Bucanero" drawn on it.

"I did that," he says. That's what Galaxy does for a living, he says. He paints signs. "Is like a Las Vegas," he says, sweeping an arm toward the commotion inside. "You like?"

Galaxy shows the way downstairs, where a bank of five glittering slot machines leads into a brightly lit, cavernous room festooned with twinkling Christmas lights. Japanese lanterns and ornate Asian fans are displayed on the high, whitewashed walls. A crowd is standing three-deep at the green-felt poker table, where the game is five-card stud and the minimum bet is 20,000 *sucres* (eighty cents).

The roulette and blackjack tables are even busier, with waitresses in white blouses and black miniskirts fetching mixed drinks and fresh packs of cigarettes for the players. Behind the metal bars of the cashier's cage in the corner, a redheaded woman hands out cups of slot-machine tokens and poker chips to a line of men waiting for their turn to play. Above the din, out of stereo speakers mounted up near the ceiling, drifts the sound of a love song—the theme from *Titanic*.

"Here you are, my friend, please," says a small Korean man, holding out a glass of iced Coca-Cola. "Free, for you."

The man is the casino's manager and part-owner, which explains the décor on the walls. The mayor's connection to this business is unclear. The Korean man shrugs and won't answer when asked. He just smiles and asks if you'd like a refill on your Coke.

Winter is winding down, spring is coming on, and *Carnaval* has arrived with its tradition of soaking passersby with buckets or jugs of cold water. The locals all know at this time of year that they're in for it if they venture outside during the day. They take the precaution of wrapping some plastic around anything they don't want to get wet. They walk the backstreets, avoiding the busier thoroughfares, where the kids and teenagers lie in wait to ambush their prey.

The tourists are the primary victims of the dousings, which have taken a nasty turn in recent years. Used motor oil and sacks of flour are dumped on the unsuspecting pedestrians, as well as on their cameras and belongings. Still, things are not nearly as vicious here as they are on the mainland. Walk down the wrong street in Guayaquil during *Carnaval*, and you're apt to get battery acid thrown at you. Or a bucket of urine. Or worse.

The mainland is in a state of suspension right now, with the *Indios* maintaining their threats to Noboa, and Noboa still pushing ahead with the dollarization, although it's become clear after a mere six weeks in office that he's no trailblazer. He's just an interim figurehead, a bridge between the coup two months ago and the next presidential election two years from now. Noboa's always been a survivor, and that's what he aims most to do between now and that next election—survive.

But it won't be easy. The political stakes are rising each day. Not only are the *Indios* continuing to turn up the heat, but the Colombians are pushing to force Noboa's hand as well. Everyone knows it was the Colombians who were behind the mail bomb that blew up two weeks ago in the office of a Guayaquil newspaper reporter and former politician named Rafael Cuesta. A group calling itself the People's Liberation Army claimed credit for the bombing, which sent Cuesta to the hospital with face and hand wounds. The group says it's Marxist, says it's Ecuadorian, but the leaflets it mailed out following the incident read like a laundry list of the Colombians' agenda, with a pointedly anti-American tone. *"No U.S. citizens can circulate quietly in the country,"* the leaflets proclaimed. The U.S. Embassy in Quito has responded by issuing yet another warning to American travelers to stay clear of Ecuador.

That's put a bit of a damper on tourism in Quito and in the Amazon, but oddly enough numbers are up around the Tungurahua volcano—"Little Hell," as the people who live in its shadow call it—which has been erupting for weeks now, prompting an entirely new tourist market. Even as thousands of Ecuadorians who live in the volcano's shadow have been evacuated, hundreds of foreign visitors have arrived to hike up the mountain and even camp overnight on its slopes. Tour companies are now packaging trips to the craters of Cotopaxi and Chimborazo as well. "A whole volcano industry appears to be developing," one newspaper recently reported, quoting a Quito tour agency selling the Tungurahua climbs. "It's a pure adrenaline experience," said the agency's spokesman, "to feel the earth rumbling and hear rocks falling down the sides of the ravines."

No matter that the Ecuadorian government is advising all travelers to beware in this region, warning that they might be killed on the slopes by rock slides, lava, or raining debris. Despite the danger—or because of it—business is booming.

It's booming in the Galápagos as well. Academy Bay is packed as the tourist season peaks with this first week of March. The boats anchored out in the harbor are almost completely booked. There are more private yachts passing through than have been seen since last spring. And more tour boats as well—ninety at last count.

Just this morning one of the newer ones pulled in, a gleaming 210-footer with three eggshell-white decks stacked like a sandwich on its navy-blue hull. The *Eclipse* is its name. On board is the American movie star Michael Douglas with his partner, Catherine Zeta-Jones, who is seven months pregnant. They were in town this morning, hiking up Darwin Avenue just like any other tourists. There was no mob scene, just a couple of nervous requests for autographs from a group of Americans. When the pair got to the Station, Roz Cameron gave them a personal tour. They were both "lovely people," says Roz. "Very pleasant, very down-to-earth. She didn't even bother with makeup."

At this peak-season time of year, a boat like the *Eclipse* charges each of its forty-eight passengers between $3,890 and $4,475 for a six-day stay in one of its twenty-seven cabins. It's that kind of cash that Braden Escobar—who's still running his hunting expeditions in defiance of the Park Service—will tell you is behind everything that is happening in the Galápagos these days. Everything.

The hammer finally came down on Escobar just one week ago. He arrived in Puerto Ayora on a morning flight from Quito with a couple of American customers, a husband and wife named MacCollum from Phoenix. The husband was a surgeon in his late sixties. He'd been to Africa a half-dozen times, and he'd hunted in Mongolia, and Spain. But this was his first trip to the Galápagos. He'd read about it in *The Hunting Report* and booked this vacation for himself and his wife.

The day they arrived, the doctor, his wife, Escobar, and a few local men took off in a boat for the northeastern part of the island. After a morning of shooting they headed back toward town for some lunch. Halfway there, they were stopped by a boat carrying Park Service wardens and Ecuadorian naval personnel. The doctor thought it strange that Escobar and the others scrambled to stow their rifles and spearguns as the government speedboat approached. And he was a little upset when the wardens asked to see his and his wife's papers right there on the boat.

But what really aggravated the doctor was when he and his wife got into town and were taken, albeit politely, to the Naval Station down near the wharf, where their bags and equipment were searched. By then the doctor was wondering if this Escobar fellow was on the up-and-up. When the authorities let the doctor and his wife go back to their hotel—although they held on to the doctor's rifle for the night—the couple noticed that Escobar wasn't released. He was under arrest. Or so it appeared.

"It *felt* like an arrest," says Escobar. "Actually, I was just detained by the navy. They put me in a room, but after they saw I was no criminal, I just hung around outside and slept on the beach." He's not apologetic at all. And he's not afraid of the Park Service or their laws. "If we want to get nasty," he says, "I could tell you some stinking shit about Eliecer Cruz."

Escobar doesn't say what that "shit" might be. He's happy to talk about his agribusiness degree from Louisiana State University, about his childhood in New Orleans, where he was born, and about Ecuador, where he's spent most of his twenty-seven years and where he makes his home today. He's eager to describe his outfitting business, the hunting and fishing tours he leads on the mainland. And he'll tell you that his motivation to start such tours in the Galápagos is "with the sincerity of wanting to help." Help the local people who need jobs and money, he says. Help get rid of those goats and wild pigs that breed in the highlands like rats. But he also admits he's in this to make money.

"The Galápagos isn't what people make it out to be," says Escobar. "All this stuff about saving the animals, that's bullshit. It's all about money. The big boats, the tour companies, the Park Service. It's a moneymaking machine, that's what it is."

His overnight stay—call it an arrest or a detention—doesn't deter Escobar one bit. He says he was "set up" by Cruz and his people, by Johannah Barry and those bleeding-heart conservationists with the Darwin Foundation. "She called me herself and pretended she was a tour operator wanting to get her clients lined up with me," he says. "I had no idea it was a trap." Barry says that's ridiculous, but Escobar insists that it's so.

Cruz has warned Escobar and hopes that will be enough. Cruz doesn't need the hassle of a full-scale arrest any more than Escobar does. The Park Service has much bigger fish to fry. But Escobar says he has no intention of stopping, no matter what Eliecer Cruz does.

"He can throw me in jail as many times as he wants," says the young businessman, "and I'll keep going."

And so comes the spring. March turns to April, and finally Jack Nelson returns home from Thailand—alone, without Forrest.

Jack had thought this might happen. He knew before going that the old man had no desire to leave Chiang Mai, even though he could hardly stand anymore because of the arthritis riddling his knees. But Jack had hoped he might be able to convince his father to face the facts once Jack arrived, to acknowledge that both Ken Calfee and Forrest were close to the point where they could no longer care for themselves. As Forrest himself put it more than once in recent conversations with Jack: "The only problem with living so long is you get so damned old."

This was the third time Jack had visited his father since the old man had moved to Chiang Mai, but this was the first for the purpose of bringing him back to the islands. When Jack got there, however, and saw once again the life his father had carved out, the same kind

of charming, idyllic retreat Forrest had created with the Hotel Galápagos so many years ago, Jack could see it wasn't going to be easy to
pry the old man away. One look at the flower-festooned compound
Forrest and Ken had built on their own *rai* of land—a small, tree-
shaded estate 120 feet on each side, each man with his own deck-
rimmed geodesic home linked by a common veranda, with ferns and
hibiscus and a private fishpond out back, and even an in-ground
swimming pool, where the Thai kids from the orphanage two doors
down came every day to the delight of both Forrest and Ken—one
look at all this, and anyone could see Forrest Nelson had found just
what he was looking for when he'd fled the Galápagos fifteen years
ago. Books, music (Ken had his own radio program on a local Thai
station, playing Beethoven and Bach CDs one hour a week), and a
circle of friends, most of them female; young, neighborhood women
who would visit with Ken and Forrest each day, sharing food, drinks,
and laughter. Who in his right mind would leave something like that?

Not Forrest. Jack made the most of the visit. He saw a bit of Chiang
Mai, enjoyed the time with his father, then flew back to the islands
knowing chances were good that it wouldn't be long before he'd have
to make this same trip again, under less pleasant circumstances.

Meanwhile, the Galápagos are changing at warp speed. In late
March, while Jack was making his journey to Thailand, Margaret
Wittmer passed away. Not long after that, Steve Divine flew his
mother, Doris, to Guayaquil, where she moved in with some
friends while Steve and his wife and kids prepared to make that
move to the United States—not to Arkansas, after all, but to Plantation, Florida, near Fort Lauderdale.

By late spring there are BellSouth pay phones along Darwin
Avenue, an oddity that puzzles more than a few townspeople.
Many have never seen such machines, and the phones take only
U.S. quarters, not *sucres*. There are now cell phones as well, with a
new satellite linkup activated just for the Galápagos. Some guides
have taken to carrying the cellular phones with them on boat tours
to keep track of families and friends back in town. The tourists are
discouraged from using theirs, though a few can't resist, checking

their voice mail back home in Munich or Montreal while riding one of those *pangas* to shore.

Out in Academy Bay, visiting yachtsmen are facing an odd little crime wave: the theft of their anchors. Eight yachts have had anchors stolen in the past two weeks. Word is spreading among traveling boatsmen to keep someone on watch if they visit this port or to simply steer clear of the Galápagos altogether.

The town has a new mayor. Franklin Sevilla was defeated in April's election by a man named Alfredo Ortiz. There's actually hope that Ortiz, a fairly sensible sort who may actually have the balls to stand up to the fishermen, might turn a few things around.

Fanny Uribe, meanwhile, kept her congressional seat. There's a new port captain now, who's been handing out fishing permits and tour-boat licenses as if they were candy. Jack's convinced the guy's either corrupt or "just doesn't give a shit." Either way, the "pickle-heads," as the *pepiñeros* have come to be called, are having their way. And still they want more, threatening each day to take drastic action if the gates to the cucumbers—and the sharks, and the lobsters—aren't thrown wide open.

In late May the government-sanctioned *pepino* season begins. Within five weeks six divers are dead and dozens more are permanently disabled by decompression accidents.

In mid-July comes word that Ken Calfee has passed away. Forrest is in emotional shock when Jack speaks to him on the phone. The old man is fuzzy about the facts, but apparently he and Ken had a group of friends over and were getting ready to go out. Ken went to lie down for a few minutes to rest. When Forrest checked on him, Ken was sprawled out on the floor in his bedroom.

From that point on, Forrest's story gets disjointed. All Christy and Jack know is that Ken was cremated a few days ago, his ashes scattered on Chiang Mai's Ping River. Now Forrest is all by himself, with only a Burmese woman named Pin to care for him. Pin has worked for Ken and Forrest for ten years now, riding through the city each morning on the motorbike Forrest bought her. She comes at dawn, sweeps the yard, cleans the house, runs errands, and cooks before leaving each afternoon to go home and tend the bar her family runs in the house where she lives. Pin has been like a niece to Forrest, and now she's all he's got left in Chiang Mai. Still, he won't even talk to Christy or Jack about the idea of leaving.

Not until August, that is, when Jack gets a late-night message from Thailand, from a friend of Forrest's, a New Zealander, who tells Jack that Forrest is in the hospital. It seems he slipped in the bathroom, fell and broke his pelvis, cracked it almost clean through.

Five days later, Jack is at Forrest's hospital bedside, setting up a couch right there in the room. He sleeps there for the next five nights, watching the Thai nurses and attendants lift his father—who's near-delerious, wearing diapers, unable to even roll onto his side—in and out of the bed like a large sack of rice. Forrest can't stand it, the helplessness. But it's going to be this way from now on. If he's able to stand on his own legs again, it will be with the help of a cane or crutches or a chrome walker.

Now there's no question Forrest will come home with Jack, whether the old man likes it or not. It takes two weeks after Forrest is released from the hospital to pull things together in Chiang Mai, to gather Forrest's essential belongings and see that everything else will be taken care of. Then it's on to Bangkok, where Jack learns Forrest's U.S. visa has expired (he took Ecuadorian citizenship back in 1969). Father and son check into a Bangkok hotel where they stay for three days while Jack wrangles with government officials. Three times a day he wheels Forrest down to the hotel's dining room for his meals.

By the time Forrest's papers are ready, it's September. The journey back home goes smoothly, except for a stop in Costa Rica where the plane is refueled, new passengers come aboard, and Forrest's wheelchair is thrown off. The weight of the archaic Russian-made chair, airline officials explain to Jack, is too much for the aircraft to safely take off.

When they finally arrive home in mid-September, Christy has set up a room behind her own house for Forrest, a studio apartment where Corina stays when she visits. The place is quite spacious, with gleaming hardwood floors, high, expansive windows flooded with sunlight, and the emerald glow of the surrounding foliage. It's only a hundred yards or so up the road to the hotel, where Forrest will now take his meals every day. But the only way to get there, until his new wheelchair, bought during their stopover in Guayaquil, is assembled by Jack, is by taxi. Three times a day by cab, seventy-five cents each way: That's almost five dollars a day, complains Forrest. Unbelievable, he tells Jack. That's a hundred and fifty dollars a month.

That *is* a lot of money just to get back and forth for such a short distance for something to eat. But the money doesn't bother Jack half as much as hearing about it over and over and over. Then again, Jack knows what's going on. The old man repeats himself now. He's straight on some memories, completely lost about others. He knows where he is, how much things have changed in this town, on these islands. But it all kind of hovers around him, a bit cloudy, like vapors that don't seem quite real. And so Forrest doesn't quite feel it, the sharp sting of just how different this place is from the small, sleepy settlement where he lived a half-century ago.

By October, the refitted wheelchair is ready to roll, and now three times a day Forrest greets his "pusher" at the apartment's front door—one of the young Ecuadorian men on Jack's hotel staff who comes over and rolls Forrest to and from the dining room at mealtimes. Forrest chuckles at the term "pusher"; he came up with it himself.

The guests at the hotel's dining room tables, tourists studying their guidebooks while they're eating their food, have no idea the old man sitting over there by himself with that thistle of soft, white hair, that delicate, pink skin, and those amazing blue eyes is the person who built this place half a lifetime ago.

November arrives, and on a bright Friday morning in the middle of the month, Christy rushes up the stairs to the small office above the Bodega Blanca, sits down at José's computer, and types out an e-mail dispatch to a long list of addresses all over the world:

From: Christy Gallardo
Sent: Friday, November 17, 2000, 10:15 a.m.
Subject: Disaster in Galapagos

Dear Friends of Galapagos:

Today we have the worst news of years, for both obvious and more subtle reasons. The "fishermen" in Isabela are "protesting" limits on lobster fishing in the same way as they did against limits on sea cucumber fishing, plus other matters they do not agree with. They have destroyed both National Park and Darwin Station offices, cars, equipment, records, removed all the tortoises (we don't know to where) from the Centro de Crianza (tortoise raising center), and even rammed dinghies full of tourists to prevent landings (so far as I know, no injuries). Of course, the State Department has already been informed and will undoubtedly issue a travel advisory against any Americans coming here, which affects absolutely everybody EXCEPT the fishermen, including all conservation projects (because the funding disappears almost immediately). My news is only a couple of hours old, at most, so I will try to revise as more comes in, and I cannot yet guarantee all details, but I will.

In the long term, I would say the effects are even worse than they first appear. If the President of the Republic himself is not willing and able, at this point, to send in the troops to haul these criminals off to the continent and pitch them in the pens, it will be yet another lesson to them, one in a long line of EXACTLY the same lessons, that they can get whatever they want by acting against the law. There is nobody left at a lower level, UNLESS IT IS THE INTERNATIONAL COMMUNITY, who can undo these lessons because all other authorities right up to his level are heavily compromised by the industrial fishing sector. The local authorities—our own mayor, our own deputies to con-

*gress—have fishing boats and march and protest right along
with the fishermen, supporting them in EVERY way, right
up to using the trucks of the municipality to block the
roads. If any among you know of anyone at all who might
raise his voice—in the newspapers or anyplace else, be my
guest. Tourism, and our own business, will be shot regard-
less, so I am only hoping to see some radical action which
will be a help five or ten years down the line. I only have
another hour now before we close the store so our family
and employees can go form up with the few others who
understand what is happening and have our own little
protest march, but it is useless. I cannot TELL you how
many of these bleeding marches I have participated in, and
the result so far has been DIDDLY SQUAT.
Sincerely Yours, Christy*

The protest march ends up canceled. Those who planned to take
part have been threatened, even a group of schoolchildren who
wrote a letter to Ecuador's minister of the environment criticizing
the fishermen. The children were promptly denounced as "puppets
of the scientists and conservationists" by none other than the
Galápagos' provincial director of education, one Clemente Vallejo
Velasco, who demanded that the names of all teachers involved be
turned in to him. The next morning, Christy types out yet another
dispatch.

*From: Christy Gallardo
Sent: Saturday, November 18, 2000, 9:43 a.m.
Subject: Update*

Dear Friends of Galapagos:

*Yesterday I promised to update you all. So here it is, and it
is only worse. The terrorism in Isabela yesterday took place
mostly around midnight. The marines were flown in to
Isabela, but did not arrive until about 4 am, too late. And,*

of course, they are only there to prevent further obvious depredations, but no arrests so far as I know, by the police or anybody else. The damage was far more extensive than I had thought—even the private homes of the directors of park and station operations were totally destroyed, right down to breaking up the toilets and burning all their clothes and distributing the Christmas presents (that were stored in one of their homes) to everybody in the streets. The Park sent a couple of boats over there to rescue their employees, and this was totally necessary—they had been hiding in the mangroves and actually had to swim out to the boats. In other places, including at Hood, divers and tourists have been prevented from landing or leaving their boats by the flotillas of terrorist-"fishermen." I still have no reports of injuries. We are without regular phone connection to the mainland because the repeater on Cristobal has been damaged, so the cell phones are in heavy use. Here on Santa Cruz we have escaped the worst of it because we have the largest population, outnumbering the "fishermen" by far, and also larger numbers of police and navy and so on. Still, it has not been pretty. I have no idea whether anything will be done to the perpetrators of all this, but the track record indicates that it will NOT. We have not seen the last of it. I will keep you all posted, if I can. Please pass it on. Christy

None of this surprises Jack. He's watched the number of licensed fishermen in San Cristobal and Villamil nearly double in the past year—from 500 to over 900—courtesy of the new regime of local authorities. The fishermen—many of them recent arrivals from tough towns on the mainland coast—feel the strength of their numbers and have become more aggressive than ever. "Storm troopers," Jack calls them. They've never directly threatened tourists before, but tour *pangas* were actually rammed during this Isabela attack, with Ecuadorian naval personnel firing tear gas to push the protesters back. A ramming even took place here in Acad-

emy Bay, an assault described in a report sent to the Galápagos
Tour Operators Association by a tour group from Ithaca College:

> *A group of 11 tourists and 2 crew left our boat on our panga to*
> *go to the Darwin Station to see giant tortoises, the Station, and*
> *then take a bus trip into the highlands. But that was the morn-*
> *ing the local fishermen went on strike. A fast motorboat of 4 or*
> *5 fishermen then swooped over to cut us off, partially rammed*
> *us (side-swiped us with a hard hit), and grabbed the rope of our*
> *panga to pull us over to a place along the shore where they*
> *wanted to take us. Our boatman realized what was happening*
> *and reversed the outboard motor enough for us to pull the rope*
> *free, leaving a fisherman with rope burns. We quickly pulled in*
> *the rope, turned around, and returned to our boat midst lots of*
> *yelling in Spanish.*

Local civic leaders brave enough to raise their voices against
these "lobster mobsters," as some townspeople have taken to calling the fishermen and the professional thugs brought in by the fishing companies in Manta to support them, have received death
threats. As Thanksgiving passes and the month comes to an end,
the renegade fishermen are enjoying their celebrity. They've
become front-page news as far away as Great Britain. At least four
of them were captured clearly on videotape burning and looting
Park and Research Station property in Villamil. Thirteen arrest
warrants were issued based on witness reports and photographic
evidence. But only one arrest has actually been made. In fact, the
government's response, rather than prosecution, has been appease-
ment: The lobster season has now been extended through the end
of the year, and catch limits have been raised.

As Christmas approaches, word comes from the United States
that reinforcements are about to arrive, the ecocavalry, as it were,
riding down to the rescue.

The Sea Shepherd, it seems, is now on its way.

Godfrey Merlen's been working on this for some years now, quietly,
behind the scenes. For nearly a decade, he and another longtime

scientist with the Station, an Englishman named David Day, have been exchanging letters and e-mails with a Canadian named Paul Watson, founder and director of the Sea Shepherd Conservation Society, the oceangoing vigilantes famous for ramming and sinking illegal fishing vessels all over the globe. Godfrey and Day, along with Eliecer Cruz and his Park Service staff, have been exploring the possibility of bringing what Eliecer calls "an international voice" to the Park Service's battle with the islands' illegal fishing fleet.

Godfrey has known all along that it's a dicey decision asking a man like Paul Watson to come help the Galápagos. On the one hand, Watson is not unlike Godfrey himself—a creature of action, impatient with words. Anyone with even a passing interest in the history of environmental activism knows Paul Watson cofounded the Greenpeace organization in 1972, then quit five years later because the group had become too bureaucratically meek for his taste—"Avon ladies of the environmental movement," is what he called them—Watson subsequently turned to the ocean, creating the Sea Shepherd in his own image with a hell-bent-for-leather, ecovolunteer crew of bearded young men and braided young women. They took an overhauled fishing trawler, rechristened it the *Rainbow Warrior,* and began going *mano a mano* against the world's pirate industrial fisheries.

The Sea Shepherd's motto, printed on T-shirts its crew passes out wherever they drop anchor, is "Sailing Into Harm's Way." This is all well and good, but this cottage-industry kind of success and the massive celebrity that comes with it worry some here on the islands. Wherever Watson goes, the press follows, and frankly he loves it—some say a little too much. Just last year *Time* magazine declared Paul Watson an environmental hero of the twentieth century. Just last month, it was announced that Paramount Studios will begin production this summer on a $60-million film about Watson and the Sea Shepherd, starring Billy Bob Thornton, Aidan Quinn, and Paul Watson's real-life pals, Martin Sheen and Pierce Brosnan. Rumor has it that Quinn, in the name of research, is at this very moment aboard the Sea Shepherd vessel *Sirenian,* bound for the Galápagos with Watson and a volunteer crew.

Four days before Christmas, the ninety-five-foot *Sirenian*, with a nine-member crew aboard, pulls into Puerto Ayora, dropping anchor in Academy Bay not far from the Park Service patrol boat, the *Guadalupe River*, just off the point where the Hotel Galápagos sits. Aidan Quinn is indeed aboard, but he jets off immediately upon arrival. Paul Watson, however, hangs around town for three weeks, doing some diving with Matías' Scuba Iguana staff and spending a few nights holding court at the newest hot spot in town, a place called the Bongo Bar, up a flight of stairs from the Panga Discoteca. When Watson takes off in mid-January, he leaves behind the ship and one crew member and an autographed photo of himself for the Bongo Bar's owners to hang on their wall.

The crew member's name is Sean O'Hearn Giminez, a twenty-seven-year-old Sea Shepherd volunteer and former Wall Street computer engineer from Brooklyn. O'Hearn looks fittingly Irish: pale skin burned bright pink by the sun, close-cut coppery hair. But he speaks fluent Spanish—with a Caribbean lilt, no less—thanks to a childhood spent in Puerto Rico. "Deception by perception," he says, introducing himself with a well-practiced smile.

For the next God-knows-how-many months, O'Hearn will be the face and voice of the Sea Shepherd Society in the Galápagos. The arrangement hammered out with Eliecer Cruz and the Ecuadorian government is that the *Sirenian* will be "loaned" to the Park Service for five years. It will be manned by a Park Service crew, with Ecuadorian naval personnel aboard, and with O'Hearn riding along as an "objective observer" (O'Hearn's term). The idea is to raise the ante in this war with the poachers, adding muscle to the Park Service resources—a speedy, agile patrol boat—as well as providing the international spotlight that follows the Sea Shepherd Society wherever it goes. O'Hearn is poised to tap out a slew of e-mail press releases following each raid and capture.

It's a nice concept, but O'Hearn and, from a distance, his boss Watson soon learn it won't be quite that easy. The Park Service may want the Sea Shepherd here, but the powers-that-be on the mainland—government officials with ties to the fishing magnates in Manta, even some of the top brass with the Ecuadorian Navy and the Merchant Marine themselves—are not so excited. They can't simply throw the foreign interlopers out; too many people are watching, and the Park Service is within its legal rights to bring the *Sirenian* here. But the authorities can certainly make things difficult for these outsiders.

Before the *Sirenian* is allowed out on patrol, it must be inspected by Ecuadorian naval officials. Is it any surprise that it flunks the initial inspection? Or that the ensuing paperwork takes weeks to process? And then comes another inspection, and another denial. There is no portable water pump to be found on the ship, although no one was told such a pump is required. The labels on the control panel are written in English, not Spanish, although again no one was told such translation is needed.

O'Hearn can see he's being sandbagged, and he's furious. As the days pass, he bides his time, handing out Sea Shepherd T-shirts all over town and hanging out at the Bongo Bar, where a Sea Shepherd videotape—provided by O'Hearn—has replaced the standard surf tapes as a favorite on the bar's TV sets. The video, titled "Blue Rage," mixes shots of ship-rammings with footage of extreme sports—snowboarding and surfing. The crowd—tourists and locals alike—loves it. O'Hearn is champing at the bit to get out and go hunting, but Watson's orders are to hang loose and sit tight, at least for the time being.

And then comes the spill.

The first message sputters across marine radio channels a few minutes past ten on the evening of Tuesday, January 16. An oil tanker, the *Jessica*, radios that it has run aground at the entry to San Cristobal's Wreck Bay, eight hundred yards off the island. The vessel, owned by an Ecuadorian shipping company called Acotramar, is carrying 160,000 gallons of diesel fuel bound for a dispatch station on Baltra, and 80,000 gallons of bunker fuel to be delivered to none other than the *Galapagos Explorer II*. The *Jessica* reports that it's grounded on a sandbar but that surf conditions are calm and that no oil has spilled. Not yet.

By Wednesday, the next morning, Cruz's Park Service people have begun arriving, intent on removing the fuel from the ship as swiftly as possible before a spill occurs. Ecuadorian Navy and Merchant Marine crews arrive as well, and it soon becomes clear that they're here at the behest of PetroEcuador, the state-owned oil company to which the fuel in that ship belongs. PetroEcuador is more concerned with salvaging its product by removing the fuel and oil slowly and carefully so it's not contaminated with seawater, than with protecting the surrounding waters and land from disaster.

It's clear to Cruz's people—more than sixty of them have arrived at the scene by late Thursday morning—that they're working at cross-purposes with the Ecuadorian military personnel. By Thursday afternoon, only 20,000 gallons of fuel have been removed from the ship and now, according to the latest weather reports, rough seas are on the way.

Meanwhile, the Ecuadorian Ministry for Environment and the U.S. Embassy in Quito are hammering out details to allow a U.S. Coast Guard oil-spill emergency strike-force team to come down from Mobile, Alabama, and join in the effort. But the talks are laborious, held up by protocol, politics, and, in no small measure on the part of the Ecuadorians, by pride.

Another day passes, and the *Jessica* begins listing. The surf becomes rougher. By the time the ten-member U.S. strike team gets the green light and arrives Friday with high-capacity pumps and inflatable oil-containment barges—state-of-the-art equipment compared with the Ecuadorians' improvised gear—the tanker's cargo hold has cracked open and thick ribbons of black, viscous bunker fuel have begun oozing out into the clear turquoise Pacific.

By then, Roz Cameron's office computer is clogged with more than one thousand e-mails, offers from volunteers all over the world to come help with the cleanup. Most of those well-meaning souls, says Roz, have no idea there are twenty thousand people who live on these islands, hundreds of whom are already preparing to fan out at various beaches, readying themselves to scoop and soak up whatever oil might come their way with buckets, towels, rags, whatever they can get their hands on.

Dozens of other islanders are already making their way over to San Cristobal, by boat or by air, to do what they can to help. Matías

Espinosa shuts down his dive shop to fly over on Saturday and can't believe what he sees as he looks down at the ocean between Santa Fé and San Cristobal: The glistening, crystal-blue water is laced by inky tendrils of oil snaking northwest, directly toward Santa Cruz, directly into the heart of the archipelago. A fuel tank split here, a faulty valve cracked open there; the *Jessica* is falling apart faster than the cleanup crews can surround it. It's a blessing the spill hasn't moved east into San Cristobal. That damage would be devastating, perhaps permanent. As it is, only a handful of sea lions, pelicans, and boobies around Wreck Bay have been hit by the oil, and Park Service staff have rescued and cleaned each one of those animals. But worse could lie ahead on the other islands, depending on where the currents and winds carry the spill.

Mathias has heard that there are already quite a few foreign newspaper and television reporters over at San Cristobal, but he's blown away when he actually gets there. He's seen plenty of press come through Puerto Ayora over the years—when a volcano blows or when the El Niños hit. He got a close look at a world-class film operation when the IMAX teams dug in to make their Galápagos movie, which features Mathias himself in one of the film's early sequences. But he's never seen anything like what confronts him when he lands at Puerto Baquerizo Moreno. Reporters are everywhere in the village, interviewing everyone. Cameras on tripods are set up along the length of the waterfront. Every person who passes—locals and tourists, adults and children—is stopped and asked to comment on the catastrophe.

Mathias is stopped by a film crew from *National Geographic.* He's struck by how long the reporter, a woman, takes to prepare her makeup before giving a nod to the cameraman and beginning the interview. This is an image that will stay with him forever. Here is this horrible catastrophe, just beyond this lady's shoulder, the ocean clouded black with a carpet of oil, and all she can think of is how her lipstick looks.

The whole scene is weird to Mathias. Puerto Baquerizo's little motels, so sleepy and empty most of the time, are booked solid right now, every one of them. And that's not nearly enough. Townspeople have taken to renting out rooms in their homes to reporters. Some of them are charging fifty dollars a night, and the reporters are gladly paying it. The reporters aren't footing these bills; their bosses are. The reporters' only concern is to get the story, to deliver the drama.

"IT IS AS IF A BOMB DESTROYED THE LOUVRE," reads a dispatch in a London newspaper.

"HOW COULD WE ALLOW BLACK TIDE TO THREATEN WORLD'S FRAGILE EDEN?" trumpets a front-page Scottish newspaper headline.

"BLACK DEATH THREATENS THE UNIQUE BEAUTY OF GALÁPAGOS' LABORATORY," declares a large Irish daily.

"GALÁPAGOS IN PERIL," says the *Chicago Tribune*.

"FOR HUMANITY, SAVE THE GALÁPAGOS FROM HUMANITY," writes the *Los Angeles Times*.

Some take a different spin on the story. A Galápagan fisherman named Washington Escarabay is described in a British newspaper as angry because the spill has kept him on dry land all week. Never mind the birds and the water, says Escarabay. What about people like him, people for whom this oil spill is just one more thing getting in the way of making a living?

Others tell the reporters this whole thing's been blown out of proportion. They point out that the *Jessica*'s load was—what?—a quarter million gallons or so of fuel and oil? That's nothing, they say, compared with the *Exxon Valdez*. Eleven million gallons, that's what the *Exxon Valdez* spilled up in Alaska. Now *that* was a disaster. This is what a vice admiral named Gonzalo Vega, the director of DIGMER (an acronym for Ecuador's merchant marines), tells the press as the weekend passes and the spill slowly spreads west from San Cristobal toward the other islands. This is not a big deal, insists Vega.

By now, details have emerged about the *Jessica*'s background. The thing is a rust bucket, a decrepit twenty-eight-year-old wreck of a ship, hardly seaworthy at all. Its deck is riddled with gaping holes. Many of its valves are so corroded they cannot be closed. Some of its cargo-tank hatch hinges are rusted so badly the covers break off when opened. As the surf pounds the ship and it continues to list, the sound of its bulkheads popping can be heard from the shore. The U.S. Coast Guard team is aghast at the shape this ship is in. When they ask how the thing passed inspection, they're told by sheepish Ecuadorian officials that the ship was not inspected at all. This was interesting for Sean O'Hearn to find out, considering that the *Sirenian* is still sitting at anchor in Academy Bay, awaiting permission from its inspectors to take to the seas.

The *Jessica* wasn't even supposed to make this trip. The tanker that normally carries these oil shipments was drydocked for emergency repairs, and the *Jessica* was hastily sent in her place. The *Jessica*'s captain, a fifty-eight-year-old Ecuadorian named Tarquino Arevalo, it turns out, is certified only for coastal shipping, not for the high seas. He and his thirteen-man crew are currently under arrest at the Puerto Baquerizo naval base. Arevalo has already admitted that this is his fault, that he mistook a signal buoy for a lighthouse and steered the ship straight toward a beacon intended to warn him away.

All these facts are reported by the international press, as well as investigations into the "cozy"—as one press report puts it—relationship between the Acotramar company, which owns the *Jessica*, and the Ecuadorian Navy department responsible for inspecting all ships in these waters. Allegations of corruption within Petro-Ecuador are being explored as well; charges that the company has been routinely shipping illegally resold oil (stolen fuel secretly transferred at sea under false documentation), including the very fuel spilled by the *Jessica*.

By Thursday the twenty-fifth, a week after the spill began, a good amount of the 180,000 gallons of fuel and oil in the water has been corralled by floating booms and barricades. But tens of thousands of gallons have escaped, reaching the beaches of Santa Fé and Floreana. Slick, black ribbons of fuel can be seen from the air snaking their way toward Santa Cruz.

Sean O'Hearn's been going nuts sitting tight with the *Sirenian*, so he's understandably excited when a call comes from the Ecuadorian authorities asking him if his ship could carry a group of dignitaries over to San Cristobal. O'Hearn's been dying to get to the scene of the spill, to do what he can to help out. But his excitement abates when he learns that the "dignitaries" are a group of local musicians hired to play at an annual municipal celebration in Puerto Baquerizo. Nevertheless, the *Sirenian* goes, and so this becomes the Sea Shepherd's first action in the Galápagos: ferrying a band to a street party.

The spill does eventually reach Santa Cruz, coming ashore at the beach at Tortuga, where several hundred townspeople line the shore, wielding towels, blankets, and shovels, chasing down the thick globs of oil as the waves carry the stuff in. The townspeople do a good job, but some of the mess still reaches the shore, where it will remain for years as black layers of goo buried beneath the beach's sugary white sand.

By the end of the month, the crisis has passed. The islands have been spared the brunt of the Rhode Island–sized spill by the currents and wind, which steered most of the oil out into open seas. The fierce equatorial sun helped as well, evaporating much of the diesel fuel as it floated on the surface. Visible damage to the animals and land is minimal, although it will take thirty more months, according to the Darwin Foundation, to complete the cleanup at a cost of about $1 million. As for the effect on the ecosystem of the untold amount of bunker fuel that has settled to the ocean floor in the shallows around the archipelago's islands, only time and long-term scientific study will tell.

Of immediate concern is some kind of assurance that this won't happen again. The Ecuadorian government has agreed to rewrite its regulations to require double hulls on all merchant ships entering Galápagos waters. Others say there should be no commercial vessels whatsoever allowed among these islands, a protest that has been heard since the Galápagos were first opened to tourism. This suggestion brings the same response it always has, that the Galápagos cannot survive in today's world without tourism.

An even more extreme suggestion, which has hovered for years in the background of the debate over how to protect the Galápagos, is to finally say "enough" to this negligence and corruption and to simply take the islands away from Ecuador altogether, to put them under a United Nations trusteeship whereby the Galápagos Islands would be managed and protected by all nations and owned outright by none.

Even those who embrace this idea know it is not realistic. Fundamental rights of national sovereignty would be violated. But the very fact that this concept is even discussed—in newspaper stories that quote outraged Darwin Research Station scientists who are, understandably, not identified by name—indicates the severity of the shock of this spill.

As the spill subsides, the *Jessica*'s captain, Arevalo—the only crew member still being detained—holds an emotional press conference and takes full responsibility for the worst man-made disaster in the history of these islands. "It was overconfidence on my part," he says, his eyes shining with tears. "I am completely to blame."

Shortly after the conference, Arevalo is taken to San Cristobal's naval base medical clinic, where he is treated for what a clinic spokesman calls "nerves." The spokesman tells the press that Arevalo is "psychologically not stable." At the same time, the merchant marine admiral, Vega, has grudgingly acknowledged the spill's severity and announces he is now pursuing criminal charges against the *Jessica*'s captain. If found guilty, Arevalo faces four to five years in prison.

As February begins and the oil disperses and the newspaper headlines abate, the Galápagos is left with a new tourist attraction: the hull of the sunken tanker, which cannot be moved. The wreck is already beginning to crust over with coral, attracting perching birds and schools of curious fish.

"Over time it will become a terrific place to dive," says Captain Edwin Stanton, the head of the U.S. Coast Guard response team.

"It's a new habitat," Stanton tells a room full of reporters. "We have a new island in the Galápagos," he says with a small smile. "Isla Jessica."

FOURTEEN

Grandeur

Isla Marchena

JUNE 3, 2001

Sea Shepherd volunteers Jennifer Jacquet and Sean O'Hearn with Park Service wardens and Ecuadorian naval officers aboard the Sirenian.

It's Sunday afternoon, and Darwin Avenue is sleepy, almost silent. Just yesterday the roadway was clogged curb to curb with men, women, and children laughing and shouting, waving Ecuadorian national flags. Some were dancing and leaping; others were piled atop the hoods of slow-moving cars and trucks. The drivers gleefully blasted their horns in rhythm to the passengers' chants of "Ecuador! Ecuador! Ecuador!" as an impromptu, half-mile-long parade snaked its way along the waterfront and up through the town.

Ecuador had just beaten Peru two to one in a World Cup qualifying match that meant much more to both nations than mere soccer. National pride, at a time when both countries have precious little to be proud of, was at stake here, the bragging rights between anciently combative neighbors. Only six years ago, these two countries were at war.

Just three weeks before the match, the coach of Ecuador's national team had been beaten and shot in a confrontation with four men in the lobby of Guayaquil's Hilton Colon Hotel. One of the attackers, Joseló Rodriguez, coaches Abdala Bucaram's overweight nineteen-year-old son, Dalo, in an Ecuadorian under-twenty-year-old junior soccer league. When selections were made earlier this year for the national team that would represent Ecuador in the under-twenty World Cup tournament in Argentina in July, Dalo was not chosen.

Apparently, it was time for the coach, Hernan Gomez, of the adult team to suffer for this slight. The coach, affectionately nick-named *"Bolillo"* ("Little Ball") by Ecuador's rabid fans, was pistol-whipped in the face and shot in his right thigh after emerging from a national soccer federation meeting in the Hilton. *El Loco*'s sister, Elsa, the former mayor of Guayaquil, who is now back home in Ecuador as a member of congress, had stood up at the soccer meeting and accused Hernan Gomez of being a cocaine addict. When the gathering adjourned, Gomez was assaulted in the lobby by Rodriguez and his friends.

Rodriguez was promptly arrested and admitted to "verbally accosting" the coach, but said he knew nothing of the shooting. A manhunt was launched for the actual gunman, one of Rodriguez's bodyguards. Meanwhile, the elder Bucaram, speaking to the press at his hotel asylum in Panama, denied any involvement. "This is something we all regret and condemn," said *El Loco.* "However, it's soccer, and people get excited and take revenge."

After the bullet was removed from Gomez's thigh and his shattered nose was reconstructed by plastic surgeons, the coach considered quitting and leaving the country. More than 10,000 fans, their faces painted red, blue, and yellow—Ecuador's national colors— marched through downtown Quito to protest the assault and persuade Gomez to stay. He did, and now in this first weekend in June, he was on the sidelines for the epochal victory over Peru.

Up at the Hotel Galápagos, Jack Nelson's office manager, Carlos Acosta, can hardly speak, his throat is so sore from screaming at the TV during the game. The lobby is empty at the moment, though dinnertime is approaching and soon the tables will fill. A group of Americans—led by Daniel Fitter, in fact—checked in this morning and will be staying the night.

Jack's got a few minutes to relax, to read through the e-mails he just downloaded from his office computer. There's a message from Christy, who is in New York for a quick layover before flying on to Portugal, then England. If her trip—this year's annual art excursion—had gone as planned, Christy would already be in Lisbon. But everything changed when Gayle Davis checked into a hospital in Quito last month. Only her closest friends knew it, but Gayle had been battling cancer for the past decade. By the time she flew to Quito for treatment in May, most of those friends knew she would most likely not be flying back. Christy put her vacation on hold so she could stay in Quito, where she remained for two weeks until this past Thursday, when Gayle drew her last breath. It hit Christy hard, another dear friend dying this way, just like Mary Fitter.

Jack's almost done leafing through his other messages when the lobby's front screen door opens and in steps Sean O'Hearn with a young woman. She is a college student from America named Jennifer Jacquet, who's volunteering for the summer with Sea Shepherd. The *Sirenian* is out on patrol at the moment, and O'Hearn is livid that he's not on it. The ship lifted anchor two nights ago, with last-minute orders from none other than Admiral Vega himself prohibiting O'Hearn from coming aboard. O'Hearn has been a thorn in Vega's side ever since early March, when the *Sirenian* was finally cleared to become the first foreign-flagged vessel to patrol the Galápagos Marine Reserve. O'Hearn's account of that initial patrol, sent by e-mail to Sea Shepherd's 25,000 members all over the world, as well as to media and government officials in Ecuador and the United States, gives a good idea why Admiral Vega is outraged:

Thursday, March 8, 2001

I arrived at Baltra Airport from Lima after having gone to the Ecuadorian Embassy in Peru for my diplomatic paperwork required to remain in Galápagos over an extended period of time. The Captain of the Sirenian *was there waiting to bring me to the ship. We had received permission from DIGMER to navigate the Marine Reserve of Galápagos after a two-month waiting period that involved a major bureaucracy-go-round. We set sail within hours and were on our way to Wolf Island in the northern regions of the Marine Reserve, where there had been reports of illegal activity. I stood on the bow of the* Sirenian *and thought, "This is what being a Sea Shepherd volunteer is all about."*

It did not take long. We were approximately 22 miles Northwest of Wolf, Lat 01° 13' 011" N Long 091° 18' 618" W, chasing a potential target on the radar about 15 miles from our current position. It was approaching 10:30 P.M. when we arrived to find out it was a dense low cloud. The crew's anticipation quickly subsided and I walked out onto the bridge wing for a quick breather. We turned port side when

I noticed a light in the distance in a 10 o'clock position to our bow. I ran back into the bridge and saw the target appear on the radar screen. I advised the wheelman of the potential target and we began to pursue.

I could see the port/starboard lights and knew the ship was facing us. We were also gaining on her so I knew that she was either stopped or heading toward us. We approached to within a mile when I saw only a starboard light and knew she was changing course and fleeing. "We got her now," I said, and instructed to increase speed.

We were now in full pursuit. It was a tuna fishing boat. There are many reports that tuna boats are involved in illegal shark finning. This was no local boat, either. We turned our sirens on and began approaching her from the starboard side. We got within loudspeaker distance, sirens blazing, and began shouting in Spanish over the PA system to stop engines. The naval officer was on the radio instructing the vessel that it was within the Marine Reserve of Galápagos and that he must stop engines for boarding.

The vessel was the **San Mateo** *out of Manta, Ecuador. It was caught traversing the Marine Reserve illegally. Fishing boats from Manta are notorious for illegal fishing within the Marine Reserve. According to the Special Law of Galápagos, all vessels entering the Marine Reserve must request permission to do so. That gave the National Park the authority to board, inspect, escort to nearest port, and, if necessary, fine. The* **San Mateo** *stopped all engines. We donned our bulletproof jackets and proceeded to board the vessel.*

We walked onto the bridge and the naval officer proceeded to check the vessel's papers. After I spoke with several crew members on the bridge and inspected the paperwork, I realized that it was a Spanish-owned ship and it was clear that the Spanish were financing the operation. There were also Spanish representatives on board. It was an Ecuadorian-registered vessel, but all the catch was going to Spain.

The Park rangers then proceeded to check the fishing log for any out-of-the-ordinary positions. Of course, there were no entries of fishing activity within the Reserve. We asked the captain if he was aware that he was within the Galápagos Marine Reserve. He claimed ignorance and showed us a nautical map that had a red zone marking the Marine Reserve but conveniently had a 30-mile radius (as opposed to the actual 40-mile zone) and also did not include the northern islands of Wolf and Darwin.

We proceeded to inspect the catch but the naval officer would not allow us to check all cargo and just wanted to spot-check the cargo. We disagreed and got them to check some additional cargo holds. Since the vessel was found within the Marine Reserve, under law we could escort the ship back to the nearest port for full inspection and possible fines and sanctions. We advised the captain and proceeded to return to the Sirenian. *What I did not understand is that no one stayed on board the* San Mateo. *I was told that the naval officer was always to remain on board. As I watched the* San Mateo *being escorted by the* Sirenian *with due course to the nearest port, I thought, "If I were them, I would get rid of any illegal catch on board now since no one is there to control the situation."*

I went to my bunk for a rest, but was shortly awakened abruptly and advised that we had a serious problem. It seemed the captain of the San Mateo *had had a change of heart and had decided that we had no authority to escort him to port and that he was going to change course for Manta, Ecuador.*

Our naval officer advised him that he would be in violation of the Special Law of Galápagos and the naval authority, and that we would be forced to intercept. We followed closely behind as the San Mateo *began to pick up speed. The* Sirenian *was (a lot) faster then the* San Mateo *and the captain soon found that out. He told us that he had called the owner's lawyer and the lawyer had advised him that* they had not broken any law and that they should proceed to Manta. The vessel changed course, defying our authority, and we pursued.

The naval officer called in to the naval port of Seymour explaining the situation and they advised him to stop the vessel at all costs and to shoot if necessary. They were even willing to send in their battleship from San Cristobal's naval base to assist us.

The ship suddenly began to slow down and the captain informed us that they had engine problems and that they were shutting down their engines. We advised the captain that we were going to board the vessel and we sent a videographer, Park ranger and the naval officer.

Apparently the captain had been calling his "contacts" and it looked as though he was stalling for time. The naval officer informed me that he had been given a direct order by Admiral Vega, high admiral of the Ecuadorian Merchant Marines, to leave the vessel immediately and allow it to go. The naval officer later told me that he was speaking to the lawyer, when the lawyer handed the phone over to the admiral, and that he received the order then.

This is a blatant example of corruption within DIGMER and the Ecuadorian Navy. The National Park, knowing they had the international support of Sea Shepherd, stood their ground and gave the order to remain on board and to not allow the vessel to leave the Marine Reserve. To no avail. The naval officer left the San Mateo with their dinghy and we had no choice but to pick him up.

We informed the National Park and the director denounced the blatant abuse of power and immediately got on the phone with the minister of the environment. I was very close to giving the order of not allowing the naval officer to get back on board. Orders or no orders, he should never have left the Park rangers alone on that vessel. The captain of the San Mateo immediately threw the rangers off the bridge and locked them out. Some were threatened ver-

bally and the San Mateo *informed us that they were under way en route to Manta. They showed no respect for the authority of the National Park—not surprising due to the blatant support and backing they had from the Ecuadorian naval authorities. The National Park cannot enforce the regulations as they are authorized to do so in the Special Law of the Galápagos if they also have to fight abuse within the Ecuadorian Naval Command.*

I had a tough decision to make: Whether to leave the rangers on board the San Mateo *or take them off. My anger told me to leave them on board as they were willing to remain on board. My fear was that they informed me that their radio battery was running low and a loss of communication would be too risky for their lives. I instructed the captain to tell the captain of* San Mateo *to stop so we could disembark our rangers. We escorted the* San Mateo *to the 40-mile outer limits of the Marine Reserve, hoping we would hear some change from the minister of the environment. We wasted so much time and fuel to then be forced to escort them out of the Marine Reserve untouched, thanks to the abuse of power by the Ecuadorian Naval Command.*

I am angry and I will take out my anger by continuing these patrols and immediately informing Sea Shepherd International HQ of the situation, and I know, with the support of Sea Shepherd members, we will act and we will tell the world—and the world will tell Ecuador—that this type of abuse of power will not be tolerated, especially not in Galápagos.

The National Park officials stood their ground despite the fact that they were facing a formidable power, the Ecuadorian Naval Command, including Admiral Vega, high admiral of DIGMER. Sea Shepherd's presence in Galápagos is being felt, and we will not stand down, either. It has been a good day for us as we have uncovered what has always been the biggest obstacle to the conservation of this precious archipelago. That obstacle comes from the blatant

*abuse of power that DIGMER has shown time and again
since Sea Shepherd first arrived. It started when we were
forced to wait over two months, through dodgy bureaucracy, for a piece of paper that would allow the National
Park to use the* Sirenian *to patrol the Marine Reserve of
Galápagos.*

*Now, through national and international pressure, we
finally received the authority to patrol and in one of our
first confrontations the blatant abuse of power is shown
once again. This type of abuse, some call it corruption,
should not be tolerated by the people of Ecuador or the
international community. If the international community
has declared the Galápagos Islands a Natural World Heritage Site, then it must be willing to support them.*

The *Sirenian* seized four more ships in the subsequent three
months—one carrying more than a thousand fresh shark fins—and
each of them, like the *San Mateo*, was released upon orders from
Admiral Vega. Then, just this past week, O'Hearn was barred from
boarding his own vessel. The port captain informed him on Friday,
just before the *Sirenian* left, that he is not properly certified to sail
with it. He needs to take some kind of marine safety course, he was
told. O'Hearn had no doubt Vega was behind this decision and
rushed to Eliecer Cruz's office that afternoon to put a call through
to the admiral.

Cruz, unfortunately, was not there. He won't be for a while. He
left last month to travel to Spain, where he is said to be completing
the course work necessary to receive his master's degree in park
management. Friends explain that it's a political necessity, so that
Cruz can protect himself from political enemies who might use his
lack of academic credentials to replace him with a more "qualified" director. But rumors are flying around town, just as they did
when Cruz last disappeared from the islands in the wake of Judge
Avellan's arrest warrant during the *Magdalena* affair. People are
whispering that Eliecer Cruz is gone for good, that he's had enough
of this mess.

Whatever the case, O'Hearn wishes Cruz were still here. When the acting park director, one of Cruz's assistants, put that call through to Vega, O'Hearn could hear the admiral shouting through the phone that O'Hearn should be kicked out of the country. O'Hearn had, in the Admiral's words, "tainted an honorable institution." Vega's rant didn't bother O'Hearn nearly as much as the sheepishness of Cruz's assistant, who all but groveled at his end of the line instead of holding his ground as Cruz would have done.

Only time will tell whether Cruz is plotting a triumphant return, as he has in the past, or if he is indeed finally quitting. At the moment, the *Guadalupe River* is bobbing harmlessly in the bay rather than hunting down poachers. It was flunked just this past week by the same naval inspectors who have been hounding the *Sirenian*. Sitting beside it is a small barge—a steel-plated houseboat—painted a pale Park Service green, with a Park Service emblem displayed on its cabin. The barge is set to be dispatched to the islands' northernmost waters, around Wolf and Darwin, where much illegal fishing has been taking place lately. It will be a floating Park Service satellite base, monitoring the area and providing supplies and support to patrol boats in the region.

Or at least that's the idea. However, right now the barge is as dead in the water as the *Guadalupe River*. O'Hearn is just sick at the sight of it all. Clutched in his hand is a sheaf of messages, including an e-mail received just last night from Paul Watson in response to O'Hearn's complaint that he's been grounded. O'Hearn is fed up, ready to call in the Sea Shepherd's big gun, the *Ocean Warrior*, and begin what the group diplomatically calls "direct action," a polite term for ramming. Watson, according to his response, seems willing:

Dear Sean,
This really is unacceptable. Our contract states that you must be a part of the patrols. Unless you go out on these patrols, we will have to revoke our agreement. I would not say anything at this moment, but the Ocean Warrior *will be back in the Galápagos in August. If this situation is not resolved, we will take back the* Sirenian.

O'Hearn is excited, ready for action, as is Jennifer, his student assistant, who can't resist leaping into the conversation. "If things keep going like this," she says, tossing her tumbling red hair away from her slim freckled face, "then we'll do what we do best, ram ships."

Ram ships. Jack looks across the low coffee table at this young girl, in all her outrage, speaking these words with the eagerness of a kid climbing onto a bumper-car ride. She means well, as does O'Hearn. But this fury of theirs, it's informed by—what?—six months or so of frustration? Six months of facing the surreal swirl of bullshit the people who live here have had to deal with for decades? It could easily feel insulting, this presumption on the part of these . . . these children . . . that they know what needs to be done to save the Galápagos, and that they are the ones to do it.

Jack takes none of this personally, unlike O'Hearn, who has reduced the Sea Shepherd's conflict to a square-off between himself and this admiral. Perspective is what is called for right now. This is what Jack wants to tell these kids. Perspective and patience. He measures his words thoughtfully, just as he wishes they'd measure theirs. "It's important to allow people in a situation like this to save face," Jack says.

O'Hearn sits back, draws a deep breath, looks first at Jack, then at the harbor, then back at Jack. Jennifer leans forward, rubbing her knees with her hands.

It's not wise in this culture to draw lines in the sand. This is what Jack is saying. There are ways to get things done here, but those ways take time and vision.

But these kids don't hear him. Jack can see that. They're all *about* drawing lines in the sand. That's what the Sea Shepherd is about. And Jack has to wonder if their way might not be right. How long has he lived on these islands, learning the rules of this place, adjusting, adapting, playing its games the best way he knows how? He's watched others play them as well, in their own ways: the Station, the Park Service, tour operators, guides, the government, the locals, the outsiders, the old-timers and the newcomers. Each of them sees the Galápagos through their own eyes, their own filters,

pushing to make it the place that they want it to be, that they need
it to be. People call these islands a jewel, and they have no idea
how right they are. Like a jewel, the Galápagos has many facets,
each reflecting a different brilliance, depending on the angle with
which it's held to the light.

This is the way it always has been. The Norwegians who came
in the twenties. The whalers who came long before them. The warships with sails and the gunboats with armor. The baroness, the
Wittmers, the Americans in World War II serving their country, the
Americans after them fleeing from theirs. The men who smelled
fortunes far back in the past, and the men who smell fortunes
today: the tour operators and fisheries.

There have always been those who have come to these islands for
freedom or safety or simply a chance to make a life for themselves.
There have always been those who have come simply to behold the
spectacle of these shores and this sea. And there have always been
those who are drawn here to study, to unlock the islands' mysteries,
to probe the pulses of life that exist here so that the life of this planet,
and our own lives upon it, can be more deeply understood.

The Galápagos belongs—it has always belonged—to each person
who visits it, each in his own way. This is as true today as it was
five hundred years ago, when the Bishop first landed here. Yes, the
Sea Shepherd has arrived, and Jack's right about this: the ante's
been raised. But the ante's been rising since man first stepped
ashore on these islands. The stakes have simply become steeper as
each year has led to the next, the winnings larger, the losses more
ruinous.

When Gayle died last week, Godfrey wrote a remembrance. It was
sent out to friends, including Jack, who received a copy by e-mail just
this morning.

Gayle lived a simple, dedicated, and utterly loyal life. Her
energy was directed toward the conservation of the
Enchanted Islands with a consistency that is hard to equal.
She truly loved the animals and plants, and even when she
left the islands for the last time, she wanted to be sure that

the little scalesia plant in the garden would be watered and cared for, even before her own health.

She was not a great swimmer but cared as much for the sharks and the fish as the finches and her beloved "iggies." She had a deep awareness for the well-being of all animals and had a special rapport with those she tended. These included blue-footed boobies, shearwaters, and the wonderful Fred, a swallow-tailed gull.

And who can forget Whish? Gayle spent hours and hours in the sun and rain gathering Whish berries and caterpillars from the saltbushes. Whish changed from a bedraggled infant to a sleek, sharp-eyed, tool-using finch. She was thrilled that this bird sought the shelter of her body when the rain beat down, clutching her fingers and gently snoozing till the storm had passed. She would be aghast and furious at the news that another long-liner from Costa Rica had been released with 1,000 shark fins aboard.

Many people have already pointed out her untiring work in the library and the unstinted help offered to all who approached her for assistance. But Gayle was much more than this, and I think we should use the example of her life to promote a better future of the Galápagos.

A few weeks before her death, I drove her to the sink-holes, known as Las Gemelos, for this was one of the places that we loved most on Santa Cruz. The green canopy of scalesia trees with their nodding daisy flowers and the staccato call of the carpenter finches was a delight to her senses. At her feet doves wandered, and in the nearby trees finches and a vermillion flycatcher busied themselves, far from the rattle and concussive racket of the town, which she hated. She lay down and dozed, surrounded by this tiny heaven on earth.

Gayle truly loved Galápagos. She knew its beauty and sorrow, the conservation efforts to save it and the dark forces of destruction that threaten to destroy it. If there is one thing that we can do in her memory and to calm her

*agitated dreams, it is to redouble the conservation efforts to
preserve the one place on earth to which she gave her life
and untiring energy.*

*I do not throw this out as a platitude. She showed that
we can live in a gentle harmony with nature through a deep
appreciation of what nature really is—that it will only survive if we love it as part of our lives, both in a physical and
spiritual sense, that greed and aggression are the enemies of
peace and fulfillment.*

Godfrey Merlen
Guayaquil
June 1, 2001

It's late. The sun has moved low, across the harbor, above the
barranco. Forrest is at the lobby door in his wheelchair. His small
corner table is set for one. The other tables are set as well for the
guests who will be arriving soon, Daniel Fitter's tour group.

Jack hasn't got time right now to read Godfrey's message. There
are so many things to do. Later this evening he'll sit down with a
scotch, put on some music, and take a look at those words. Then
he'll prepare for a meeting tomorrow with the town's chamber of
commerce to iron out a new set of regulations for Galápagos
tourism, something the Chamber's been haggling over for ten years
now: workable limits on diving and sportfishing and boat tours.
After a decade of discussion, with Jack often leading the way, the
new rules—aimed as much at protecting the islands as preserving
the tour industry's profits—are just about ready to be sent to the
mainland, to the Department of Environment, then on to the president's desk for his signature.

At least that's how Jack hopes it will go. *If* the regulations get
past the cadre of fishing-industry attorneys who stand in their way.
If the Department of Environment, in all of its industry-influenced
fractiousness, approves them. *If* the president, whoever he might
be once the rules reach his desk, agrees to sign them into law.

Jack admits it's a lot to hope for. But then what was it Godfrey
said on that soft afternoon early last year, as he sat on the *Ratty*

anchored in Bud's Bay? Love, hope, and example. These, Godfrey said, are the three things man lives by. And the greatest of these, he said, must be hope.

Darwin himself would agree. *The Origin of Species* concludes with a passage that, in the face of eternal destruction, is nothing if not optimistic:

> *Thus, from the war of nature, from famine and death, the most exalted object which we are capable of conceiving, namely, the production of the higher animals, directly follows. There is grandeur in this view of life, with its several powers, having been originally breathed into a few forms or into one; and that, whilst this planet has gone cycling on according to the fixed law of gravity, from so simple a beginning endless forms most beautiful and most wonderful have been, and are being, evolved.*

Grandeur and beauty and wonder. This, in the end, is what all who continue to care for these islands believe, that the grandeur and beauty and wonder of the Galápagos will prevail.

And that the goodness of man will allow it.

EPILOGUE

Audrey Nelson looking out on Academy Bay

The day before New Year's Eve 2001, I returned to the Galápagos for the fourth time in three years. It had been almost six months since my last visit, and even as our morning flight closed in for its landing at Baltra, at least one change was apparent: A smaller number of tour boats was anchored in the cove near the airport than at any time I had been here before.

Indeed, the number of ships licensed to tour the islands had dropped during the past year from ninety to eighty. The ailing worldwide economy, which had set in during the summer, had something to do with that. The September terrorist attacks on the United States had made it even worse—the Galápagos' tourism rate had plunged thirty-six percent in the three months since those attacks. Still, according to the Park Service, the total number of visitors to the islands for this calendar year was a record-high 81,500.

Furio Valbonesi would say amen to that. His "Royal Palm Resort," now allied with a Singapore-based resort hotel consortium, had officially opened in early December with a great deal of fanfare, including a brief item in the *New York Times* and a visit from Ecuadorian President Gustavo Noboa, who arrived for the opening ceremonies as Furio's guest of honor. The Baltra airport itself now bore Furio's stamp—a newly constructed private lounge for the Royal Palm's guests, with frosted cut-glass doors opening to a tile-floored waiting room arrayed with sofas, chairs, end tables, and a uniformed, English-speaking bartender.

A week after Furio's hotel opened, President Noboa was in the news again, this time with the announcement that he would not be a candidate in Ecuador's 2002 election. Someone whose name *would* appear on the ballot, if he had his way, was . . . yes, Abdala Bucaram. Speaking from his hotel penthouse in Panama, *El Loco* announced in late October his intention to return from exile to lead his nation back from ruin. Officials of the Partido Roldocista Ecuatoriano—Bucaram's political party—were working at the moment to devise a law that would allow *El Loco* to be pardoned of the corruption charges that had led him to flee the country in 1997.

Whoever would become Ecuador's next president was going to inherit a wasp's nest of crises: with the economy, with the *Indios,* and with Colombia . . . all of which are interconnected, and all of which ultimately affect the Galápagos.

Two weeks before Christmas, the International Monetary Fund (IMF) released a $95 million loan to Ecuador, but the money came with a caution. Yes, said the IMF, Ecuador's shift to the U.S. dollar seemed to be working. The nation's rate of inflation had dropped in one year from 91 percent—the highest in South America—to below 20 percent. But the IMF warned that the country's almost complete dependence on oil exports was dangerous. The past year had been a time of healthy oil prices. If that market dropped, Ecuador's economy would again collapse.

But oil had become all Ecuador was left with—oil and bananas. The corruption and instability that continued to riddle the nation's government and business leadership since the coup nearly two years earlier had stripped its economy of just about everything else.

The *Indios* understood this, and that's why, as the year 2001 drew to a close, they were still protesting in the streets of Quito, demanding a voice in the government and a share in the control of the oil industry. The oil comes from beneath the *Indios'* land; this gives them leverage, at least as long as the international community is watching.

But the *Indios'* leverage is nothing compared with the Americans', and this is something the Colombians understand. Ecuador wants no part of a conflict with Colombia, but because it's beholden to the United States as its primary oil customer and as the financier of its shaky economy, it cannot say no when the U.S. government "requests" Ecuador's cooperation with its anti-drug operations.

As the summer and autumn went by, those operations had begun taking shape. A $61-million U.S.-funded renovation was now well under way at Ecuador's Manta air base to prepare for the arrival within months of more than 200 U.S. military personnel and a fleet of radar-equipped P-3 Orions and C-130 aircraft to fly surveillance missions over Colombia.

FARC guerrilla leaders in Colombia, who pronounced the Manta operation a "declaration of war" by the United States, had responded by stepping up their forays into Ecuador. More than twenty kidnappings of oil workers in the Amazon region were reported by the end of 2001, compared with just three the year before. Armed Colombians had become an everyday sight on the streets of Lago Agrio, prompting 150 Ecuadorian police troopers outfitted in bulletproof vests and armed with assault rifles to be dispatched there, supported by 11,000 Ecuadorian soldiers deployed to the Amazon region by President Noboa. With even more violence on the horizon, Noboa announced a plan to recruit 24,000 more policemen during the next six years, "to improve national security."

All of which would explain why the Ecuadorian government continued to ignore and even impede the laws written to protect the waters around the Galápagos. The conservation of these islands was simply not among the government's priorities at the moment. Meanwhile, there were far too many tuna and sharks swimming in those waters for Ecuador's cash-starved industrial fishing interests to ignore.

As the year 2001 drew to a close, the battle between the Galápagos National Park Service and the illegal fishing fleets had reached pitched proportions. Eliecer Cruz did indeed return from his sojourn to Spain, and by the end of the year, supported by the Sea Shepherd's *Sirenian*, the Park Service had seized sixteen fishing vessels for an array of violations.

The government's response in each case was to either release the ship and its crew, or at the most, to delay legal action. In mid-October the case of a long-liner fishing boat named the *Maria Canela II* made national news by actually appearing before Ecuador's Constitutional Tribunal—the first time such a case had reached this high court. The *Canela II* had been seized back in March near the Galápagos' Wolf Island with a twenty-five-mile line in tow. Seventy-eight shark carcasses and 1,044 shark fins were found on board the vessel. The Park Service and its supporters had high hopes for this hearing. But it wound up "postponed" at the last moment when two of the tribunal's five judges decided not to appear. As of New Year's Eve, that case had still not been heard.

Meanwhile, the *Sirenian* was now patrolling the islands without Sean O'Hearn aboard. In mid-August, Paul Watson followed through with his promise to bring down the Sea Shepherd's flagship, the *Ocean Warrior*, to support the *Sirenian*. When Watson arrived, however, the *Ocean Warrior* was detained in Academy Bay by an Ecuadorian naval gunboat armed with Exocet missiles. After an eight-day standoff between Watson and a battalion of Ecuadorian lawyers and middling bureaucrats, the *Ocean Warrior* agreed to leave the Galápagos, and O'Hearn was informed by Ecuadorian authorities that he was to leave with it. His visa, he was told, had been rescinded. When O'Hearn refused to go, he was arrested by none other than Puerto Ayora's Police Chief Proáno. After a brief detention at the town's police station, O'Hearn flew to Guayaquil to plead his case to return to the islands. As of the year's end, he was still pleading.

Some of these dramas, large and small, were subjects of the *muñecos* that began taking shape New Year's Eve day along Darwin Avenue and up into the village of Puerto Ayora. Fiddi Angermeyer's party this year would be not at his house but at a new restaurant he opened a few months ago on the "other side," not far from Gus Angermeyer's old place, right on the *barranco*. Gus no longer spent time over there. It had become too hard for him to get around. He was now living in town, staying with relatives up in the village, lying in a hammock in a dusty side yard, talking to the chickens and goats and the occasional passerby.

Fiddi's new place had become quite an attraction, with water taxis ferrying customers back and forth from the town's wharf to his restaurant's waterfront cement steps. Anchored not far from those steps, paint-peeled and rotting, sat what was now left of the *Symbol*. Bico Rosero sold the boat early in the year, and the new owners left it uncared for for months, until the mast decayed and broke, a plank or a fitting came loose in the hull, and finally, one morning in early December, the old sailboat sank to the bottom of the bay. She was refloated not long after that, but nothing more had been done. The *Symbol* was now just another derelict in a harbor speckled with the ruins of old vessels.

As night fell on this New Year's Eve and the revelers took to the streets, it was striking how sparse the crowds appeared and how few white faces were among them—nothing like two years before, when the tourists seemed to outnumber the locals.

Jack Nelson would attest to that. The reservation board mounted on a wall in his office is normally filled this time of year, not just for the holiday but for the next couple of months. This night, however, the blank spaces on that board far outnumbered the reservation tags.

But Jack's chin was still up, in spite of it all. He was excited about plans now afoot to build a new school at the west end of town, a modern academy that would extend its reach into the community, beyond just the classroom and into the lives and needs of the families on this island. The Sapienza University of Rome was behind the project, and just last month a delegation of forty people had arrived in Puerto Ayora to survey not just the educational but also the social services needed here. Forty people. And they stayed for two weeks, not just a few hours. This was not simply lip service or political window dressing. This looked like it might actually happen, something that could truly make a difference for these islands, and that had Jack excited.

So did the news that the Research Station had decided to go ahead and bring in the ladybugs to save the Galápagos' mangroves from dying. Finally, something was going to be done about the dead, blackened branches sagging from the trees shading the town's shoreline. Within the next month, the Station had promised, the Australian ladybug would be officially released to combat the cottony cushion scale insects spreading over the islands.

Good news. Meanwhile, even with all those blank spots on Jack's board, there was still business to do on this evening, guests to take care of. Some of those guests had already left for Fiddi's restaurant, to ring in the new year with an outdoor buffet. Christy and José-Luis would be there. And Jason and Monica. And Georgina Cruz and her husband Augusto. The Balfours would be there, with their son Andrew, who was now done with his studies in England. Jack and Romy had been invited, but decided they'd skip it and stay home this year.

By eleven o'clock most of the town had gathered down by the waterfront. A live band was playing, and the sound—the guitars and drums—carried across the harbor to the backyard of Jack's hotel. He stood out there, alone, in the dark, by the water, with a small box of fireworks he'd bought earlier in the week.

Half past the hour red flares began arcing from the boats in the bay and from the skyline toward town. Jack pulled one of his rockets from the box, lit it, and stepped back as the small missile shot skyward and burst high above him. He smiled, lit another, and stepped back again.

Out by the hotel's front entrance, a *muñeco* was propped by a hand-printed sign. The figure wore sunglasses and a bright blue–striped shirt. A camera hung from its neck. And a pair of snorkeling goggles. And a bottle of suntan lotion. Inscribed on the sign were the words: EL TURISTA QUE NUNCA VINO—"The Tourist Who Never Came." Jack and his staff had put the thing together that afternoon.

At a quarter to midnight, Jack walked out front. The street was deserted. A pool of white light fell from a street lamp, casting Jack's shadow on the cobblestoned road. Romy and Audrey came out to join him. He took down the *muñeco*, laid it out on the road, and splashed it with gasoline.

The countdown to midnight had begun. The chants of the crowd down in town drifted over the treetops as Jack lit a match and stepped back.

The *muñeco* puffed into flames, its sawdust stuffing glowing bright orange as its face and its clothing peeled away.

And now it was midnight, the start of another new year. Jack turned to kiss Romy, and the three of them—Jack, Romy, and Audrey—watched as the figurine lay on the stones of Darwin Avenue, surrounded by darkness, burning away.

Notes, Acknowledgments, and Sources

All scenes, incidents, and conversations contained in these pages occurred as described. In most cases, I was there to witness and record them. If I was not, they are re-created from the recollections of those who were, as well as from documented accounts.

As I wrote in the prologue, I had no idea anyone other than scientists and perhaps a few Park rangers lived in the Galápagos until my good friend David Black, who is also my literary agent, returned in the summer of 1996 from a week-long visit to the islands with his wife, Melissa. David came home with a strong sense that there was a story to be found among the Galápagos people—maybe even a book—and he challenged me to go find it. For that I can never thank him enough.

I first visited the islands in January of 1999 for a one-week scouting trip of sorts. It was during this visit that I met a number of people who would become invaluable resources for the writing of this book. They included Jack Nelson and Romy Hartmann, Christy and José-Luis Gallardo, Jason Gallardo, Roz Cameron, Gayle Davis, Godfrey Merlen, Eliecer Cruz, Steve Divine, and Daniel and Tina Fitter. During this initial visit and during my subsequent stays on the islands, these people not only provided me with their personal experiences shared through hours of interviews, but they also invited me into their homes and lives, puting into my hands various journals, diaries, notes, photographs and letters written over the years by both themselves and loved ones. I will always be grateful for their generosity and trust.

Several of these people, in their professional capacities, were able to provide or point me in the direction of reliable documentation and research materials: books, magazine and newspaper articles, government reports, scientific studies, photographs, and other valuable sources of information. Most notably, Gayle Davis gave me access to the rich holdings of the Charles Darwin Research Station library; Roz Cameron provided reams of material on the Station, on the Charles Darwin Foundation, and on the Galápagos National Park; Eliecer Cruz and his staff were most cooperative in sharing Park Service records and documents; and Christy Gallardo and Jack Nelson were more than generous with the contents of their personal collections of Galápagos-related material.

In November of 1999, just prior to my second trip to the islands, I visited Johannah Barry at her Charles Darwin Foundation office in northern Virginia, where she graciously shared even more information about the Foundation and its work. I then returned to the Galápagos in late December of 1999 and stayed for three months, through the end of March 2000. During that time, I lived in the town of Puerto Ayora on the island of Santa Cruz. I also visited the Galápagos' three other principal communities: Puerto Baquerizo Moreno on San Cristobal; Puerto Villamil on Isabela; and Puerto Velasco Ibarra on Floreana. Besides the journeys on the *Symbol* and on the *Galápagos Explorer II* described in the book, I made several trips among the islands aboard cargo ships (a common and inexpensive way for many Galápagans to get from one island to another) and by small airplanes. A little more than a year after that three-month stay, I returned to the islands, in June of 2001, to do additional reporting, then made one final trip at the end of that year.

Besides those individuals whose names appear in the text, I must thank a number of people for their advice, assistance, and encouragement. They include my editor at HarperCollins, Megan Newman, along with Greg Chaput and Megan's assistant, Matthew Benjamin; Gary Morris, Susan Raihofer, Joy Tutella, and Carmen Rey at the David Black Literary Agency; Dave Addis, Don Naden, Erika Reif, Earl Swift, Lawrence Jackson, Bill Tiernan, and Bob Voros at the *Virginian-Pilot*; John Hutchinson, Joel Martin, and Hospital Corpsman First Class (and retired Baltra veteran) John H. Peck in Norfolk; Bill Morris in Brooklyn; Wil Haygood at the *Boston Globe*; Chris Lamb at the College of Charleston; Dr. Andrew Spencer and Dr. Theresa Longo at the College of William and Mary; Dr. J. Hamilton Brown at Old Dominion University; Barry Boyce of Galápagos Travel in San Juan Batista; Doris Welch of the Galápagos Network, Inc., in Miami; Don Causey of *The Hunting Report* in Miami; Odette Morillo, Joel Rivera, and Eduardo Borja of PromoTravelSouth in Quito; and in the Galápagos, Henri Schaeffer, Fabio Peñafiel, Elena Alvarado, Edgar Muñoz, Desirée Cruz, Marta Romo Leroux, Carlos Acosta, Monica Plaza Mejia, Paola Luqué, Bitinia Espinoza, Yvonne Baskin, Richard Polatty, Silvana Martinez, Anita Salcedo, Jim Anderson, Alfredo Guggenheim, Fiddi Angermeyer, Fernando Grodsinsky, Danny Torres Sarmiento, Manuel Soriano Echevema, Isabel Romero Holst, Julio Gallo Cabrero, Juan Berrera, Ramiro Tomála, Juan Manuel Quinchiguango, Antonio and Rosa Angrango, Kleber "Pony" Hida, and Dora Werder.

Finally, a variety of books, magazine articles, institutional reports and studies, newspaper articles, and Internet publications provided insight and information about the Galápagos, Ecuador, and related subjects. They are listed below.

Books

Angermeyer, Johanna. *My Father's Island.* New York: Viking Press, 1990.

Beebe, William. *Galápagos: World's End.* New York: G. P. Putnam's Sons, 1924.

Black, Juan, and G. T. Corley Smith. *The Path of Conservation,* pt. 1 and 2. London: Pergamon Press, 1984.

Boyce, Barry. *A Traveler's Guide to the Galápagos Islands.* San Juan Bautista: Galápagos Travel, 1994.

Bowlby, John. *Charles Darwin: A New Life.* New York: W. W. Norton & Company, 1990.

Brockman, Walter, with Dore Strauch. *Satan Came to Eden.* New York: Harper & Brothers, 1936.

Buchanan, Chris T., and Cesar Franco. *Independent Traveler: Galápagos Handbook.* Guayaquil: Flying Fish Publications, 2000.

Conway, Ainslie and Frances. *The Enchanted Islands.* New York: J. P. Putnam's Sons, 1947.

Darwin, Charles. *On the Origin of Species.* New York: Random House, 1979.

———. *Voyage of the Beagle.* New York: Penguin Books, 1989.

De Roy, Tui. *Galápagos: Islands Born of Fire.* Toronto: Warwick, 1998.

———. *Galápagos: Islands Lost in Time.* New York: Viking Press, 1980.

De Soto, Hernando. *The Other Path: The Invisible Revolution in the Third World.* New York: Harper & Row, 1989.

De Witt, Meredith. *Voyages of the Velero III.* La Crosse, Wisc.: Brookhaven Press, 1939.

Glantz, Michael H. *Currents of Change: El Niño's Impact on Climate and Society.* Cambridge: Cambridge University Press, 1996.

Gordilló, Jacinto. *Guide to Villamil, Isabela, Galápagos.* Puerto Villamil, Ecuador: Municipal Council of Puerto Villamil, 1995.

Gould, Stephen Jay. *Ever Since Darwin.* New York: W. W. Norton, 1977.

Hickman, John. *The Enchanted Islands: The Galápagos Discovered.* Shropshire, U.K.: Anthony Nelson, 1991.

Hurtado, Gustavo Vasconez. *Isle of the Black Cats (Galápagos).* Quito, Ecuador: Libri Mundi, 1993.

Jackson, Michael H. *Galápagos: A Natural History.* Calgary, Canada: University of Calgary Press, 1993.

Kane, Joe. *Savages.* New York: Vintage Books, 1996.

Lopez, Barry. *About This Life: Journeys on the Threshold of Memory.* Westminster: Alfred A. Knopf, Inc., 1998.

Melville, Herman. *Great Short Works of Herman Melville.* New York: Perennial Library, 1969.

Moorehead, Alan. *Darwin and the Beagle.* New York: Penguin Books, 1969.

Merlen, Godfrey. *Field Guide to the Fishes of the Galápagos.* London: Wilmot Books, 1988.

Pearson, David, and David Middleton. *The New Key to Ecuador and the Galápagos.* Berkeley, Calif.: Ulysses Press, 1996.

Philbrick, Nathaniel. *In the Heart of the Sea: The Tragedy of the Whaleship* Essex. New York: Viking, 2000.

Perry, R., ed. *Key Environments: Galápagos.* London: Pergamon Press, 1984.

Porter, David. *Journal of a Cruise.* Upper Saddle River, New Jersey: The Gregg Press, 1970.

Porter, Eliot. *Galápagos: The Flow of Wildness*, vols. 1 and 2. New York: Sierra Club/Ballantine Books, 1970.

Quammen, David. *The Flight of the Iguana: A Sidelong View of Science and Nature.* Westport, Conn.: Touchstone, 1998.

_____. *The Song of the Dodo: Island Biogeography in an Age of Extinctions.* Westport, Conn.: Touchstone, 1997.

Robinson, William Albert. *Voyage to Galápagos.* San Diego: Harcourt, Brace and Company, 1936.

Schofield, Eileen K. *Plants of the Galápagos Islands.* New York: Universe Books, 1984.

Steadman, David W., and Steven Zousmer. *Galápagos: Discovery on Darwin's Islands.* Washington, D.C.: Smithsonian Institution Press, 1988.

Treherne, John. *The Galápagos Affair.* New York: Penguin, 2001.

Weiner, Jonathan. *The Beak of the Finch.* New York: Random House, 1995.

Wittmer, Margaret. *Floreana.* Shropshire, U.K.: Anthony Nelson, 1989.

_____. *What Happened on Galápagos? The Truth of the Galápagos Affair As Told by a Lady from Cologne.* Abridged and translated from the German *Was Ging Auf Galápagos Vor?* by Sydney Skamser. Los Angeles: Archives of the Allan Hancock Foundation, 1936.

Magazine Articles

"Back to Nature: Mild Life in the Raw in Two Retreats." *Time,* October 6, 1934.

"Beachhead on the Moon." *Time,* July 15, 1946.

Benchley, Peter. "Galápagos: Paradise in Peril." *National Geographic,* April 1999.

Bensted-Smith, Robert. "A Pig-Free Santiago: Is It a Dream or on the Horizon?" *Noticias de Galápagos,* April 1998.

_____. "The War Against Aliens in Galápagos." *World Conservation,* April 1997.

Carlton, James T. "Bioinvaders in the Sea: Reducing the Flow of Ballast Water." *World Conservation,* April 1997.

Cash, William. "Shell Game." *The New Republic,* May 30, 1994.

Causey, Don. "Two More Reports on Galápagos Islands Hunt." *The Hunting Report,* May 2000.

R. S. Chase and J. P. Hailman. "Two Views on Conservation in the Galápagos." *Bulletin of the Philadelphia Herpetological Society,* July-December 1963.

Coblentz, Bruce E. "Strangers in Paradise: Invasive Mammals on Islands." *World Conservation,* April 1997.

Davies, David. "Kill a Pinta Goat a Day." *Nature,* June 28, 1974.

de Groot, R. S. "Tourism and Conservation in the Galápagos Islands." *Biological Conservation,* December 1983.

Dillard, Annie. "Innocence in the Galápagos." *Harper's,* May 1975.

Eliasson, Uno. "An Incident with Feral Dogs on Volcan Cerro Azul, Isabela." *Noticias de Galápagos,* April 1982.

Emory, Jerry. "Galápagos: What Price Success?" *Pacific Discovery,* Winter 1990.

_____. "Managing Another Galápagos Species—Man." *National Geographic,* January 1988.

_____. "Tourism and Tension in the Galápagos." *The World & I,* February 1989.

Faris, Robert E. L., William R. Catton, Jr., and Otto N. Larsen. "The Galápagos Expedition: Failure in the Pursuit of a Contemporary Secular Utopia." *Pacific Sociological Review,* April 1963.

"Fernandina: Flank Eruption Slows but Was Continuing on March 19." *Bulletin of the Global Volcanism Network,* February 1995.

"Fernandina: Lava Escapes on SW Flank and Flows 5 km to Enter the Ocean." *Bulletin of the Global Volcanism Network,* January 1995.

"Fernandina: Now-Cooling Lava and the Eruption's Impact on Plants and Animals." *Bulletin of the Global Volcanism Network,* August 1995.

Fitter, Julian. "Darwin's Islands" (letter to the editor). *New Scientist,* October 1995.

Freeman, R. B. "Darwin in the Galápagos." *Noticias de Galápagos,* No. 42, 1985.

"Galápagonistics." *Time,* May 25, 1936.

"Galápagos: Mystery and Death Come to a Tropical Paradise." *Time,* December 15, 1934.

Golden, Frederic. "Visit to the Enchanted Isles." *Time,* June 26, 1978.

"Good-Neighborly Bases." *Time*, September 2, 1942.

Gould, Stephen Jay. "Dorothy, It's Really Oz." *Time*, August 23, 1999.

"Guagua Pichincha: Magmatic Outbursts; Unprecedented Seismicity; Explosions Up 2-fold." *Bulletin of the Global Volcanism Network*, September 1999.

Heyerdahl, Thor. "Archaeology in the Galápagos Islands." *California Academy of Sciences*, September 1961.

"In Darwin's Footsteps." *Newsweek*, January 20, 1964.

Jameson, Kenneth P. "Crisis in Ecuador: Who's in Charge Here?" *Common Weal*, April 11, 1997.

Jenkins, Peter. "Re-Joining the Continents." *World Conservation*, April 1997.

Jervis, Maria Helena, Jose Rodriguez Rojas, Carlos De Paco, and Jim Thorsell. "Galápagos Goldrush." *IUCN Bulletin*, July–September 1994.

Johnson, Irving, and Electa Irving. "Lost World of the Galápagos." *National Geographic*, May 1959.

Kane, Joe. "Moi Goes To Washington." *The New Yorker*, May 2, 1994.

Kennedy, Robert F., Jr. "Amazon Cruder." *The Amicus Journal*, Spring 1991.

Kingett, Robert P. "Chess Run to Galápagos." *Motor Boating*, July 1956.

Kramer, Peter. "The Galápagos: Islands Under Siege." *Ambio*, Vol. 12, No. 3-t, 1983.

_____. "Wildlife Conservation in the Galápagos Islands." *Nature and Resources*, October/December 1973.

Laurie, Andrew. "Santa Fé in an El Niño Year." *Noticias de Galápagos*, December 1999.

Lewin, Roger. "Galápagos: The Endangered Islands." *New Scientist*, July 1978.

Lundh, J. P. "A Brief Account of Some Early Inhabitants of Santa Cruz Island." *Noticias de Galápagos*, July 1995.

McGirk, Tim. "A Carpet of Cocaine." *Time*, August 9, 1999.

Matthiessen, Peter. "In the Dragon Islands." *Audubon*, September 1973.

Mauchamp, Andre, and Maria Luisa Munoz. "A Kudzu Alert in the Galápagos: The Urgent Need for Quarantine." *Noticias de Galápagos*, August 1996.

Mendez, Sixto, Jennifer Parnell, and Robert Wasserstrom. "Petroleum and Indigenous Peoples in Ecuador's Amazon." *Environment*, June 1998.

Merlen, Godfrey. "A Dawn of Despair: Journey to Alcedo." *Noticias de Galápagos*, July 1992.

_____. "Use and Misuse of the Seas Around the Galápagos Archipelago." *Oryx*, April 1995.

Meyer, Richard. "First-Hand Report on Galápagos Island Hunt." *The Hunting Report*, May 1999.

Moore, Alan W. "Tour Guides as a Factor in National Park Management." *Parks*, April/May 1981.

Pearce, Fred. "Galápagos Tortoises Under Siege." *New Scientist*, September 1995.

Peterson, Roger Tory. "The Galápagos: Eerie Cradle of New Species." *National Geographic*, April 1967.

Pinson, Jim. "Electronic Mail Comes to the Galápagos." *Noticias de Galápagos*, July 1995.

"RFC in the Galápagos." *Newsweek*, August 4, 1941.

Robertson, George. "Schooling Hammerheads of the Galápagos: Threatened Natural Treasure of the World." *Ocean Realm*, June 1994.

Rosenberg, Tina. "The Great Cocaine Quagmire." *Rolling Stone*, April 12, 2001.

Schimpff, J. F. "Floreana Island." *American Weekly*, 1932.

Schofield, Eileen K. "Hope for the Galápagos." *Garden*, January/February 1981.

Smith, G. T. Corley. "A Brief History of the Charles Darwin Foundation for the Galápagos Islands." *Noticias de Galápagos*, June 1990.

Snell, Howard, and Solanda Rea. "The 1997-98 El Nino in Galápagos: Can 34 Years of Data Estimate 120 Years of Pattern?" *Noticias de Galápagos*, December 1999.

Stoppard, Tom. "This Other Eden." *Noticias de Galápagos*, No. 34, 1981.

Sulloway, Frank J. "Darwin's 'Dogged' Genius: His Galápagos Visit in Retrospect." *Noticias de Galápagos*, No. 42, 1985.

"Taps at Galápagos." *Newsweek*, July 15, 1946.

"Tortoise Isles." *Newsweek*, September 21, 1942.

"Tungurahua: Elevated Seismicity and SO2 Fluxes Led to an Eruption on 5 October." *Bulletin of the Global Volcanism Network*, September 1999.

Wetterer, James K. "Alien Ants: Spreading Like Wildfire." *World Conservation*, April 1997.

Wingo, Walter. "A Fragile Land Where Man Is Greatest Enemy." *U.S. News & World Report*, April 27, 1981.

Woram, John. "Who Killed the Iguanas?" *Noticias de Galápagos*, No. 50, 1991.

Reports and Studies

Bensted-Smith, Robert, Eliecer Cruz, and F. Valverde. "The Strategy for Conservation of Terrestrial Biodiversity in Galápagos." April 1998.

Bustamante, R., K. J. Collins, and R. Bensted-Smith. "Biodiversity Conservation in the Galápagos Marine Reserve." April 1998.

CDF Task Force. "Charles Darwin Foundation Task Force." Evaluation. 1998.

Fundacion Natura and World Wildlife Fund. "Galápagos Report: 1998/1999." 1999.

MacDonald, Theodore. "Conflict in the Galápagos Islands: Analysis and Recommendations for Management." Prepared for the Charles Darwin Foundation, January 1997.

MacFarland, Craig. "Case Study: Biodiversity Conservation and Human Population Impacts in the Galápagos Islands, Ecuador." Charles Darwin Research Center, 1995.

National Ecuadorian Police Report. "Putumayo: Sacrifice and Courage." Authored by Fausto A. Fuentes Garcia. Report on violence along the Putumayo River border of Colombia, 1993.

"Operation Plan of the Charles Darwin Research Station," 1999.

U.S. Army Report. "Report of Searching Expedition on Pinzon Island, 30 October, 1943." Documents the search for wreckage of U.S. bomber that crashed on Galápagos' Pinzon Island on July 30, 1942.

Newspaper Articles

"Accord in Ecuador Can't Hide Woes," *New York Times*, March 21, 1999.

"AIDS in Latin America—A Special Report: In Deception and Denial, an Epidemic Looms," *New York Times*, January 25, 1993.

"A Luxury Resort in Pristine Galápagos," *New York Times*, December 30, 2001.

"Andean Countries Face Painful Financial Reconstruction," *Financial Times* (London), June 30, 1999.

"Angry Ecuadorians Clash with Army Looters: Residents Forced to Flee Rumbling Volcano," *The Ottawa Citizen*, January 4, 2000.

"'A Pirate? Of Course I Am,'" *The Daily Telegraph* (London), April 19, 2001.

Associated Press report on discovery of wreckage and bodies of IMAX film crew, July 1, 1998.

Associated Press report on missing IMAX film crew, June 26, 1998.

Associated Press report on search for IMAX film crew, June 29, 1998.

"As U.S. Military Settles In, Some in Ecuador Have Doubts," *New York Times*, December 31, 2000.

"A World Apart," by Tui de Roy, *The Press-Enterprise*, June 6, 1999.

"Banks in Ecuador Reopen After Week's Closing, but Taxi Strike Aggravates Tensions," *New York Times*, March 16, 1999.

"Bitter Indians Let Ecuador Know Fight Isn't Over," *New York Times*, January 27, 2000.

"Black Death Threatens the Unique Beauty of Galápagos 'Laboratory,'" *The Irish Times*, January 25, 2001.

"Board for Kansas Deletes Evolution from Curriculum," *New York Times*, August 10, 1999.

"Can Paradise Be Pulled from the Brink?" *The Ottawa Citizen*, April 4, 1999.

"Causes for Concern in Latin America," *The San Diego Tribune*, July 16, 1999.

"Clashes with Protesters, Police Leave 19 Injured in Ecuador," Associated Press report, March 11, 1999.

"Colombia Is Reeling, Hurt by Rebels and Economy," *New York Times*, July 18, 1999.

"Colombian Rebels Quitting Safe Haven As Peace Talks Fail," *New York Times*, January 14, 2002.

"Colombia's Drug War Spills into Ecuador," *The Chicago Tribune*, February 13, 2001.

"Corruption Charges Swirl Around Ecuador's President," *Miami Herald*, March 9, 1998.

"Corruption, Substandard Tanker Fleet of Ecuador Exposed," *The Business Times* (Singapore), April 3, 2001.

"Could-Be Inmates Run for Asylum: Sanctuary for the Deposed Is an Old Tradition Honored in Panama," *The Houston Chronicle*, August 31, 1997.

"Coup Is Over, but Ecuador's Indians Aren't Going Away," *The Christian Science Monitor*, January 26, 2000.

"Critics Call for Mahuad to Quit As Currency Hits Record Low," *Financial Times* (London), January 7, 2000.

"Damage Is Limited in Galápagos Fuel Spill," *New York Times*, February 25, 2001.

"Darwin vs. Design: Evolutionists' New Battle," *New York Times*, April 8, 2001.

"Day of Rebellion Ends with Ouster of Ecuador Leader," *New York Times*, January 22, 2000.

"Death Is Better Than Tyranny, Ecuador's Indians Say," *The Scotsman*, January 13, 2000.

"Dollar Policy Is Praised," *The Miami Herald*, November 13, 2001.

"Ecuador Afraid As a Drug War Heads Its Way," *New York Times*, January 8, 2001.

"Ecuador Battles to Perserve Spell of the 'Enchanted Isles,'" *Financial Times* (London), August 9, 2001.

"Ecuador Chief Issues Decree to Limit Crisis," *New York Times*, March 10, 1999.

"Ecuador Chief, the Populist, Is Anything but Popular," *New York Times*, January 11, 1997.

"Ecuador Coach Shot after Not Selecting Player," Associated Press, May 10, 2001.

"Ecuador Congress Votes to Oust President for 'Mental Incapacity,' " *New York Times*, February 7, 1997.

"Ecuador: Darwin's Family and Other Animals," *Independent on Sunday* (London), May 13, 2001.

"Ecuador Declares State of Emergency," *The Gazette* (Montreal), January 7, 2000.

"Ecuador Ends Emergency After Accord With Indians," *New York Times*, July 19, 1999.

"Ecuador Hopes Volcano Is Only Letting Off Steam," Reuters, October 2, 1999.

"Ecuadorian Centrist Claims Win: Quito Mayor Appears to Be Next President," *Chicago Tribune*, July 13, 1998.

"Ecuadorian Coup Shifts Control to No. 2 Man," *New York Times*, January 23, 2000.

"Ecuadorian Indians Flex Political Biceps," *The Christian Science Monitor*, January 24, 2000.

"Ecuadorian Indians Fuel Uprising," *Chicago Tribune*, January 22, 2000.

"Ecuadorian Journalist Injured by Mail Bomb," *The Orlando Sentinel*, February 17, 2000.

"Ecuadorian Leader Won't Step Down," *The Ottawa Citizen*, January 22, 2000.

"Ecuadorian Police Fight Protesters in 3 Cities," *The Washington Post*, January 7, 2000.

"Ecuadorian President Told to Step Down; Army Backs Indian Protesters," *The Washington Post*, January 22, 2000.

"Ecuadorian Protesters Tear-Gassed," *The Washington Post*, January 18, 2000.

"Ecuadorian Protests Swell," *The Gazette* (Montreal), January 21, 2000.

"Ecuadorian Rebels Sent Home As U.S. Sways Army," *The Times* (London), January 24, 2000.

"Ecuadorian Revolution Has Been Bloodless—So Far; but Indians Warn of Violence If Demands Aren't Met," *The Dallas Morning News*, January 30, 2000.

"Ecuadorians Rally in Drive to Oust President," *New York Times*, February 6, 1997.

"Ecuadorians See New President as Same Old Story: Little Hope Poverty, Corruption Will End," Associated Press, January 24, 2000.

"Ecuador in Crisis: A Risky Bargain," *The Plain Dealer*, April 11, 1999.

"Ecuador Indians Give New Leader 6 Months' Grace: Ecuador's New President Battles Economic Woes," *The Guardian* (London), January 27, 2000.

"Ecuador: Indians Break Off Talks," *New York Times*, April 13, 2001.

"Ecuador Indians Fight for Forests," *The Christian Science Monitor*, June 16, 1993.

"Ecuador in Turmoil As Mobs Storm Congress," *The Independent* (London), January 22, 2000.

"Ecuador Names a New President, Ending Crisis," *Los Angeles Times*, January 23, 2000.

"Ecuador Oil Crew Taken in Ambush, Flown to Colombia," *The Washington Post*, October 13, 2000.

"Ecuador on the Verge of Anarchy As Indians Revolt," *The Independent* (London), January 14, 2000.

"Ecuador Pays Heavy Price for Strikes," *Financial Times* (London), July 20, 1999.

"Ecuador: Pilot Tries to Land at Wrong Airport," *The Gazette* (Montreal), June 25, 1999.

"Ecuador Prepares for Indian Protests," *New York Times*, January 15, 2000.

"Ecuador President Pegs Currency to Dollar," *New York Times*, January 10, 2000.

"Ecuador President Resists Army Coup," *The Times* (London), January 22, 2000.

"Ecuador President Won't Seek Re-Election in 2002," *Los Angeles Times*, December 20, 2001.

"Ecuador Qualifier for First World Cup," *The Miami Herald*, November 8, 2001.

"Ecuador Rallies for Coach," Associated Press, May 11, 2001.

"Ecuador Reluctantly Joins U.S. War on Cocaine," *St. Petersburg Times*, February 21, 2001.

"Ecuador Sentences Tanker's Captain," Associated Press, May 3, 2001.

"Ecuador's 3 Top Central Bankers Quit over Dollarization," *New York Times*, January 12, 2000.

"Ecuador's Armed Forces Deny Rumors of a Coup," *The Orlando Sentinel*, January 9, 2000.

"Ecuador's 'Crazy One' Plans Comeback: Ousted President Faces Treason Charges on Return," *The Toronto Star*, September 21, 1997.

"Ecuador's Currency Falls As the Government Examines Its Options," *New York Times*, January 5, 2000.

"Ecuador's Desperation," *The Christian Science Monitor*, January 27, 2000.

"Ecuador's Military Says 'Junta' Is in Charge," *Los Angeles Times*, January 22, 2000.

"Ecuador's Richest Man is Wild Card in Presidential Race," Associated Press, May 27, 1998.

"Ecuador, Swept by Inflation and Unrest, Brakes the Economy," *New York Times*, March 13, 1999.

"Ecuador's Troubles Seen as Threat to Drug War; Poor Indians Bid for Social Reform," *Chicago Tribune*, February 26, 2001.

"Ecuador Taxi Strike Causes Emergency," Associated Press, July 5, 1999.

"Ecuador: Volcano Rumbles," *New York Times*, September 29, 1999.

"Ecuador Worries About 'Wild West' Northern Border," *Financial Times* (London), July 6, 2001.

"El Loco Dodged Hotel Bill," *The Guardian* (London), May 17, 1997.

"El Loco Still Calls the Shots from Outside Ecuador: Ousted President Highly Influential in Sunday's Vote," *The Ottawa Citizen*, May 28, 1998.

"El Niño Gives Darwin's Finches a Breeding Frenzy," *Chicago Tribune*, September 17, 1998.

"El Niño Lands Reefs in Hot Water," *The Daily Telegraph* (London), September 26, 1998.

"El Niño's Victims Teeter on Edge of Disaster in Ecuador," *Associated Press*, March 12, 1998.

"Eruption over Ecuador Volcano," *The Boston Globe*, February 3, 2000.

"Europe Dominates Survey's Top 10 Least-Corrupt Countries," *New York Times*, October 4, 1998.

"'Fishing' for Ransom, Colombian Rebels Cast Net Wide," *New York Times*, June 3, 1999.

"For Humanity, Save the Galápagos from Humanity," *Los Angeles Times*, January 24, 2001.

"Fragile Islands Under Pressure from Nature-Loving Travelers," *The Christian Science Monitor*, August 19, 1991.

"Futility on the Front Lines of a Drug War," *The Boston Globe*, March 12, 2000.

"Galápagos Islands Face New Peril As More Oil Spills from Tanker," *New York Times*, January 25, 2001.

"Galápagos Islands: Out of the Frying Pan, into the Fire," *The Jerusalem Post*, July 22, 2001.

"Galápagos Looks Beyond the Spill," *The Guardian* (London), January 27, 2001.

"Galápagos Sea Lions Butchered," *The Scotsman*, July 19, 2001.

"Galápagos Turmoil: Tortoises Dragged into Fishing War," *The Guardian* (London), December 30, 2000.

"GOP Plans Funding Boost for Military, Drug War," *The Washington Post*, March 8, 2000.

"Governments vs. Journalists: Latin News Media, Hard-Pressed," *New York Times*, October 5. 1997.

"Guagua Pichincha Report," *El Comercio*, February 18, 1999.

"Harvard-Educated Mayor Fails to Win Majority in Ecuador Election," Associated Press, June 1, 1998.

"Health Alert Issued As Ecuadorian Volcano Spews Huge Ash Cloud," *The Ottawa Citizen*, October 8, 1999.

"Here Are the Latest Foreign Office Warnings," *The Herald* (Glasgow), July 3, 1999.

"How Could We Allow Black Tide to Threaten World's Fragile Eden?" *The Scotsman*, January 24, 2001.

"Human Intrusion Bodes Ill for Galápagos Creatures," *New York Times*, February 13, 2001.

"Indians, Farmers Seek Share of Oil Profits," Associated Press, November 24, 2999.

"IMF Loans 95 Million to Ecuador with Warning," *The Miami Herald*, December 12, 2001.

"In Ecuador, No Money, No Soup," *The Gazette* (Montreal), January 12, 2000.

"In the Shadow of a Volcano," *The Irish Times*, February 19, 2000.

"Isles Rich in Species Are Origin of Much Tension," *New York Times*, January 27, 2001.

"It's a Fact: Faith and Theory Collide over Evolution," *New York Times*, August 15, 1999.

"It's My Fault, Says Oil Spill Captain," *The Times* (London), January 26, 2001.

"Kidnapped American's Body Found in Ecuador," *The Miami Herald*, February 2, 2001.

"Kidnappers Are Blamed for Bombings in Ecuador," *The Miami Herald*, January 30, 2001.

"Latin America's Contagion: Where Taxes Aren't So Certain," *New York Times*, March 21, 1999.

"Latin America Scrambles to Prepare for Year 2000," *New York Times*, April 19, 1999.

"Leader Defies Ecuador Army Call to Quit," *The Scotsman*, January 22, 2000.

"Life after the Oil Spill in the Real Jurassic Park," *The Observer* (London), February 25, 2001.

"Local Sailor Dies at Sea Near Galápagos Islands," *The San Diego Tribune*, February 11, 2000.

"Lonesome Beast," *Daily News*, November 29, 1998.

"Losing Battle to Contain Galápagos Spill," *The Scotsman*, January 23, 2001.

"Military Installs New President," *The Boston Globe*, January 23, 2000.

"Neighbors Fear Fallout of Aid to Colombians," *New York Times*, August 25, 2000.

"New Horizons in Ecuador, but Paralysis Sets in Early," *New York Times*, April 3, 1997.

"New Leader in Ecuador Promises Jobs, Homes," *New York Times*, August 11, 1998.

"No Peace for Pirates," *Sunday Times* (London), April 1, 2001.

"Oil Danger Gone, Grounded Ship to Become New Galápagos Reef," *Chicago Tribune*, January 29, 2001.

"Oil in Troubled Waters," *The Guardian* (London), January 24, 2001.

"Oil Spill Endangers Wildlife," Associated Press, January 23, 2001.

"Oil Spill Highlights Hazards of Galápagos Isles' Growth," *The Washington Post*, January 27, 2001.

"Oil Spill Moves to Center of Galápagos Ecosystem," *New York Times*, January 23, 2001.

"Oil Spill's Shift in Course Aids Galápagos Mop-Up," *New York Times*, January 24, 2001.

"Oil Tanker Spillage Threatens Wildlife on Galápagos Islands," *The Daily Telegraph* (London), January 22, 2001.

"Oil Threatens Galápagos," Associated Press, July 2, 1999.

"Oil Threat to Darwin's Isles," *The Observer* (London), January 21, 2001.

"Oil Workers Are Freed in Ecuador; Kidnappers Grab Ransom," *The Miami Herald*, March 2, 2001.

"100,000 Goats to Die for Island's Giant Tortoises," *Sunday Telegraph* (London), July 16, 2000.

"On Patrol in Jungle 'Danger Zone,'" *Sun-Sentinel* (Fort Lauderdale), October 4, 2001.

"Panama Cools Its Welcome for Exiles," *The Philadelphia Inquirer*, October 28, 2001.

"Peru and Ecuador Agree to Put Border Dispute in Outsiders' Hands," *New York Times*, October 18, 1998.

"Peru and Ecuador Leaders Seal Border Treaty," *New York Times*, May 14, 1999.

"Peru's Drug Successes Erode As Traffickers Adapt," *New York Times*, August 19, 1999.

"Petty Politics Muddies Ecuador's Democracy, Image," Associated Press, May 7, 1998.

"Pirate Patrol: Illegal Fishing Threatens the Galápagos," *The Guardian* (London), September 19, 2001.

"Political Madness in Ecuador," *New York Times*, February 11, 1997.

"Populist's Victory in Ecuador Worries the Elite," *New York Times*, July 22, 1996.

"Protests Mount as Ecuador Teeters on Brink of Collapse," *The Scotsman*, January 10, 2000.

"Pullout from Panama Hampering Drug War," *Los Angeles Times*, February 5, 2000.

"Quito: Life under the Volcano," *The Toronto Star*, October 12, 1999.

"Real Lives: Birthplace of the Evolution," *The Guardian* (London), January 23, 2001.

"Rugged, Ragged and Richly Rewarding," *The Irish Times*, July 17, 1999.

"Rumble in the Jungle," *Sunday Telegraph*, April 8, 2001.

"Runoff to Decide Ecuadorian Race," Associated Press, June 1, 1998.

"Rusting Oil Tanker Was 'Stand-In' on Galápagos Route," *The Independent* (London), January 26, 2001.

"Ruthless Crooks Raise Risks for Oil Workers," *Rocky Mountain News*, February 6, 2001.

"Saving the Galápagos," *The Christian Science Monitor*, November 28, 1972.

"Saving the Islands," *Daily News*, November 29, 1998.

"Sea Shepherd off to Galápagos Islands," *Seattle Post-Intelligencer*, November 26, 2000.

"77 Die in Crash of Cuban Jet in Ecuador," *New York Times*, August 30, 1998.

"Ship Carrying Elderly Americans Sinks off Galápagos Islands," Associated Press, June 12, 1998.

"Shooting Takes On a New Meaning in Ecuador's Football," *Financial Times* (London), May 12, 2001.

"Short-Lived Junta Yields Reins to Vice President in Ecuador," *The Houston Chronicle*, January 23, 2000.

"Singapore Resort Heads to Galápagos," *The Straits Times* (Singapore), August 4, 2001.

"So This Is What We Call Evolution," *The Scotsman*, January 24, 2001.

"Spill from Oil Tanker Imperils Rare Wildlife in the Galápagos," *New York Times*, January 21, 2001.

"Spills and Thrills," *The Daily Telegraph* (London), April 7, 2001.

"State of Emergency Is Back in Force in Ecuador," *The Orlando Sentinel*, July 15, 1999.

"Surfing the Net: Tech-Wary Board Riders Find the Web Isn't All Wet," *San Francisco Chronicle*, August 26, 2000.

"Survival on the Galápagos: It's Tourism vs. Tortoises," *The Christian Science Monitor*, April 14, 1982.

"Tanker Captain Called 'Not Stable,'" Associated Press, January 26, 2001.

"Tanker Wreck in Galápagos Will Be a Habitat for Marine Life," *The New York Times*, January 29, 2001.

"Terrorist Threats Move U.S. to Close Embassy Indefinitely," *New York Times*, December 18, 1999.

"Texaco and Ecuador," *New York Times*, February 19, 1999.

"'This President Is Killing Us': 'Dollarized' Economy Offered No Hope to Millions of Poor Ecuadorians," *The Gazette* (Montreal), January 23, 2000.

"Three U.S. Embassies in South America Temporarily Closed," *The Miami Herald*, April 18, 2001.

"To Colombians, Drug War Is Toxic Foe," *New York Times*, May 1, 2000.

"Top Military Leaders Say Nation's Future in Doubt," *The Orlando Sentinel*, November 21, 1999.

"Tortoises Held Hostage As Lobster War Turns Nasty," *The Independent* (London), November 18, 2000.

"Tourist Ship Sinks Off Galápagos; 1 Dead and 3 Missing," Associated Press, June 12, 1998.

"Tourist Ship Sinks Off Galápagos Islands," Associated Press, June 11, 1998.

"Travel: On the Crater's Edge," *The Independent* (London), July 24, 1999.

"Travel: The Lure of Lava," *The Daily Telegraph* (London), February 5, 2000.

"Troubled President Tries to Win Back Ecuadorians' Hearts," Associated Press, April 20, 1999.

"Turtle Rescue: Evacuation Defies Natural Selection," *The Guardian* (London), October 2, 1998.

"U.N. Foundation Awards $21 Million to 11 Projects," *The Atlanta Journal and Constitution*, May 20, 1999.

"Unions Strike in Ecuador As President Declares Emergency," Associated Press, March 10, 1999.

"Unnatural Selection: Rampaging Galápagos Fishermen Put Islands and Creatures at Risk," *San Francisco Chronicle*, December 10, 2000.

"Upheaval in Ecuador Shows Clout of Indians," *The Washington Post*, January 27, 2000.

"U.S. Defends Aid to Wage Drug War in Embattled Colombia," *Chicago Tribune*, July 27, 1999.

"U.S. Drug Chief, in Colombia, Speaks of 'Regional Crisis,'" *New York Times*, July 27, 1999.

"U.S. Plans Big Aid Package to Rally a Reeling Colombia," *New York Times*, September 15, 1999.

"U.S. Seeking New Bases to Offset Panama Loss," *New York Times*, December 2, 1998.

"U.S. Team Gets Ready to Clean Up an Oil Spill in Galápagos Islands," Associated Press, January 21, 2001.

"Vacationing Attorney Didn't Return From Scuba Dive: Others Searched Near Galápagos Islands for Hours," *The Courier-Journal*, April 28, 2001.

"Volcano Ash Kills One Man in Ecuador, Injures Four Others," Associated Press, October 6, 1999.

"Volcano Covers Quito in White Ash," *The Guardian* (London), November 27, 1999.

"Warning over Galápagos Fish Protests," *Financial Times* (London), December 13, 2000.

"Weave of Drugs and Strife in Colombia," *New York Times*, April 21, 2000.

"Where Darwin Mused, Strife over Ecosystem," *New York Times*, December 27, 2000.

"Where the Wildlife Is Free to Flourish," *The Times* (London), March 31, 2001.

"Why Lonesome George Needs a Mate," *The Financial Times* (London), May 8, 1999.

"Will Science Come to Aid of Galápagos Bachelor? Tune In," *New York Times*, November 9, 1999.

"Winds Dispel Fuel, Ease Fears of Disaster in Galápagos Islands," *The Washington Post*, January 25, 2001.

"With Each Year, Galápagos Faces New Perils; Oil Spill Only the Latest of the Islands' Woes," *Chicago Tribune*, January 30, 2001.

Internet Publications

"A Narrative of Four Voyages," by Captain Benjamin Morrell, 1823, *www.galapagos.to*, July 4, 2000.

"Australian Ladybug Released in Galápagos to Control Invasive Insect," *www.darwinfoundation.org*, January 25, 2002.

"*Canela II* Decision Delayed," *www.seashepherd.org*, October 23, 2001.

"Canine Distemper Virus Threatens Wildlife of Galápagos," *www.darwinfoundation.org*, March 15, 2001.

"CDRS Suffers Vandalism and Threats of Violence at the Hands of Local Fishermen," *www.darwinfoundation.org*, November 17, 2000.

"Census Data Complete for Galápagos," *www.naturalist.net*, April 25, 1999.

Charles Darwin Foundation press release about Research Station takeover and tortoise abduction, www.naturalist.net, November 15, 2000.

"Costa Rican Vessel Detained by *Sirenian*," *www.galapagos.to*, March 22, 2001.

"Ecos del Oriente," by Nick Drake, *www.qsl.net*, 1998.

"Ecuador Concedes to Fishermen's Demands," *www.galapagos.to*, November 16, 2000.

"Ecuadorian Presidential Visit to Galápagos," *www.darwinfoundation.org*, November 28, 2001.

"Fishermen Harass Tourists," *www.galapagos.to*, November 28, 2000.

"Galápagos Corruption Reaches a New Level," *www.galapagos.to*, March 17, 2001.

"Galápagos Fishermen Demand Quota Increase," *www.galapagos.to*, November 17, 2000.

"Galápagos Fishermen on the Attack," *www.galapagos.to*, November 17, 2000.

"Galápagos Fishermen Smash Up Conservation Offices," *www.galapagos.to*, November 22, 2000.

"Galápagos National Park Director Takes On an Admiral," *www.galapagos.to*, March 20, 2001.

"Galápagos National Park Wardens Association Sends Ultimatum to President," *www.naturalist.net*, November 27, 2000.

"Galápagos Oil Spill," *www.galapagos.to*, January 17–20, 2001.

"Galápagos Oil Spill—A Preliminary Overview of the Impacts on the Ecosystem," *www.darwinfoundation.org*, January 23, 2001.

"Galápagos Update," *www.naturalist.net*, November 27, 2000.

International press release—Committee of Concerned Galápagos Citizens, *www.naturalist.net*, November 21, 2000.

"Intimidation of Children and Teachers by Government Authorities," *www.galapagos.to*, November 16, 2000.

"Margaret Wittmer Dies," *www.naturalist.net*, March 21, 2000.

"Merchant Marine Orders Another Illegal Fishing Boat to Be Released," *www.galapagos.to*, March 18, 2001.

"Message from Elicecer Cruz," *www.darwinfoundation.org*, March 21, 2001.

"New Protests and Violence by Galápagos Fishermen—Government Backs Down Again," *www.naturalist.net*, November 17, 2000.

"*Ocean Warrior* Gets Deadline to Leave Galápagos," *www.seashepherd.org*, August 29, 2001.

"*Ocean Warrior* Held by Ecuador Navy in Galápagos," *www.seashepherd.org*, August 27, 2001.

"Rights Violations in the Ecuadorian Amazon," The Center for Economic and Social Rights, *www.cesr.org*, March 1994.

"Sea Shepherd Captures Three More Poachers in the Galápagos," Charles Darwin Foundation Web site *www.darwinfoundation.org*, March 16, 2001.

"Sea Shepherd Liaison Officer Sean O'Hearn Giminez Has Been Arrested and Is Being Held by Police in Puerto Ayora, Galápagos," *www.seashepherd.org*, August 31, 2001.

"Sea Shepherd Officer Released," *www.seashepherd.org*, September 4, 2001.

"Sea Shepherd Patrol Boat *Sirenian* Confronts Illegal Activity Within Marine Reserve of Galápagos," *www.seashepherd.org*, March 8–11, 2001.

"Ship Is Caught Fishing Illegally inside the Galápagos Marine Reserve," *www.darwinfoundation.org*, November 25, 1999.

"The Curse of Lago Agrio," by Jeff Conant, *www.narconews.com*, September 25, 2000.

"The *San Jacinto* Wreck," *www.galapagos.to*, February 18, 2001.

"Tortoises Held Hostage by Angry Fishermen," *www.naturalist.net*, May 31, 2000.

"Urgent Action Needed for the Galápagos," *www.seashepherd.org*, March 18, 2001.

Personal Notes, Essays, Journals

Fitter, Mary. "Mum's Diary." Diary of 1969 sail from England to the Galápagos.

Gallardo, Christy. "Galápagos Is a Nice Place to Visit, But . . ." Autobiographical essay, March 1987.

_____. "The old motor-sailer . . ." Autobiographical essay, February 1987.

_____."Streets filled up with water . . ." 1973 calendar notations.

Nelson, Jack. "The Gringo's Opinion," Essay, November 1999.

_____. "Guides in the Tourist Market." Essay, May 2001.

_____. "Holothurans." Essay, June 1999.

_____. "National Interest and Sovereignty in the Galápagos Islands." Essay, August 2000.

_____. "I was born in Lockport . . ." Autobiographical essay, February 1999.

_____. "Many changes are coming soon . . ." Essay on the Special Law, January 1999.

For information on "Friends of the Galápagos," write to:

Charles Darwin Foundation, Inc.
407 N. Washington St.
Suite 105
Falls Church, VA 22046

Or e-mail:

comments@galapagos.org

All photographs courtesy Michael D'Orso except the following:

Puerto Ayora, Santa Cruz Island, *page xiii*, by Stuart Franklin, Magnum Photos.

Norwegian settlers, 1920s, *page 76*, courtesy of Charles Darwin Research Station library.

Dr. Ritter and the "baroness", *page 194*, courtesy of University of Southern California, on behalf of the Hancock Foundation Archive, Archival Research Center.

Wreck of the *Jessica, page 278*, by Heidi Snell. *Sirenian* crew, *page 304*, courtesy of Sean O'Hearn Giminez.